Solving On-the-Job People Problems

115 TOUGH CHALLENGES AND SMART SOLUTIONS

Solving On-the-Job People Problems

115 TOUGH CHALLENGES AND SMART SOLUTIONS

PRENTICE HALL

MARY ALBRIGHT • CLAY CARR

Library of Congress Cataloging-in-Publication Data

Albright, Mary.
  Solving on-the-job people problems : 115 tough challenges and smart
solutions / Mary Albright, Clay Carr.
    p. cm.
  Includes index.
  ISBN 0-13-043311-X
  1. Supervision of employees.   I. Carr, Clay, 1934–   II. Title.

HF5549.12.A527 2002
658.3′14—dc21   2002023264

Acquisitions Editor: John Hiatt
Production Editor: Eve Mossman
Interior Design: Shelly Carlucci

Printed in the United States of America

10 9 8 7 6 5 4 3 2 1

ISBN 0-13-043311-X

ATTENTION: CORPORATIONS AND SCHOOLS

Prentice Hall books are available at quantity discounts with bulk purchase for educational, business, or sales promotional use. For information, please write to: Prentice Hall Special Sales, 240 Frisch Court, Paramus, New Jersey 07652. Please supply: title of book, ISBN, quantity, how the book will be used, date needed.

PRENTICE HALL
Paramus, NJ 07652

http://www.phdirect.com

We affectionately dedicate this book to

Bryan Carr
Heather Arsham
Lisa Conant
Chris Erdman
Lynn Marker
Michael Fletcher
and
Matthew Fletcher

Introduction

"Well I'll tell you. If I were in charge, things would work a lot better around here!"

How many times have you heard that refrain? Maybe you even said it yourself—back when you *weren't* in charge. But as even the briefest experience in management demonstrates, being in charge isn't always all it's cracked up to be.

And why not? It's all those *people*! Employees to supervise, customers to please, peers and suppliers to negotiate with, and perhaps higher level managers to satisfy. That's exactly what a manager's job is all about: people. Management has been defined as the art of accomplishing work through other people. Those people include staff in other parts of the company, outside suppliers, consultants, and contractors—but mostly they include your own group of employees, the work unit you supervise.

Often, though, it seems to be a lot harder to accomplish work through other people than it is to do it yourself.

Your employees don't have exactly the same set of skills you do—and so may make mistakes in accomplishing the work. They don't necessarily share your work values or your goals, and so they occasionally focus on different aspects of the work than you want them to. They often don't work at the same speed you do—they may be faster (and maybe make more mistakes), or they may be slower (even interminably slow). And sometimes they're ornery, and grumpy, and just downright difficult to get along with.

But your employees also bring fresh new perspectives to the job. They often have skills you don't have. They can approach problems from a different angle and may be able to find a better solution than you could. Because they've had a different set of experiences in their lives they can relate to some customers better than you might be able to. In a well run organization, managers are able to leverage their resources—working through the diverse members of their staffs to perform better and more effectively than they ever could with a unit of clones.

So the task of accomplishing work through other people, your primary job as a manager, is both rewarding and frustrating—sometimes both at the same time—and always challenging.

That's where *Solving On-The-Job People Problems* can help. It addresses many of those challenging day-to-day issues that you probably never learned about in basic management training, and may never have thought about until you were faced with them yourself. The book was previously released as *The Manager's Troubleshooter*. Tens of thousands of managers have read and benefited from the previous editions as we helped them deal with some of the thorniest challenges they face as managers.

In the years since the previous editions were published, there have been shifts in organizational focus–often away from people issues and more toward the bottom line. As a result, both managers and employees report greater stress, longer hours, and less satisfaction in their careers.

But in spite of the emphasis on dollars and statistics, managing people remains the most challenging part of managing an organization, and what most first-level managers spend the greater part of their days wrestling with.

The specific problems managers encounter differ depending on the environment in which they work. So *Solving On-The-Job People Problems* contains sections on changing employee expectations, addressing issues such as flexible work schedules and flexible work sites as well as empowerment and teamwork, use of technology, and corporate restructuring. Chapter 1 contains many ideas to help you with the problems that can arise in making the transition from outdated hierarchical structures to a culture of teamwork and empowerment. The challenges described in this chapter include working with employees who don't want to be part of a team or who think that being in an empowered environment means they can do whatever they want. The chapter can also help you meet the challenge of nudging your own company's structure into a more empowered, self-directed mode. Several aspects of the very delicate balance between accommodating your employees' requests for increased autonomy regarding when and where they accomplish their work and optimizing the company's performance are covered in Chapter 2.

In Chapter 6, we discuss how to improve employee performance. Chapters 3, 5, and 7 provide insight on how to handle "attitude" challenges, such as how to get employee buy-in to the job and the company's goals, how to foster cooperation among your staff and between your own unit and others, and how to address employee misconduct. Managing the use of technology in the workplace is covered in Chapter 11. And to ensure that none of your concerns will be neglected, in Chapter 13 we take a careful look at your all-important relationship with your own boss.

The challenges addressed in *Solving On-The-Job People Problems* include some of the toughest situations you'll encounter as a manager–from performance issues, to personal concerns, to problems with your boss. We attack head-on issues such as substance abuse, workers who try to beat the system, workers who can't keep up with the team, and maintaining morale even during a company's uncertain times.

Solving On-The-Job People Problems gives you the tools you need to handle the most challenging, continuously relevant management issues you're likely to encounter. It focuses on practical solutions to problems every manager is likely to face. This specific, step-by-step guide to analyzing and conquering "people" challenges is an invaluable aid for every manager—one you'll want to keep close at hand.

How To Use This Book

How many times have you had to read pages and pages—perhaps even chapters and chapters—to find a solution to a challenge you faced? You won't have to do that with *Solving On-The-Job People Problems*. Designed as a practical, easy-to-use manual to help you handle the daily management challenges you face, this book will help you find the cause and determine the right response to your specific issue quickly and easily.

HERE'S HOW TO USE IT:

- The manual describes *115* management challenges, grouped into 13 different chapters. Each chapter deals with a specific theme (such as "Promoting Empowerment and Teamwork" or "Encouraging Good Workplace Ethics"). This helps you zero in on the right topic and the right specific issue in a hurry.

- Find the chapter that deals with the type of issue that you're facing. Then take a look at the list of challenges in that chapter. Find the challenge that sounds closest to yours and turn to it.

- Each challenge begins with a brief description or vignette. Read the description carefully. If it describes a situation similar to yours, keep going.

- But what if it isn't similar? Look at other challenges in that chapter, or even in other chapters. Find the challenge that's most like yours. If it isn't quite the same, don't worry—many challenges suggest similar challenges you might want to look at.

- Once you've found the right challenge and read its description, read about its possible causes. We spell out the most common causes for each situation we've described. It's important to read this carefully. Why? Because situations that look the same at first glance can have very different causes—and your response may be very different depending on the cause. You have to find just what caused the situation before you can respond to it successfully.

- Once you understand the cause of the situation you've encountered, you need to know how best to respond. That's the next part of each section. It's also the longest, because we talk you through all the steps you need to take. If you've identified the cause of your management challenge and follow these steps, you're on your way to conquering it.

- In most cases, there are two or three different sets of steps to take, depending on the cause of the situation. Read and think about each set carefully before you decide which one to use. Then use it.

- What if a challenge described in the book sounds like yours, but turns out to be not quite the same? You're not stuck. We've also included a number of checklists in the back of the book that you can use instead of, or in addition to, the steps described for a specific challenge. You might look on these checklists as general problem-solving processes. There are eight checklists: a General Checklist that can be used with any management issue and seven specific checklists for issues such as poor performance and substance abuse.

- What if the challenge you're faced with is beyond the scope of your expertise? You'll see that it's not uncommon for us to suggest that you consult with other experts as you work your way through management issues. Often, there are legal implications of what you do. There may also be medical or psychological issues, or other aspects of the situation that most lay people aren't equipped to address. This is not a law book; it's not a medical book; it's not a psychology text. We've tried to give you the information you need to analyze the situations that you encounter and to identify those times when you need to go to someone else for help. Those sources of help include human resources professionals, training providers, employee assistance counselors or other mental health professionals, lawyers, and technology experts. Being a good manager doesn't mean you always have to go it alone; it also means you know when it's time to call in the reinforcements!

A FINAL SUGGESTION

This is *your* book, and it will help you solve your people management challenges efficiently and effectively. It's written around specific situations and challenges, and its goal is to help you meet these challenges, but we'd like to give you this hint:

When you resolve a people problem, don't settle just for restoring things to the status quo. Use the situation to make things *better* than they were before. What does that mean?

- It might mean resolving the situation in a way that increases the trust between you and your employee. The more you trust each other, the easier it is to resolve other issues as they arise–and before they become bigger issues.

- It may mean resolving a situation in a way that helps workers manage themselves more effectively. The better your workers are at managing themselves, the fewer the situations that will come to you.

- It may also mean resolving a problem in a way that increases your employee's sense of responsibility for and commitment to the job. A strong commitment to the job prevents many problems from occurring at all.

You can think of more ways to improve things as you resolve the management issues you encounter. The important thing is to keep looking for ways to make the situation better and the worker more effective. The more you do this, the fewer problems there'll be for you to solve in the future, and the more positive the challenges you'll be able to address.

Mary Albright
Clay Carr

Contents

CHAPTER 1
Promoting Empowerment and Teamwork

CHAPTER 2

Keeping Up with Evolving Employee Expectations

CHAPTER 3

Improving Your Employees' Approach to the Job

CHAPTER 4

Overcoming the Personal Problems of Your Employees

CHAPTER 5

Building Win-Win Relationships with Employees

CHAPTER 6
Helping Your Employees Succeed

CHAPTER 7
Encouraging Good Workplace Ethics

CHAPTER 8

Corralling the Free Spirits in Your Company

CHAPTER 9

Maintaining Morale in Uncertain Times

CHAPTER 10

Surviving and Thriving During Corporate Restructuring

CHAPTER 11

The Human Side of Technology

CHAPTER 12

Working Through Your Own Issues

CHAPTER 13

Getting It Right with the Boss

Solutions Checklists

Promoting Empowerment and Teamwork

No. 1 Rebellious Subordinates

Your employees think that being empowered means they don't have to listen to you

THE SCENE

"Hannah, I don't understand what's happened here. I asked you last week to call the Supero Group and apologize for our having taken so long to finish their order. I see that they've sent back their customer satisfaction questionnaire and said that we took too long and did superficial work. I thought you were going to try to mend our relationship with them. You reported back last week that everything was taken care of."

"Well, everything is taken care of, Hannah replies. When I passed your request on to the team, they decided that because Supero was such a pain to work with, we'd be better off without them. Why, is that a problem? You told us we were empowered to handle our own accounts!"

POSSIBLE CAUSES

Your employees may not have a clear understanding of the limits of their authority.

They may truly believe that they're entirely on their own, and you may have contributed to their misunderstanding by the way you've delegated assignments to them.

1

Your employees may be testing their limits.

They're not sure how far empowerment extends, and dealing with a challenging customer seems like a good opportunity to find out—particularly if this customer doesn't seem that important to them.

Your employees may not want to be "empowered" and think that ignoring your request will force you to take charge again.

If your employees have been accustomed to a fairly structured environment, the idea of taking charge of their own assignments may not be all that appealing.

> ***Hint:*** For empowerment to work, there must be a high degree of trust between you and your workgroup. If the relationship is strained or uncertain, the notion of empowerment must be introduced more slowly— maybe without even saying the word "empowerment" at all until the group is more accustomed to accepting responsibility for its decisions. If your attempt to empower employees begins to resemble anarchy, consider whether you're moving too fast. Allow the group enough time to assume the increased responsibility that comes with empowerment.

YOUR RESPONSE

If your employees don't have a clear understanding of the limits of their authority:

It's not too late to fix the misunderstanding. You just need to back up a little and offer extra guidance.

Empowerment, just like any form of delegation, is not all or nothing. Employees can be empowered at several different levels. For example:

- At one level, your employees are empowered to handle "routine" cases (and you will define *routine* for them), but are expected to come to you for direction for more complicated or sensitive matters.

- At a higher level of empowerment, your employees handle all routine cases as well as some more difficult ones and come to you with recommendations for handling the most troublesome situations.

- At the highest level of empowerment, your employees handle virtually everything themselves, coming to you with recommendations and seeking approval only in unusual cases.

At all levels, your staff is expected to keep you sufficiently informed so that you don't get blind-sided. In addition, at all levels, you have ultimate "veto" power to override the team's decisions.

It is up to you to decide at what level of empowerment you expect your group to operate and at what level the group is capable of operating. Because "empowerment" implies a level of autonomy higher than traditional "delegation," ultimately you will want to have as many people as possible operating at the highest level of empowerment, or at least the middle level. But not all employees are ready to make that leap. So how do you start?

- Begin by assessing your staff members' strengths and weaknesses and your own comfort level with each level of empowerment.

- Meet with your workgroup to explain exactly what you mean by "empowerment," including what level of autonomy they'll have to begin with and where you want to end up. Explain the kinds of issues they have authority to resolve themselves, and give them specific examples of what they can and cannot handle without consulting you.

- Explain how you'll know when it's time for them to assume the next level of authority (if you've decided that there is a "next" level). Don't just tell them you'll "know it when you see it." Take time for a bit of introspection so you can offer clear measures of the group's readiness for increased autonomy.

- Finally, turn them loose, but monitor their performance, especially in the first few weeks (or months, if necessary). Work with the group to establish performance expectations. Meet with them on a regular schedule, perhaps weekly or biweekly to review their performance and their decision-making. Give frequent feedback on what your goals are and how well they're meeting those goals. As soon as the group members have demonstrated that they can competently handle routine issues according to your quality and quantity standards, it's time to move to the next level of empowerment.

It's important that you not throw employees into unfamiliar waters too quickly and before they've built up your trust in their judgment. But it's also important that employees be recognized for the progress they make and that you allow them to operate with a higher level of authority as soon as they've earned your trust. If you hold them back too long, they'll doubt that you're sincere about empowerment and they'll begin to work around you.

If your employees are testing the limits of their authority:

Let's begin by assuming that your employees really do know what they're empowered to do and what they're not. They understand their limits, but they want to push further.

Your first task is to figure out why they feel the need to test limits. Are they capable of working at a higher level of authority, but limited by your rules? Do they think you're being arbitrary and autocratic in not giving them greater autonomy? Or is the opposite true—do they see you as a weak leader who will buckle under pressure or simply not react to their bid for more power?

How do you know whether they're capable of assuming a greater level of authority? Ask yourself two questions: Do they successfully handle the things they are delegated authority to handle? Do you trust them to handle more difficult or more sensitive issues appropriately? Keep in mind that trusting your employees doesn't mean that you trust them to handle more difficult issues the way you would. It's only necessary that you trust them to handle matters in a way that's consistent with your policies and corporate values. Part of empowerment is trusting that other people's judgments can be good ones, even when they're not exactly the judgments you would make.

So, if you can answer "yes" to both questions, then it's time to give the group greater responsibility and authority. Holding them back will only stifle their initiative and cause them to test you even more often.

On the other hand, if the group sees you as a weak leader who can be run over by a show of independence, you can easily reinforce the limits you've set: Call the group's attention to the delegation discussion you had with them when you first established the limits of their authority. Don't overreact by being too stern or authoritarian; they'll recognize that for the mask of insecurity that it often is. Instead, calmly and reasonably point out that they've overstepped their bounds. Then explain why it's important to ensure that *all* customers are satisfied, even those you don't particularly want to cultivate. Express your confidence that your employees will follow your guidance in similar situations in the future and wait to see what happens next time.

If the group complies with your guidelines and begins to come to you with recommendations, listens to your suggestions and follows your explicit directions, then members are moving in the right direction and may be getting ready to jump to the next higher level of authority. But if you have a repeat of the problem, then it's time to move down to a lesser level of empowerment (of course, after you've explained why) until they can rebuild your trust and confidence in their judgment.

If your employees are trying to undermine your attempts at empowerment:

Recognize that not all workgroups will embrace the idea of empowerment. Although empowerment is discussed in management literature in terms of the increased authority and autonomy it gives employees, it also shifts to employees increased responsibility for the consequences of their actions. Many of your employees won't want that increased responsibility, either because they are fearful of making mistakes or because they don't want the added burdens.

SOMETHING TO THINK ABOUT

There is one level of delegation that's even lower than those we've described here (and doesn't even deserve the title "empowerment"). At that level your employees make recommendations to you for almost every decision they make and very seldom take an independent action, no matter how small or insignificant.

If your workgroup is operating at this level, it's likely that you either have a very inexperienced group or you have somehow made it clear to them that you want to work this way. Making all the decisions yourself isn't healthy in the long term—for you, for your workgroup, or for the organization.

Get the most from your group by:

- Making sure they have the tools they need to work on their own. Those tools may be equipment or resources, or they may be skills that they'll develop by training.
- Giving them the appropriate level of authority to take actions on their own initiative.

If you examine your own management style and leverage your resources, you'll multiply your group's productivity immensely.

If your workgroup is to successfully negotiate the transition from a traditional authority-based structure to an empowered-team structure, you will need to be sensitive to this reluctance, and guide your employees through the transition by taking the following steps.

- Look again at the levels of empowerment described earlier. Notice that at each level the workgroup assumes a little more responsibility and gains a little more autonomy. Where is your workgroup most comfortable? Find that level (a decreased level, if necessary) and begin again.

- Explain to your workgroup that you believe that it will benefit both them and the organization for them to operate as an empowered team, but that you realize that you have to move one step at a time. Then once again describe the level of empowerment at which you'll start—what decisions they can make on their own, which ones they need to get approval for first, and which ones you will make. If you're decreasing the level of authority and responsibility at which you'll require them to operate, make it clear that this decrease is only *temporary* and that your goal is still a fully empowered group.

- As the group gets comfortable with the starting level of empowerment, begin to move them toward the next level. Encourage them.

- Reward employee's successes and help them learn from their mistakes, but don't punish mistakes. Learning involves risk, and when you punish errors, you discourage the risk-taking that is necessary for employees' growth. Support your team members, but don't allow them to use you as a crutch. And that's a fine line to draw.

No. 2 Uncooperative Employee

You're having trouble getting cooperation on a joint project

THE SCENE

"How do you want to handle getting the Haversons' business incorporated?" you ask Frances Powell, your tax expert. "I can get started on the incorporation documents, but we'll need to talk to them about tax elections. Would you be available in the next week or so to meet with them?"

"Oh, just go at it however you want," Frances replies. "I'm pretty busy right now, so why don't you just get started with them and then we'll talk."

"Well, that's going to make it tough if we don't both participate in deciding how they should be handling their tax issues. I'm not that strong on all of the implications of C-corp vs. S-corp status and I was counting on your expertise. Let's see if we can work something out around your schedule."

As you put the telephone receiver in its cradle, you muse that this isn't the first time you've felt like Frances was stonewalling you.

POSSIBLE CAUSES

Frances may really not have the time or resources to devote to the project.

It may be an area in which she'd really like to be involved, and she may be the sort of person who usually comes through, but you just caught her at a bad time.

Frances may want to make you look bad by failing to produce on this joint project.

She seems to think you're not capable of handling the work, and wants others in the company to think so, too.

She may think that her reputation is strong enough to ensure that you'll be blamed for any problems that crop up. Then she'll feel vindicated, because she'll have proof that you're not doing your job.

> ***Hint:*** You know from your experience with your own internal work-group that when a project is executed poorly, the *whole* team looks bad, not just the one or two people who contributed most to the failure. Frances may be able to make you look bad on this project, but she won't come out smelling like a rose either. And even if you want to see that Frances gets her just desserts, sabotaging the project won't accomplish your purpose. Regardless of the cause of Frances' lack of cooperation, it's up to you to make sure the work is done well and on time. Revenge is not sweet when you're damaged in the process.

YOUR RESPONSE

If Frances doesn't have the time to devote to the project:

Talk to Frances about what she's able to do. Define clearly at the beginning what Frances can contribute and what she'll have to leave up to you. If she can't come to meetings or devote her personal time to the assignment, is there someone else available who could carry information back and forth (or even do part of the work she was responsible for)? Can she feed you information that you can put together in the final product? Can she give you some ideas on how to approach the work, which you can then carry out on your own or delegate to others?

Because Frances is someone whom you can trust to do what she says she'll do, we'll assume that she follows through on what she's promised, or at least makes arrangements for someone else to do the work. Take what she's given you and do the best job for the clients you can. If there are areas you can't finish without additional input from her, get back to her with *specific* questions.

Allow Frances an opportunity to monitor the work you're doing as you progress through different stages. Let her know how you plan to advise the clients and give her copies of documents you've prepared. But give her a "drop dead" date after which you'll consider that, if you haven't heard anything to the contrary, she agrees with the approach you're taking.

Let her know in advance also that hers is a technical review only. If the material is technically correct and she simply disagrees with the way you're presenting it to the clients, she can make suggestions, but you're not going to feel bound by them. By declining the opportunity to be more involved, and by depending on you to put together the final project, she implicitly agreed to defer to your judgment.

If Frances is as trustworthy a person as you think she is, she'll give you top billing and lots of credit for the success of the project. If not, you'll know the next time around how unreliable she is and treat her accordingly. (See below.)

If Frances consistently takes advantage or wants to discredit you:

Keep track of the attempts you've made to collaborate with Frances on the project. Identify the parts of the project you think you should be responsible for and the parts that only Frances has the knowledge or information to handle. Give the list to Frances and try to get her agreement. Chances are you won't get disagreement—just no response at all. In that case, keep a copy of your memo to her, annotated with the attempts you've made to discuss issues with her, and start working. Document all your attempts to get Frances' support as well as your attempts to schedule meetings with her.

Once you've completed as much as you can without Frances' input, go back to her again to get the information you need. If she still refuses to cooperate, put together a draft proposal or action plan. Make it as complete as you can, but identify clearly the information that's missing and its possible impact on the validity of the final product. Give Frances a copy of your mock report with fair warning that if she doesn't do her share you'll have to go elsewhere for assistance. Chances are pretty good that she'll finally come through.

And if she doesn't? Follow through on your promise to get the help elsewhere. Someone else in the company may have the expertise to help, or you may need to go outside for consultation. Your goal is to prepare the best product you possibly can. But in no case can you allow your clients to suffer because of a lack of cooperation internally.

Whether Frances finally comes through or not, be sure that your peers know what a struggle you've had to get the assignment finally completed. A well-placed word to the other people you work with will get the message across. Keep in mind that Frances' failure to help you is probably not an isolated incident. If she hasn't cooperated on your joint project, she's probably let others down too, including her superiors.

Finally, be sure that when you're asked to work with someone else on a joint project, even someone you don't particularly care for, you don't follow Frances' example. Your cooperation with others will demonstrate that if there was any flaw in the way the prior project was executed, the fault surely wasn't yours.

SOMETHING TO THINK ABOUT

There are only so many things you can do to get your peers to cooperate with you. While good peer relations are critical to your own success as a manager, you'll inevitably run into others who don't want to play fair. When that happens, try your best to work things out with them. But if your attempts fail, do whatever you must to protect yourself. Don't let an unsuccessful worker take you down with her.

No. 3 Blind Faith in Management Fads

Your manager wants self-managed teams, but offers no guidance on how to do it.

THE SCENE

"You're one of the most intelligent managers I know, and certainly one of my most intelligent people. I just can't understand why you keep fighting me on this self-managing team issue!"

"Mr. Garcia, I'm not fighting you. I just don't have any idea how to go about making my workgroup a self-managing team."

"For someone as smart and experienced as you, that's no excuse."

"Then you tell me—how do I go about it? Where do I begin?"

"That's your job, and I'm not going to do it for you. Now go and get started."

POSSIBLE CAUSES

Mr. Garcia has been told to create self-managing teams; he has no idea how to do it either.

Many organizations attempt to implement teams by issuing a mandate to managers to do so, sometimes with minimal training, sometimes with no training at all.

Mr. Garcia understands the basics, but he wants you to exercise the necessary initiative.

He may believe that the team will be much more effective if you create it according to the group's needs, rather than a cookie-cutter structure. He may also be testing to see if you're willing to take the initiative.

Mr. Garcia needs greater productivity from your workgroup and this is how he believes he can best get it.

Teams have been endorsed by management "gurus" as the way to increase productivity, and Mr. Garcia sees self-managing teams as a real positive step for you and your workgroup and for himself.

> *Hint:* It doesn't really matter what the cause is—this could be a great opportunity for you and your workgroup. Approach it that way, no matter what the obstacles may seem to be.

YOUR RESPONSE

If Mr. Garcia has been told to create self-managing teams and has no idea how to do it:

If Mr. Garcia doesn't understand much about teams, starting to make your workgroup a self-managing team may raise his anxiety level in a hurry. He may well feel that he's losing control, and managers never like that feeling in the least. So what do you do?

- Keep him posted at every turn. He will get educated along with you and the workgroup. If possible, have him attend the training with the group. If you think he would find that insulting, get an executive summary of the training for him from your training provider. Schedule frequent conferences with him to keep him updated on what you're doing.
- Explain to him—over and over if necessary—how the team's greater autonomy is going to boost production and make him look good. Don't attempt to move the group any faster than he's willing to go.

  Continue with the steps in the next response.

If Mr. Garcia understands the basics, but wants you to exercise the necessary initiative:

This should mean that you can spend less time educating him and more time educating the group. Start by looking at the characteristics that make teams most effective, described in the next response. Make sure that your workgroup has or can develop these characteristics. Find a good book or two on self-managing teams and read them. Make sure you understand the basics and know what you need to do. Then take the following steps.

- Arrange for the workgroup to receive training in the essentials of self-managing teams as soon as possible. The entire workgroup should attend the same training, either at the same time or at successive sessions. Needless to say, you must attend the training with them.
- Immediately following the training, hold a discussion session or two with your workgroup to compare notes on what everyone learned and begin to plan the transition to a self-managing team. You should also identify training in team-building and conflict management and schedule the team for it.
- If the organization has trained team facilitators available, arrange to get one of them to help the team get started.
- By this point, you and the team should have a good idea of what you need to do. Establish a clear mission, one that each member of the team is committed to. Begin finding ways to share leadership among team members. And you're on your way.

If Mr. Garcia needs greater productivity from your workgroup and this is how he believes he can best get it:

Teams have been oversold. They do not always improve productivity. In fact, they are not always as productive as a traditional workgroup. And if an individual can do a job independently, a team attempting to do the same job will always be less efficient.

How can you tell whether teamwork will help your unit? There's no simple answer, but here are two key points:

- Be sure that the team has a clear mission, one that every member considers important and worthwhile. Teams work only when each individual member is committed to the team mission.
- The team will be most effective if the team has unity of purpose, which is easiest if the team produces a single product or service, manages a single process, serves a single customer or group of customers, or combines two or all three of these. Each team member can contribute a different skill (the

team can be multi-functional), or each can learn all of the skills required (the individuals can be multi-skilled).

If, after you analyze your workload, you decide that a self-managing team will actually improve your group's productivity, then follow the steps outlined in the two responses above to create a team.

If you decide that teams aren't likely to help productivity and may even slow down the operation of your unit, then come back to Mr. Garcia well-prepared. Find a couple of articles from management periodicals or your local library that describe the work situations that are likely to benefit from teams and make copies for Mr. Garcia.

But knowing what *won't* help isn't enough. If your workgroup's performance needs to improve, it's up to you to figure out how to make that happen. Look at the challenges described in Chapters 3 and 6 of this book to see if they offer any more suitable solutions to your productivity problems.

You should approach Mr. Garcia only after you've figured out why teams won't improve your productivity and what will improve it. You'll need to work through both of these issues fairly quickly so he knows you're not stalling. As soon as you have a positive recommendation to offer, get together with him and make your case. If you've proven yourself a capable manager in the past, chances are he'll be receptive to your ideas.

SOMETHING TO THINK ABOUT

The opportunity to help a workgroup become a self-managing team often is an opportunity worth seizing. But be aware of a critical point: Your role will change dramatically. You will move from being a supervisor to being a leader, then to being a teacher or coach. Depending on the degree of self-management the organization will tolerate, you may even end up as consultant and coordinator for a large group of teams.

If your workgroup is headed for self-management, get some training for yourself as well as your group—so you can adapt to your own new role quickly and successfully.

No. 4 Boss Won't Back the Idea

Your boss overrules you every time you try to empower your workgroup

THE SCENE

"I don't understand what the problem is, Mark. Empowering my group doesn't mean I'll let them just fly off on their own. I'll still . . ."

"I know perfectly well what empowerment is, and I don't like it. You're in charge of this group, and I expect you to act as if you're in charge," Mark replies.

"But they're a good group, and they do good work. If they had a little more authority to make decisions on their own, we could get a lot more done. Our productivity can always stand a boost."

"No, this isn't going to work. I supervise you, and you supervise your group. And we both know what that means . . ."

POSSIBLE CAUSES

Your boss may not understand what you mean by "empowerment."

Even though Mark says he knows what empowerment is, he may think this is just a way for you to make supervision easier for yourself.

You and your boss may have different ideas about what a supervisor's job really is.

Your discussion with him indicates that he's focused on what a supervisor does. Empowerment is more about what a supervisor can accomplish.

Your boss may be concerned that the group's work will deteriorate without your close supervision.

He may not be as convinced as you that the group will do good work on its own.

> ***Hint:*** The three causes can be summarized as disagreements about what to do, how to do it, and what it means to be a supervisor. Whenever you and your boss disagree about something, chances are good that the bottom line is one or the other of those causes. So you might want to gener-

alize the approaches we've described below for solving the problem; they apply to a multitude of situations.

YOUR RESPONSE

If your boss doesn't understand what you mean by "empowerment":

"Empowerment" is one of those popular terms that mean different things to different people. For some managers, empowerment means allowing employees to do as much as they can as independently as they can, but with continuing management responsibility for ensuring the overall adequacy of their work. But for some others, empowerment *does* mean making their own lives easier by passing off the responsibility for getting the work done, while keeping much of their authority.

So, before you resume your discussion with Mark about why empowering your employees is a good thing, you need to decide what it is that *you* mean by empowerment.

In its best form, empowerment is a way to "leverage your resources." It's a way to allow your workgroup to exercise as much responsibility and authority as it can competently handle. By delegating some of the decision-making power in your group, you don't have to be involved in every decision group members make. So, instead of the unit's productivity being limited by your capacity, it's limited by the capacity of the group, which is much greater than yours alone.

In its most advanced form, an empowered workgroup operates with the authority to make all routine decisions and many more difficult decisions. However, they will *always* be responsible for consulting with their supervisor on issues that are particularly complex or particularly sensitive. How many of those complex or sensitive issues they must get guidance on depends mostly on the competence of the workgroup. The more practice they get in handling issues and the more comfortable the supervisor is with their judgment, the less often consultation will be necessary.

Empowerment is not about making anybody's life easier; it's about getting the most out of the resources you have. And it's a two-edged sword: It confers both authority and responsibility. The workgroup not only has the ability to make decisions, but they are accountable for those decisions. Any successful empowerment initiative has to include consequences, both good and bad, for the decisions the workgroup makes.

And it's not just a bowl of cherries for the manager either. In some ways managing an empowered workgroup is *more* difficult than traditional supervision. You're still responsible for what the group does, but you don't have the same level of control you used to.

So, if after thinking about what you mean by empowerment and considering our suggestions you still want to empower your workgroup, what should you do to convince your boss?

- First, work out a specific plan for how you intend to empower your employees. What will be the extent of their authority? What will you do to ensure that quality and quantity aren't adversely affected? How will you review their decisions? How will you decide whether they're ready to move from one level of authority and responsibility to the next? What will be the rewards to the group for successful exercise of their authority? What will be the consequences for inappropriate exercise of their authority?

- Then schedule an appointment with your boss to present your proposed plan in some detail. This should take about an hour. Begin by explaining what you see as the benefits to the organization; then go through the implementation steps. Let your boss interrupt all he or she wants. Be prepared to answer the tough questions such as, "What's this going to do for me?" and "If your group is so empowered, what do I still need you for?"

- Don't press for approval right away. Make this an information presentation, not a decision-making session. Give your boss a couple of weeks to think about empowerment as you've presented it and to come up with any other objections. You might even want to consider not referring to your plan as "empowerment" at all. That's a pretty radical term in some circles. It might be better to talk about "delegation" or a "responsibility matrix" instead.

- After some time, go to your boss to explain how you plan to proceed, planning to take the first steps slowly. This also is not a decision-making meeting—it's an information meeting for your boss. Unless your authority to organize the work of your group is restricted, you're probably in a position to decide who has authority to do what within the group. So when you talk to your boss about your first steps, do it in the context of passing information, not asking permission.

- As your group assumes greater authority successfully, continue to delegate more authority and responsibility to it. Keep your boss informed and stay within the limits of your own authority, but maintain a positive, active approach—and your strategy will probably never even be questioned.

- Recognize that there are probably some "sacred cows" assigned to your workgroup that you may *never* be able to delegate. Those are the issues or projects that your boss has such a personal interest in that you need to know exactly what's happened on them and be actively involved in making decisions about them. Similarly, your group needs to recognize that you probably have your own one or two "sacred cows" that you consider to be so sensitive or visible that you can't delegate them. Those issues don't destroy your entire empowerment initiative; they're just minor exceptions to your general practice.

If you and your boss have different ideas about what supervision really is:

Recognize that you're not going to change your boss's ideas and he or she is probably not going to change yours (although he may change the way you implement them). Acknowledge that you understand what your boss says about a supervisor's role. Identify for yourself the areas where you agree and disagree. Then decide whether the span between your views is too great to bridge.

If not, then prepare the detailed implementation plan described in the preceding response and present it to your boss, with special sensitivity to what you know about the differences in the way each of you views supervision.

If you de-emphasize the notion of "empowerment" and talk instead about delegation and the continuing control you'll exercise over a broader delegation of powers, you probably won't get strong resistance to your plan. You should at least be able to implement it on a trial basis. Then your work-group and your boss (and you) can have some time to see if you're all really ready for your group's greater autonomy.

If the differences between your ideas of supervision and your boss's are too great to span, you must decide whether you want to back off or take a strong stance (recognizing that it may cost you political capital or even your managerial role). You can compromise, or back off completely for a while, and then offer a compromise proposal. Most managers are in favor of increasing their units' productivity; their concern is largely with the perceived lack of accountability of an "empowered" workforce.

If your boss is concerned about deterioration of your unit's work without close supervision:

Again, the detailed implementation plan described earlier is one of the most powerful tools we've found. But don't march into your boss's office and try to steam-roll his acceptance of your proposal. For many managers, the notion of empowerment seems like a big change. But, at base, it's much the same concept as "delegation" or "authorization"—progressively greater authority with progressively more powerful consequences.

- Show your boss how you will phase in decision-making authority as the group demonstrates the ability to handle the more extensive autonomy. Explain, also how you'll reduce group members' authority if they consistently fail to handle it well. Emphasize the parts of your plan that address your continued monitoring of the group's performance and your intention to intervene if necessary. Assure your boss that you'll keep in touch with the work, but that the rewards for delegation of much of the decision making and responsibility will be greater productivity and efficiency.

- Then, begin your implementation slowly and without fanfare. Your goal is not to announce to the world that you've "empowered" your workforce. Your goal is to leverage your resources by delegating responsibility.

- Follow through on the phased-in implementation you promised your boss. As the group achieves successes, and your system of controls and reviews becomes established and routine, let your boss know how well it's working. Your successful implementation of early steps is the best guarantee that you'll be able to see the empowerment process through to the end.

SOMETHING TO THINK ABOUT

Often negative reactions to new initiatives are as much an emotional response to the words used as to the ideas being proposed. Unless you're working with a management group that's on the cutting edge of management theory, be sure the proposals you make to your boss are as free of jargon as possible. Focus on what you want to accomplish and what it will do for the organization. Leave the jargon for your write-up in the business magazines.

No. 5 Reclusive Group Member

A "loner" won't work with fellow team members

THE SCENE

As you leave for a staff meeting, you hear one of your group members call to another, "Hey, Walter, want to see this demo Carlene brought back from the applied learning conference last week?"

"No thanks," Walter replies, "I'm busy on the graphics for next week's class in Houston."

Following the group down the hall, you hear them remarking on how aloof Walter is and speculating that he thinks he's better than they are.

POSSIBLE CAUSES

Walter may simply be more comfortable working alone.

Some individuals aren't comfortable in groups or just don't choose to spend their time with others.

Walter feels like an outsider.

He may not want to be a loner, but believes that the group doesn't really like him or want him to be part of its activities. This may happen because the individual belongs to a different racial or ethnic group from the others, or is a different gender, but it can also happen when the individual has a different level of education from his peers, or comes from a different background, or just has different interests.

The group is uncomfortable with Walter.

He feels like an outsider because that's how the group considers him. This is also particularly common when the "outsider" is different in race, ethnic background, or gender.

The group may be discriminating against him.

There's a fine line between being "uncomfortable" with another and discriminating against him. It's important to know if that line's been crossed.

> ***Hint:*** Although not "fitting in" hasn't always been much of a problem, and in the past workers who did a good job but weren't team players were still valuable employees, that's not nearly as true today. Restructuring and the requirement to do more with less, combined with the "flattening" of organizations make it essential that every worker in the company be able to function as part of a team. So, while you may be tempted to put Walter in a corner and leave him alone, don't.

YOUR RESPONSE

No matter what the cause is:

It's always important to know and understand your employees, and this is one of the times when it's particularly important. You may not know Walter well, but you should know all the people who've been with you for months or years. You should have a good idea whether they're excluding Walter or he's choosing to be isolated.

To confirm your own perceptions, you might talk with one or two of your trusted workers to see how they view the situation. Have they really tried to get Walter to join them, or are they waiting for him to come to them? When you know the answers to these questions, you'll be ready to handle the situation.

If Walter seems to prefer being alone:

Take Walter aside for a few minutes to talk to him about his work style. Explain that you value his accomplishments and understand that much of what he does requires individual effort, but also stress the importance of working as a part of a team to accomplish larger projects, to combine the expertise of several people, to help solve complex problems.

Give him specific examples of work your unit has done in the past year or so that *couldn't* have been accomplished without team effort. Let him know that it is your expectation that he will begin to include himself in group efforts, that it is a part of the job for which he will be held accountable.

Consider also developing guidelines or performance criteria for your whole group that stress teamwork over individual effort. Link consequences to workers' participation in group projects, especially positive rewards for working and contributing to team efforts.

Lead by example. Do you work together with other group leaders to solve problems or develop work processes that cross unit lines? If you have such team success stories to tell, share them with Walter and the rest of the group. If you don't, why not? Demonstrate your commitment to team efforts by assembling teams within your group to work on specific projects and join in those team efforts when it's appropriate.

If Walter appears to feel like an outsider:

Don't rush things. Walter may be very careful and cautious about the group and may want to be sure he's really comfortable with them before he makes overtures to participate with the group. Even though he may want to belong, pushing him can have the reverse effect from what you or he intends.

Get to know Walter well yourself. Your goal is to know him better—in the process, you may also learn why and how he feels like an outsider. If Walter has certain mannerisms that separate him from the group, sensitively discuss these issues with him. And if there are things in the way the group acts that he doesn't understand, you can help him.

Stay in touch with the group and their feelings about Walter. When both they and Walter are ready to move closer together, help the process. You might want to suggest going to lunch together or stopping for a drink after work.

If the group seems uncomfortable with Walter:

Again, don't rush things, but take the time to get to know Walter better yourself.

Listen to what your workgroup is saying about Walter. If necessary, ask several of them what they're uncomfortable with in Walter. They'll probably talk in generalities, such as "He's unfriendly," "He's just *different*." Push them (gently) for specifics. You may, for example, discover that group members consider him too loud, or a know-it-all.

Now, as you talk with Walter, help him understand how the group is and how they see him. Where possible, tactfully point out the mannerisms and habits that bother them. Don't push him to change, just help him understand how they see him. If Walter gets defensive, don't get defensive yourself. Just stay friendly and objective and help him understand.

As you get to know Walter better, help your other employees understand him. Encourage them to talk with him, to understand him better, and to help him understand them. Don't push—just try quietly to help Walter and the others become more comfortable with one another. When the time is right, you might want to suggest a group activity that will include Walter.

If they are genuinely discriminating against Walter:

This is clearly unacceptable behavior and the earlier suggestions no longer apply. Talk to one or two people in the workgroup who seem to be most determined in their rejection of Walter. Remind them that discrimination in the workplace is illegal and you as their supervisor are dedicated to ensuring that no one in your workgroup discriminates against another.

Then follow through. Assign Walter to projects that require group work and hold the entire group accountable both for the quality of the results and for the quality of their team efforts. Impose whatever consequences are appropriate (written reprimand, dismissal, and so forth) for continued discriminatory behavior.

Be sure that nothing in your own words or behavior might lead your group to believe that you'll tolerate discrimination.

SOMETHING TO THINK ABOUT

Much of the problem we've described here is best solved by recruiting and selection procedures that weed out applicants who lack good teamwork skills. While it won't solve your problem with Walter, you can avoid other "Walter" problems in the future if you look for evidence of good (or poor) interaction when you interview applicants or when you check their references.

Ask each applicant you interview whether he or she prefers to work alone or with other people. Ask applicants to describe a particularly challenging "people problem" they've faced, and how they resolved the situation. When you talk to former supervisors (and talk to at least one!), inquire about the applicant's interaction skills in each of those jobs.

No. 6 SUBVERSIVE SUBORDINATE

An employee won't tell you when something's bothering her, then disrupts the group

THE SCENE

There goes Darla again! You *knew* she wasn't happy about your sending Glenda on the trip to Phoenix with her. She wanted to spend time visiting relatives, and now she'll feel obligated to socialize with Glenda at least part of the time they're out there. But did she say anything to you about it? No, of course not. She complained to Ken, Tricia, and Curt about how insensitive and biased you are. This would have been bad enough a year ago, but now that you're trying to emphasize teamwork and cooperation it's even worse. How are you going to get your group working as a team when Darla complains to everyone about you, and never comes to you with the problem?

POSSIBLE CAUSES

Darla may dislike your decisions but may not believe she has a good enough reason to challenge them.

She doesn't think she can persuade you to change, but she at least wants someone to sympathize with her tough break.

Darla may believe that complaining to you won't do any good.

Have you established a relationship with your employees in which they trust you to listen to their concerns and act on them? If not, then they won't come to you when they're unhappy. They'll try other tactics.

This may simply be how Darla learned to deal with conflict.

She never learned how to deal directly with individuals who upset her. Because managers often don't like workers to complain to them, Darla's habit may have been reinforced at past jobs.

> ***Hint****:* While this kind of situation is rarely a serious problem in itself, it can lead to more serious problems, particularly if it gets out of hand in a workgroup that needs to work closely together. Darla and one or two others may habitually complain about your decisions at first, leading to some grumbling in the ranks. Then there seems to be slightly less cooperation among the group. Finally, the group begins to have significant trouble working together, and productivity begins to suffer. It's best to identify the initial problem and deal with it before it grows out of control.

YOUR RESPONSE

If Darla dislikes your decisions but doesn't believe she has a good enough reason to challenge them:

It's inevitable that you, as a manager, will make some decisions your employees won't like, even if they agree that they're reasonable decisions. But if an employee is unhappy simply because a decision you've made, sound though it may be, inconveniences him or her, there's not much you can do to change that.

If Darla limits her grumbling to ordinary, everyday griping and doesn't really disrupt the group, it's probably better to let her express her feelings, work through them with her peers, and get back to work. If that's all that's involved, you can ignore most of her grumbling.

Nonetheless, give Darla an opportunity to express her feelings to yous too. Even if the decision is one you can't change, she needs to know that you, as well as her co-workers, empathize with her and that you'll listen to her with an open mind. She also needs to be aware that, whether she comes to express her concerns to you directly or not, you'll likely find out what she's saying to the group.

If Darla believes that complaining to you won't do any good:

There are several steps you could take:

- Look first in your own backyard. Is there anything you've been doing in your relationship with Darla that would make her believe you won't listen? Or that you'll listen, and make empty promises to fix things? If so, fix your own problem before you approach Darla. Unless you change what you're doing so that employees believe that coming to you will make a difference, it won't matter how much you talk about having an open door. Your door may be open, but is anybody really home?

- If you're not aware of anything you're doing to discourage Darla from coming to you when something's bothering her, approach her about the problem directly. Ask her why she doesn't feel free to talk with you about her dissatisfaction. Listen carefully to what she says; don't argue or disagree with her.

- Because Darla has a specific concern, is there something you can do to resolve or minimize the problem? Could you offer to let her out of this trip entirely, since it's not working out the way she'd like? Maybe you could send Glenda for just part of the time. Or perhaps you could let Darla take some extra vacation time once the work is completed so she can mix business and pleasure. Try to find a way to demonstrate that you hear her concerns and that you're prepared to do what you can to help her.

- Make sure Darla knows you're aware of how she's been dealing with her dissatisfactions and that you don't think she's using the most productive methods to resolve them. Encourage her to come to you directly in the future, and explain that you can only fix problems you know about—that there's not much you can do in response to vague grumbling. And make sure she knows the impact her griping to others can have on the workgroup's ability to work together.

- It may take a few attempts before Darla gets the message. But once she sees that coming to you really does yield results—maybe not every time, but often enough—she'll change. She may even encourage others who complain to her to come to you instead.

If this is how Darla learned to deal with conflict:

Darla has learned to deal with conflict not by dealing with its source but by *avoiding* its source. Of the three causes, this is by far the most serious and the hardest to manage effectively. What should you do?

- Begin by establishing, publicizing, and then living by an open-door policy. Make it clear that if someone in the workgroup is dissatisfied with a decision or action of yours, you want the individual to come to you with the dissatisfaction—and to come to you promptly. Then demonstrate that you'll listen and, whenever possible, deal with the individual's dissatisfaction. Give everyone, including Darla, the chance to use this open door.

- Now if Darla persists in complaining to other group members, you can challenge her on it. (They may get tired of it, and challenge her as well.) This won't make everything right, but it will start to put pressure on Darla to change because she now has another clear alternative.

- If she continues to complain to others, and particularly if her complaints disrupt the group, you need to begin counseling her. Make sure she understands the damage she can do to the workgroup, and that you will not permit this damage.

- If Darla still doesn't change, make sure her lack of teamwork is reflected in her next performance appraisal. And if she continually disrupts the group with her complaints, counsel her that you may have to let her go. (Yes, when close teamwork is required, constantly disrupting the group could get serious enough to merit termination.)

SOMETHING TO THINK ABOUT

When workgroups were more or less loose collections of individual workers, teamwork wasn't required. In today's business environment, though, the individuals in many workgroups must work closely with one another to get the group's job done. Even when a group isn't called a team, it performs more and more like one.

In these circumstances, the ability to bring up and resolve conflict is a survival necessity. Conflict will always occur. Individual workers will always have dissatisfactions with your decisions and with the decisions or actions of other workers. It won't work to cover up the conflict by encouraging everyone to keep a "positive mental attitude" that prevents individuals from acknowledging the conflict.

What will work? Respect for the feelings and thoughts of everyone on the team and the willingness to deal with employees openly and frankly on any matter that concerns them. As the manager, you take the lead by demonstrating this attitude in your own performance, and you get the workgroup the training they need to practice it themselves.

No. 7 High-Maintenance Colleague

A staff member refuses to deal with anyone in your workgroup but you

THE SCENE

You sigh as John Wolensky closes the door behind him. You've just taken 20 minutes to clear up a problem for him. That's 10 minutes longer than it should have taken. More important, it should never have happened at all. John's refusal to deal with anyone but you was bad enough before, but now that the organization is stressing teamwork it's even worse. John should have dealt directly with the person in your unit who really does this work, person to person. Not only did he waste the time you spent playing go-between, but he caused you to interfere with employees' ability to deal directly with each other. But John won't bring his problems directly to the folks in your unit. How do you get him to change?

POSSIBLE CAUSES

John doesn't have confidence in your people.

His dealings with your workgroup in the past haven't been satisfactory from his point of view. He doesn't believe that he'll get the response he needs if he goes directly to your workers.

He isn't comfortable with the team idea and is still working as though you headed a traditional workgroup.

One of the ways he can feel he's retained his status and authority as a senior staff member is to refuse to deal with anyone he considers "beneath" him.

Your workgroup hasn't matured to the point that they can manage their contacts yet.

They're accustomed to getting all of their directions from you, and they still need to pick up the skills required to deal effectively with other staff members.

YOUR RESPONSE

No matter what the situation is:

Have an informal talk with John. Find out why he wants to deal with you. This may take some tact; John may or may not be willing to level with you. And you certainly don't want to seem unresponsive to him. Be patient. If he begins to tell you that he thinks you or the workgroup fall short, don't argue or get defensive. Listen. You may believe he's wrong, but this is not the place to tell him so.

Maybe you can get an idea of what his reasons are. Perhaps it's your unit's shortcomings as he sees them; perhaps it's his attempt to preserve his traditional senior role. Make your best guess about the cause and use the information in the response below, but be prepared to switch to another tack if the first one isn't working.

If John doesn't have confidence in your people:

Talk to John again if necessary and get all the details you can. Ask him to give your people a chance to provide directly what he needs.

Then meet with your group and go over what he said. The group may be tempted to argue or get defensive. Let them, but don't let them stop there. Help them move through their emotional reaction to planning how to meet John's needs. Then see that they do so.

An effective way to help your workers establish some independence of action and at the same time see that they perform effectively is to help them schedule follow-ups with John. If your workgroup is continuing to fall short of John's expectations, group members will be more apt to listen carefully and take the criticism seriously if it's coming directly from John, not from John and then through you to your unit.

If John isn't comfortable with the team idea and still wants to preserve his own sense of status and seniority in the company:

You may have found this out when you talked with John. Dealing directly with you may be important to him, particularly if he holds strong beliefs about protocol. Dealing directly with your subordinate staff may appear inappropriate. And no matter what other reasons he may have, he believes that if he has to go to your workers for help, he's demeaning himself.

Remember, whatever his reason, and no matter how inconvenient his behavior is, this is an honestly held belief. You're not going to get him to change it by attacking it. So what can you do?

More than anything else, you can model the appropriate behavior. Let him see that you trust your workgroup to deal with others directly. If the occasion arises, mention how you prepared the unit to do this and how you follow up to ensure that it's done effectively.

What will be more persuasive than anything else, though, is your own understanding of your new role as a coach, teacher, and mentor for your unit. Have you gained this understanding? If you haven't, then you need to make it a top priority for yourself.

Then show this understanding in your everyday actions and demonstrate to John that he doesn't have to hold on to his old role. Be patient, though. This will take time, probably for both you and John.

If your workgroup hasn't matured to the point that they can manage their contacts yet:

In this case, you and John should be able to agree that this is the situation and that you will work together to help the group develop.

Try this. When one of your employees has an issue to be worked out with John, meet with the employee and make sure that he or she understands the issue clearly and has devised an effective way to present it. Then schedule a meeting that includes you, your employee, and John. Although you'll be sitting in on the meeting, don't intervene unless your worker is clearly over his or her head. Two or three sessions like this should develop your employees to the point that they're ready to schedule and manage the meetings on their own.

SOMETHING TO THINK ABOUT

It's extremely important for your people to be able to deal directly with their customers—whether they're external or internal customers. If you keep acting as an intermediary, their job commitment will start fading, as will their productivity. Discipline yourself to deal only with the most unusual and complex situations. Let your workgroup handle all the others.

No. 8 Defensive Colleague

Another manager accuses your unit of undermining her authority

THE SCENE

"Just where do your people think they get the authority to screw up my workgroup?!" Myra Sanderson glares at you across your desk.

"I have no idea what you're talking about."

"What do you mean? You're the one who lets them get away with it, and for all I know you put them up to it!" Myra accuses.

"At least tell me what they've supposedly done."

"There's no 'supposedly' to it. I called in Denzil, my senior worker, and told him I needed to get together with him to plan what to do about the joint visit to Global Insurance next week. He told me it was already taken care of, that he and a couple of other members of my workgroup had met with some people from your workgroup and planned the whole thing out. That's my job, and I don't want your people or anyone else interfering with it. You tell your people to back off."

POSSIBLE CAUSES

Myra is willing for her unit to become more self-managing, but isn't ready for this step yet.

She may be taking it more slowly than you are, either because of her personal preference or because her unit isn't as ready as yours was.

Myra expects her people to operate like a traditional workgroup with her as the supervisor, while you've helped your workgroup become much more of a self-managing team.

Individually and collectively, the members of your workgroup have more freedom and authority than the members of her workgroup do.

> *Hint:* When an organization is stressing teamwork and encouraging independent, even self-managing teams, this kind of stress can easily develop. Some supervisors and their workgroups will move toward autonomy and self-management faster than others. It's almost impossible to avoid this. The key is to minimize the conflict it causes as much as possible and to overcome the stress as quickly as possible.

YOUR RESPONSE

If Myra is willing for her unit to become more self-managing, but isn't ready for this step yet:

You can hope that this is the cause, because it's much easier to deal with than the next cause, but you won't know until you listen to Myra at greater length.

If this is why she still holds her workgroup in, tactfully offer to work with her, or let your people work with hers, to develop her group. Schedule one or two joint meetings in which the workers in the units carry most of the responsibility, but the two of you sit in and take over if the groups begin to lose their way.

If it helps her feel more comfortable with the situation, have your group prepare an agenda for the meeting that you and she agree on and revise as necessary before the meeting.

Myra expects her people to operate like a traditional workgroup with her as the supervisor, while you've helped your workgroup become much more of a self-managing team:

If this is the case, you and Myra—and your workgroups—have a serious conflict in the way you want to operate. To begin with, your group will have to back off some. They can do all of the work they would normally do, but then they'll have to let you arrange any meetings with Myra's unit. They may also need to let you meet with Myra instead of the two units meeting. Make sure they understand that this isn't what you want to do and that you're working to improve the situation.

Another important factor to consider is the strength of your company's commitment to teams. Is "team" just another name for the traditional workgroup, so that you and Myra are both expected to manage as you always have, perhaps with a bit more emphasis on cooperation? If that's the case, you'll have to work closely with your unit to minimize any future confrontations with Myra or any other supervisors who want to remain in the traditional role. You and your unit should try to find a few other units whose supervisors are willing to let them have some autonomy and work as closely with them as possible.

Suppose, though, that the company is really serious about strong teams with a great deal of autonomy. That means you and your team are doing what the organization wants. You can be more aggressive in trying to help Myra change. Work actively with her to let her unit have as much autonomy as possible when dealing with your own team. (She can hold the reins in her unit's relations with other teams, if she wants.) Keep reminding her, as gently as possible, that what you're advocating is what the organization expects from both of you.

Keep demonstrating your understanding of your new management roles. If you genuinely see yourself as a coach, teacher, and mentor and help Myra understand what this means, she may become more willing to move out of her traditional role.

Remember, though, that you're trying to make progress in team self-management at the same time that you're trying to maintain good relations with Myra and other traditional supervisors. Don't concentrate on one to the exclusion of the other.

SOMETHING TO THINK ABOUT

When an organization decides to make use of highly autonomous teams, first-level supervisors often see this as a threat. In one sense, it certainly is. Not only will the organization not need traditional supervisors, it will need fewer managers of any kind. First- and second-level managers often respond to this by opposing and even attempting to sabotage the transition to teams. In turn, this often leads organizations to fire these managers—a kind of self-fulfilling prophecy for the naysayers.

How do you prevent this? Even when an organization depends heavily on teams, it needs some managers to oversee the teams, coordinate their activities, and ensure that the teams are going in the direction higher management wants. As teams are being established, successful managers become teachers, coaches, and mentors. As teams become more effective, managers keep these roles to a certain extent, but also learn how to coordinate the activities of these autonomous teams.

The moral? Be prepared to change. Find out whether your company is willing to give you training and support in your new roles. If not, find the training for yourself and learn how to perform your new roles effectively—even if you have to learn on your own time.

CHAPTER TWO

Keeping Up with Evolving Employee Expectations

No. 9 Child Care Complications

An employee brings his son to work whenever the baby-sitter isn't available

THE SCENE

You look up from your papers to see a freckled little face peering around the door frame.

"I know you. You're Saul Freeman's son. Did your dad bring you in to help around the office?"

"Yeah. My babysitter's sick, so Dad said I could come spend the day with him. Whatcha doing? Can I watch?"

POSSIBLE CAUSES

Saul may have his son infrequently and so not have regular baby-sitting backup arrangements.

Even though Saul's baby-sitter seems incredibly unreliable, he brings his son to the office only every few months—it just seems like more often.

Saul may not have adequate child care arrangements for his son and thus brings him to work frequently.

If the situation occurs often, or if your work situation is particularly inappropriate for children (for example, because it requires work around machinery

31

or direct customer contact), you'll need to take a much more directive approach with Saul.

> *Hint:* Some companies (although not many) do have specific policies about bringing children into the work environment. Places where children are almost *never* allowed include production lines in factories, warehouse and transportation facilities, health-care facilities, high-security environments, and workplaces that involve regular customer contact. Even offices and retail stores may have specific rules about when and how often children may visit. Check with your personnel department to see if your company has such rules.
>
> Note, too, that many companies now have on-site day care for workers' children. In that case, the company probably does have policies governing children in the work areas—and, for the most part, workers would be expected to bring their children to the day care facility rather than the work environment.

YOUR RESPONSE

Regardless of the cause:

Whatever your policy or your company's policy about employees bringing their children to work, whenever children are allowed to visit, you must have a *standard* set of rules for their behavior. Some children—regardless of their ages—don't know how to behave in a professional environment. They roam the halls, walk unannounced into workers' offices, whine for money for the snack machines, and generally disrupt the entire office.

Make it clear to your employees that children are welcome only if they use their "company manners." You can acknowledge that children, especially young children, are incapable of acting like little adults, but make it clear that their parents are responsible for ensuring that children who are brought to work cause as little turmoil to the rest of the staff as possible. And keep in mind that not all of your workers will necessarily jump for joy at the idea of little ones prancing through the aisles. Adults who are not accustomed to having children around aren't always prepared for the playful sounds of even well behaved children. Your rules should be sensitive to the needs of all your workers, parents and non-parents alike.

As we mentioned earlier, it's important that you have a *standard* set of rules for children's behavior. If you allow some children to roam the halls, but require that others stay in their parents' offices, or if you allow some children to congregate in the snack room, but not all children, you're inviting hard feelings from the parents whose children are excluded. And it's best to let your workers know in advance what your expectations are. That way, parents whose children aren't capable of conforming to the rules will know (hopefully) to keep them at home—or at least you'll be able to gently remind them of the rules when the children cause a nuisance.

If Saul brings his son in only infrequently:

Unless there are specific reasons for *not* allowing Saul to bring his son to the office occasionally (such as those we mentioned earlier), there's probably no harm done, as long as the child is well behaved. Let Saul know what your expectations are for children's behavior and how often you can tolerate having children in the office (and for how long at a time).

The decision regarding how often is too often for Saul to bring his son to work is a judgment call and is very much dependent on the specific environment in which you operate. In an office setting where workers have their own private work spaces, with few outside visitors or customers, it's probably acceptable to allow school-aged children to come to the office *briefly* on a fairly frequent basis. Many children are expected to call their parents when they get home from school, and a visit of 15 to 20 minutes every week or so is no more of a distraction. However, younger children should be allowed to visit the office only infrequently. Their activity level and the need for more attention make their visits much more disruptive.

How long is too long is also a judgment call. In general, we suggest that children be allowed to visit for only an hour or so at a time. On special occasions, such as designated children-at-work days or for a company picnic, longer visits are acceptable. But children tire much faster than adults, and the strain of extended "company manners" is often more than they can handle. Further, you must avoid creating the impression that the work site can substitute for regular day care by allowing extended visits.

If Saul brings his son in fairly frequently:

Talk to Saul about the disruption to the work (his and others') caused by having his child in the office. You can empathize with his baby-sitting dilemma, yet remain firm on your position that children do not belong at work. Emphasize that, even if his son is well behaved and relatively self-sufficient, you cannot reasonably draw a line between allowing his son to come regularly to the office and not allowing others to bring their children. Work out with Saul a timetable for making reliable baby-sitting arrangements. Explain that, if he's still bringing his son to work after the deadline has passed, he'll have to take his son home and care for him there. Then follow through.

If company policy allows, and if Saul's work assignments are appropriate, you might explore with him the possibility of working at home occasionally. If this alternative is a useful one, you'll want to work with him to determine the amount of time he can work at home (for example, a limit on the number of hours each week) and to establish performance expectations for his work-at-home assignments. If his work is repetitive, the expectations can be standard (such as seven documents processed for every hour of home work time). If his assignments vary or if his work can't be measured quantitatively, you'll need to define your expectations more flexibly. (Of course, if Saul is a marginal worker who needs closer supervision even when he's at work, work-at-home is *not* a good idea.)

SOMETHING TO THINK ABOUT

Child care, as well as "elder care," are important concerns to a large percentage of workers. If your company does not have on-site day care facilities and you have a significant number of employees who have young children, suggest that your human resources department look into establishing a partnership with a nearby provider. This need not involve any outlay of company funds and need not include subsidies for the day care costs. Many providers will be willing to offer at least nominal discounts to employees in return for your publicizing their facilities in your company newsletter, or providing transportation from the company to the facility, or donating occasional time or talent. This very small investment can give your workers security and peace of mind that will allow them to concentrate on the work at hand, rather than worrying about the welfare of children or parents.

NO. 10 POST PARTUM EMPLOYMENT GAP

A request for six months maternity leave puts you in a bind

THE SCENE

You lower the paper in your hands and stare in disappointment at Wendy. "Six *whole* months?" you ask.

"Well, yes," replies Wendy. "You know when Josh was born, I needed to get back to work right away because we had just moved into the new house and we had so many other bills. But I really missed spending the time at home with him. With the new baby, I'm in a position to be able to take some time off, and I really think the whole family will be better off for it."

You can't fault her reasoning, but this sure puts you in a pickle.

POSSIBLE CAUSES

The cause seems simple enough: Wendy wants to have some time at home with her new baby, and perhaps also have more time to spend with her older son.

You really can't fault her reasoning, but there are several things you need to determine before you can respond to her request:

YOUR RESPONSE

Before you can respond to Wendy's request, you'll need to consider the following issues.

- What are your company's policies about extended leave—for maternity purposes or otherwise? (It's likely that there are either rules or past practice, but also likely that exceptions have occasionally been made in the past.)
- How good a worker is Wendy? Is she someone you want to retain, someone you'd just as soon have stay home permanently, or somewhere in between?
- How likely is it that Wendy will return to work after the six months are up? You'll need to talk to Wendy about her future plans, and get a commitment, if possible, that she'll be back on the job. A related issue is whether, when Wendy does return, she'll be ready to work full-time again or whether she'll want to switch to a part-time schedule for some period. (The next Challenge can give you some ideas about how to respond to a request for part-time work.)
- Can you accommodate Wendy's request and still accomplish the work your unit is charged with? Although we've left this question until last, it may be the most important one you have to answer. If Wendy does the same kind of work as other people in your unit or if her work doesn't require specialized skills or training (or it requires skills or training other people in your unit already have), the answer isn't too difficult. But if she's in a one-of-a-kind position, you've got a harder problem.

Next, find out what your company's policies are. Many companies do have standard policies for granting maternity leave. Not too many years ago, six to eight weeks was the "normal" amount of time workers were given for maternity leave, and whether that leave was paid or unpaid depended on the company's policies and, often, on how much sick leave and vacation time the employee had accrued. Since 1993, however, the policies of many companies have been altered as a result of the Family and Medical Leave Act.

The Family and Medical Leave Act (FMLA) includes provisions that define which employers are covered and which employees are entitled to leave under the Act. In general, the Act requires covered employers to grant up to 12 weeks of *unpaid* leave in each 12 month period to eligible employees for the birth of a child or placement of a child for adoption or foster care, for the care of an immediate family member (including spouse, child, parent, and certain other individuals), or for the employee's own serious health condition. Early in your planning, be sure to consult your company's personnel department or legal counsel to determine the Act's applicability and requirements in your specific situation. In addition to the FMLA requirements, your own company or your state's laws may provide for more generous entitlements.

In Wendy's situation, however, you're facing a request for considerably more leave than an employee is entitled to under the FMLA, so we'll assume that you have some flexibility in responding to her request.

If your company's policies could accommodate an absence of six months:

Decide whether you can afford to spare Wendy for that long and whether you *want* to in light of her performance and contributions to the unit. If you can let her have the leave and she's been a good employee, then grant the time she's requested. Have Wendy make a detailed list of the tasks she performs, whether on a regular basis or only occasionally, and determine which of your other employees will cover each item. Establish in advance a date by which she'll return to work.

If Wendy waffles about when she'll be ready to come back to the company, then, as a condition of granting her leave beyond her entitlements, you might want to have her sign a resignation letter which says that, if she's not returned by the agreed-upon date, the company is to consider her continued absence as notice of resignation. You can provide that the letter of resignation can be renegotiated, but having the letter in your files will save you from having to terminate Wendy later if she decides not to return to work at the agreed-upon date after all.

If you can't accommodate Wendy's request, then explain to her what the obstacles are and try to negotiate a compromise. The next response contains several suggestions.

Be creative in looking for solutions. Perhaps you can borrow an employee from another unit who has skills comparable to Wendy's—either on a full-time basis for part of Wendy's absence or for occasional assignments throughout that period. Perhaps you can arrange for coverage through a temporary placement agency. In larger metropolitan areas, there are agencies that accommodate staffing needs even for professional services such as medical, legal, and accounting.

Perhaps you could even cover some of Wendy's work yourself if you have the skills and if Wendy's retention is that much of a plus to your unit.

SOMETHING TO THINK ABOUT

If one of your workers is planning an extended absence, whether for maternity leave, sabbatical, or some other reason, do as much as you can during that absence to keep the employee tuned in to what's happening back at the company. If your company has a newsletter or other "people" publication that emphasizes human interest stories rather than technical information, make sure your employee still gets copies at her home, along with any notices regarding social functions, such as the company picnic or Christmas party. Invite the employee to lunch occasionally as well as to attend occasional office meetings, especially those that may include important announcements, such as new product lines.

The better you are at staying in touch with your absent employee, the more he or she will still feel like a valued member of the team—and the more likely the employee will want to return.

If your company's policies won't accommodate an absence of six months:

If keeping Wendy on your staff is important to the success of your unit, talk to the policy makers—either your boss or the people in your human resources department—about making an exception to the policies to allow Wendy to have the time off she's requested. If no exception is possible, then try to negotiate with Wendy some alternate arrangements. Ideas you might consider include:

• Grant Wendy the time off work she's entitled to, but then have her come in part-time for a longer period or let her work at home as part of her regular work schedule. (Other challenges in this chapter discuss each of these options.)

- Work out a "consulting agreement" with Wendy under which she agrees to be available (after a few weeks at home with the baby) to help out with specified assignments, either by doing them herself or by assisting another worker.

- Assign Wendy responsibility during the last few weeks she's on the job to identify sources of coverage for her work while she's gone—either within the company or outside. Agree that, if she can find adequate resources, she can have the full six months at home with the baby, but, if she can't arrange for adequate coverage, she'll need to be prepared to come back to work.

And if you don't really care whether Wendy ever returns or not, then, of course, your response should be to grant her only as much leave as you're required to and let her make her own choice about whether or not to return.

No. 11 Putting Baby First

A mother-to-be wants a part-time schedule after the baby comes

THE SCENE

"I've been thinking a lot about how things will change when the baby is born," Nicole begins, "and I really think I want to be able to spend some time at home with her—not just when she's a newborn, but as she begins to interact, too. I want her to know her mom not just as that lady who leaves every morning and comes home and drops into the armchair every night, but as somebody who's there when she needs her. So I've decided that when I come back from maternity leave, I'd like to switch to a part-time schedule. Maybe I could work just a couple of days a week, at least for a while. What do you think?"

What you think is that this is going to be really hard to arrange. Nicole is a very good employee, but with all the cuts in the company lately, losing half the production of one of the workers you've managed to retain is going to hurt.

POSSIBLE CAUSES

As with the preceding challenge, the cause here seems clear, but handling it can be tricky.

You need to weigh the pluses and minuses of granting Nicole's request, looking at the same kinds of factors examined in the earlier Challenge: Nicole's contributions to the company, how unique her skills and talents are, the workload in your unit, and the length of time Nicole wants to be on a part-time schedule. This analysis will result in one of four possibilities:

- Nicole's not a very good worker, and you don't have any reason to accommodate her request.
- Nicole makes a real contribution to the company, and her work *can* be covered by other employees. However, this will require several employees to take on more work than they're accustomed to.
- Nicole's work can't realistically be covered by the rest of your unit, either because no one else has the skills and training needed to do the job or because everyone else is so busy that they can't absorb Nicole's work too.
- Nicole makes a contribution to the company, but her work can be covered by other employees without much sacrifice.

YOUR RESPONSE

If Nicole isn't a very good worker:

Nicole's request could be a real blessing. Of course, your response will be to tell her, pleasantly and regretfully, that you're just not in a position to move her to a part-time schedule. Her response to that will either be to come back to work at the end of her maternity leave (in which case you're probably no worse off than before the maternity leave) or to decide she'd rather be at home full-time and give you notice of her resignation (in which case you're probably better off than before the maternity leave).

Be aware that even though Nicole says that she'll come back to work, that doesn't mean she will actually return. She may very well hedge her bets by job-hunting while she's home with the baby, so you may not know her real answer until the maternity leave expires.

If Nicole is a good employee and her work could be covered by other employees in the unit, albeit with some difficulty:

Grant Nicole's request. If some of the work she'll be transferring to others is work with which they're not familiar, set aside time in the last few weeks before her maternity leave for her to train the employees who are picking up her assignments. Make sure Nicole and the other employees know that she'll be available on a continuing basis after her return to assist with unusually heavy workload or problem situations.

This may also be an excellent opportunity for you to engage in some process improvement work in your unit. Call together the staff members who'll be asked to cover some of Nicole's assignments and ask them to examine the full range of their job duties. Have them prioritize, according to their understanding of the job, the work they're responsible for. Then review the priority lists with the group to determine whether there are tasks that don't need to be performed at all, tasks that could be assigned elsewhere, or tasks that could be given less time and attention. In accommodating Nicole's request, you may be able to improve the efficiency of the entire unit.

If Nicole's work can't realistically be covered by the rest of the unit:

Let Nicole know what the problems are in granting her request and enlist her aid in figuring out a solution that will ensure that the work is covered but allows her to work part-time. Some options you might consider are:

- Negotiating a schedule with Nicole that doesn't reduce her hours as drastically as she's requested. Perhaps if she'd be willing to work three or three and a half days a week instead of two, as she requested, she could perform her most critical assignments and the rest could be absorbed elsewhere.
- Explore a job sharing arrangement. Perhaps there are other people in the company, or elsewhere in the community, who have the skills necessary to perform Nicole's job and who would also like to work less than a full-time schedule. Job sharing schedules need not be full-day schedules. Perhaps both Nicole and her job partner could each work several hours each day instead.
- Talk to Nicole about working a part-time schedule temporarily rather than on a permanent basis. If she'd be willing to work part-time for a few months (or even a year or so), but agrees to revert to a full-time schedule at the end of that time, you may be able to find temporary help to fill the gap. The company could hire a part-time worker on a temporary basis, or you could arrange for assistance through a job placement agency.
- Determine whether Nicole could do some of her work at home. She wouldn't have as much free time to spend with her child, but she would be more available to him and, depending on the kind of work she does, might have more flexibility in scheduling when she does her work.

If you just can't figure out a way to accommodate Nicole's request, let her know that as soon as possible. Encourage her to stay with the company, but recognize that she now has a tough choice to make.

If Nicole is a good worker, but her assignments can be covered by the rest of your unit without much sacrifice on their parts:

Grant Nicole's request, but recognize that you may be faced with a more significant management issue than the question of whether to allow one worker to switch to a part-time schedule. Unless your unit is a large one, so that the amount of work to be picked up by each of your other workers isn't that great, being able to do with a part-time worker in place of a full-time worker is likely to give your boss the impressions that your department is over-staffed. Make sure your boss knows that you're monitoring your staffing needs and making appropriate adjustments, either by accomplishing more work or by cutting extraneous positions. Then do it.

SOMETHING TO THINK ABOUT

If granting Nicole's request to work part-time will result in significant accommodations by other employees in your unit, be sure to earmark some of the money you'll be saving on her salary and benefits to reward the employees who are affected by her schedule change. Consider making one-time awards to employees who are particularly helpful in the transition, especially if Nicole's part-time schedule is just a temporary one. It may also be appropriate to use some of the funds for permanent salary increases, particularly for employees who will need to acquire more demanding skills to accomplish the work.

But make sure that the employees who are still working their regular schedules know that you appreciate their cooperation and team spirit, and be sure to recognize their contributions in a tangible way.

No. 12 Smart Decision, Bad Timing

Your top staffer asks to go part time to attend college — just as an important project begins

THE SCENE

Why did Maria have to do this to you now? A year ago you'd have been happy to give her a leave of absence for college. Eighteen months from now, you'd be happy to give it to her. But six weeks from now, the week after you start reviewing every company operation to see whether it could be contracted out? Ow!

If it were anyone but Maria, the answer would be simple: "No." Maria, though, has been with you for five years, and she's an excellent worker. If ever anyone deserved help getting through college, it's her. How in the world can you tell her "no?" But how can you tell her "yes"?

POSSIBLE CAUSES

The causes aren't the critical elements. Whatever Maria's reasons are for wanting to go to college, you support them. Your real concerns are: (1) how you can help her get college courses without totally disrupting your operations, and (2) how useful those courses will be to the company.

YOUR RESPONSE

If Maria's education will make her more valuable to the company and you expect her to stay with you:

In this case, both you and Maria benefit and you should do everything you can to help her get her college courses. No matter what arrangements the two of you make, though, you need to keep these two points in mind:

If possible, the company should provide financial assistance. This shows your support for her ambitions and will probably help her concentrate on her studies. If the company has a program for this, use it. If not, talk with your boss and anyone else who can help arrange it.

Make all your commitments contingent upon successful performance at work and at college. The two of you should make your agreements on a quarter-by-quarter (or semester-by-semester) basis. At the end of the quarter, the two of you should take a look at how she's doing and make a decision about the next quarter.

Here are some of the options the two of you can consider:

- *Maria can convert to part time.* For instance, could she take off only a few hours each week for the courses themselves and do all of her homework at night and on weekends? This would keep her on the job, and if she's really that good she may accomplish more part time than a replacement could working full time.

You have a strong motivator working here. If Maria sees that you've really made an effort to support her college goals, she'll probably work even harder during the time she's on the job.

- *She does some work at home.* If you really need her full time, would it help if she did some of her work at home? Perhaps she could take time off during the day for college and then make it up by doing work at home at night or on the weekend.

This doesn't give her the additional time for college. It does give her more control over her schedule, and that may be enough to make it practical.

- *She attends college at night.* If you just can't spare her, can she attend college at night? This may put quite a strain on her, particularly if she has children or has to care for her own parents. Look at it carefully, though, because there are steps you can take to make it easier for her.

For instance, you might work out a flexible work schedule for her. If she has a late class, she might start work an hour or two later than normal the next day. If she needs a class that starts in late afternoon, perhaps she can start work earlier on the days she attends that class.

Working at home can also help, for the same reasons that we mentioned earlier. If she has a job that permits this, allowing her a lot of flexibility could be a major help to her.

If you can agree that she'll go to school at night, at least while the project is "hot," you should provide her as much financial assistance as possible. If she's really that good and your company will allow it, could you pay even for extra expenses such as baby-sitters and parking if that's what it takes?

- *She puts off attending college.* This is a last resort. If none of the alternatives we've looked at work, would she be willing to wait a year or 18 months to start?

Don't make the effort one-sided. If you're going to ask her to wait on something as important as this, there needs to be some commitment on your side, too. For instance, you might make a firm commitment that she can start part-time in a year, no matter what. Does that make you nervous? You've given yourself a year to plan to handle it, and that should be enough time.

If Maria's education won't make her more valuable to the company:

Suppose she wants to become a nurse, but you're an accounting firm? Or she wants to prepare herself for a job where you already have plenty of well-qualified applicants. In other words, the education she wants may pay off for her but it doesn't pay off for you.

The list of alternatives here isn't as long. One of the first is to talk with her about taking courses that *will* help the company. If you're an accounting firm and she doesn't want to become an accountant, could she study human resources management? The company might be able to use that skill.

What about reducing the number of hours she works over several years? The first semester or two, she works full time and goes at night. Then she shifts to half time for a few semesters as she trains a replacement. When she finishes her education and moves to a new career, she leaves a fully trained replacement behind her.

If these suggestions won't work, is there another way that you could support her desire for education and still act responsibly for the company? Do your best to find it.

SOMETHING TO THINK ABOUT

Education is a very precious possession in America in the twenty-first century. Employers need every college-trained person they can get. It benefits you to support Maria. Even if there's no immediate payback to the firm, it's probably worthwhile to help Maria get to college.

There's also a very practical reason to help. If you won't let Maria shift to part time (or otherwise help her), she has another option. She can leave you and go to work for a company that will help her get a college education. If she's good, that probably won't be too hard. Most firms are delighted to have employees who are putting themselves through college. It may be a hardship to shift her to part time, but is it more of a hardship than losing her?

If Maria is a valuable employee, do everything you can to support her as she works toward her college degree.

No. 13 Winking at the Rules

One of your best employees has asked you to make an exception for her

THE SCENE

"I know this is a little irregular, Ben, and I know I was off on the day after Thanksgiving last year, but I really need to be off again this year," Fran says. "It's important to be consistent, I know, and this policy of 'one year on, one year off' is a good one, but my parents are coming in this year. The kids and

I haven't seen them for three years, and I'd really appreciate being able to spend some time with them. Couldn't you make an exception, just this once?"

POSSIBLE CAUSES

If we assume that Fran's reasons for wanting you to make an exception are legitimate, then it doesn't matter much beyond that what they are. The real questions here have to do with the rule itself and the importance of applying it consistently. To decide what to do when an employee requests an exception to a work rule, ask yourself the following questions:

- *How important is the rule?* In this case, Fran's asking you to make an exception to a rule that's clearly discretionary (determining who gets to take off the day after a major holiday). But if the rule were something affecting workers' safety (like a requirement to wear a hard hat in certain areas) or if it affected the quality of your unit's products or services (like a request to skip a checking step to meet a customer's production requirements), your flexibility in granting exceptions would be more limited.

- *How much discretion do you have in granting exceptions?* Is this a rule you made, or is it a part of your labor agreement? Is it something your superiors require, that they consider "sacred" even if you don't? What are the bounds of your authority to make exceptions?

- *What message do you want to send to your employees about this rule, or your application of it?* It doesn't matter *what* kind of exception Fran is asking for, or how discreet you and she are about granting the request. You can almost guarantee that *someone* else in the unit is going to find out that you've made an exception. Is it important that you be as consistent as possible in how you treat this rule, or this particular group of workers? Will granting the exception make you look like a humane and concerned manager, or will it make you look like a wimp? Will granting this exception make it harder to enforce the rule next time?

YOUR RESPONSE

If the rule isn't critical to the success of your unit and if allowing Fran the exception won't set a precedent for the rest of the group:

Allow Fran to take the time off she's asked for. Explain to her what prompted your decision so she (and other workers who may ask the same favor) will know under what circumstances you consider the exception appropriate. If possible, arrange for Fran to reciprocate (perhaps by working another day that she would normally be permitted to have off).

If the rule itself is important, but some flexibility in your application of it is appropriate:

Ask Fran for her suggestions of ways you can meet the spirit of the rule, while still granting her the exception she wants. Maybe she could trade days off with another worker. Or maybe she could work part of the day—the hours when her presence is most critical, then take the rest of the day off. Between the two of you, you should be able to come up with some accommodation that will preserve the integrity of the rule itself, without being rigid in applying it.

If you *can't* come up with a way even to meet the spirit of the rule, then you'll need to rethink how important it is. If it's really important to conform in some measure to the requirements, then you'll have to deny Fran's request.

If the rule itself isn't that important, but it's critical that you be consistent in its application:

Consider Fran's request in light of other requests for exception you may have received. Can you make a policy decision that would permit these exceptions for all workers who meet specified criteria? Maybe employees who have seniority could be permitted to select the days they'll work or request exceptions? Maybe employees could be allowed to switch with coworkers as long as both people agree?

As above, if you can't come up with a set of criteria that you could apply across the board, then think again about how important it is to be consistent. Will it really do that much damage to your ability to enforce the rules if you grant an exception to a good employee? Are there extenuating circumstances you could cite to make it clear that *won't* you grant exceptions just to suit each employee's whim?

If the rule is one over which you exercise little or no control:

Explain to Fran that you don't have the authority to grant her request. Let her know who in the supervisory chain she should see about her request and the kind of back-up information or arguments she'll need to present to have it approved. Suggest that she route her request through you on its way to the final decision maker so that you can add your recommendation for its approval, along with a summary of Fran's contributions that illustrate why it's a good idea to accommodate such a valuable employee.

SOMETHING TO THINK ABOUT

Consistency isn't as great as it sounds. While you may think that granting a request for one employee means you have to do the same thing for others, that really isn't so. Nor is it practical in many cases to come up with a policy that will cover all the possible situations and reasons for exception that may arise. Most employees will understand why you've given someone a special exception (as long as you don't favor certain employees consistently over others) and won't try to take advantage. They'll be much more impressed with your humane, reasoned approach to requests for exception than a mechanically consistent application of every rule.

Whenever an employee asks you to make an exception to a rule, particularly a rule that affects how employees are treated rather than how the work is done, ask yourself whether it's more important to be consistent or to be understanding.

No. 14 Telecommuting Tie-ups

An employee asks to work at home two days each week

THE SCENE

When Joel brings in the drafts he just completed, he also brings in a request: "You know, I think I could be just as productive working at home part of the time as I am here. How 'bout if I work a couple of days a week at home and the other three here at the office?"

POSSIBLE CAUSES

As with many of the other challenges in this chapter, the cause isn't particularly important. What's important is Joel's performance during the time he's worked for you and the nature of his work.

In evaluating Joel's performance, you'll want to look not only at how well he performs his job duties, but also at his self-management skills. If Joel produces work of acceptable quality but you have concerns about the quantity of work or his ability to schedule and organize the work appropriately, then he should not be working at home—at least not without significant reporting requirements, and perhaps a gradual transition.

YOUR RESPONSE

If Joel has the skills he needs to work at home, but the work he's assigned isn't appropriate for at-home completion:

Look first to be sure the work can't be accomplished at an alternative work site. Often, customer contact is a basic requirement of the job that seems to preclude working at home. But how does that contact occur? If it's over the telephone, you might be able to forward Joel's calls to his home or to a cell phone he uses just for work. If he meets with customers, but primarily by appointment, he might be able to schedule his appointments only on those days when he'll be in the office.

Of course, if there's a lot of "walk-in" customer traffic, there's no easy substitute for being in the office. But even in that case, do all of your customer service employees work with customers all the time? Or are some employees performing "back-room" work while others meet with customers? Perhaps Joel and another employee can schedule themselves to cover customer contact time in such a way that Joel, and your other employee too, can work part of the time at home and part of the time in the customer contact work in the office. If Joel's a good worker, don't give up too easily.

If after diligent scrutiny, you decide that there's no way the work Joel performs can be done at home, then talk to Joel about the relative importance to him of changing his schedule and of keeping the same job he has now. Perhaps he could be reassigned to an opening in a different line of work that could accommodate the flexibility he needs.

But if Joel's committed to the work he's in now (or if there aren't any other suitable openings) and the work is not amenable to performance away from the work site, this is a request you'll have to refuse.

If the work could be done at home but Joel hasn't exhibited the ability to manage his workload well:

Although working at home is usually viewed as an employee "perk," it also places more time-management demands on the employee. It's very easy to spend those work-at-home days getting up late, puttering around the house, playing with the kids, and generally frittering away the day. If you're inclined to allow Joel to work at home but you have serious doubts about his self-management and organizational skills, try one or more of these arrangements:

- If Joel's work can be measured quantitatively, give him production quotas for the days he works at home. At least in the beginning, make sure he turns in the work after each work-at-home day rather than accumulating several days of work. That way you'll be able to assess his situation more accurately.

- Even if Joel's work can't readily be measured quantitatively, you can still require him to give you regular reports of his activities on work-at-home days. For long-term projects he may be working on at home, have him develop a schedule of the various steps in the project and estimated completion dates. You may not be able to assess his production on work-at-home days specifically, but you'll be able to monitor his progress on the project's completion overall.

- Find some training for Joel in organizational and self-management skills. Require that he attend the training and develop some positive goals for himself before he begins the work-at-home schedule.

SOMETHING TO THINK ABOUT

As employees become increasingly responsible for making decisions about how and according to what schedule their work will be accomplished, and increasingly empowered to determine their own priorities and responses to difficult situations, self-management skills of the kind required for work-at-home arrangements become more and more important even in the "traditional" workplace. There are a number of sources for training your workgroup in these skills. Find one and arrange for training everyone in your unit. Even if your employees still work under close supervision and have limited discretion in performing their work, good self-management skills can help make them more productive.

As Joel demonstrates his increasing ability to manage his workload, even when working a couple of days each week at home, you can gradually loosen the controls you've instituted. In time, you should expect to give his work-at-home days no greater monitoring than you do the days he's in the office. And the self-management skills he will have developed in order to be able to work at home will increase his productivity in the rest of his job too.

If Joel begins his work-at-home schedule with satisfactory results, but his performance later deteriorates:

Look at the suggestions in Challenge 44 for ideas about how to correct a work-at-home arrangement that's gone awry.

No. 15 Excessively Casual Attire

Your team seems to be dressing more sloppily every day

THE SCENE

You walk down the hall, intent on making it to the weekly managers' meeting. But the first person you see is Jerry, striding along in khakis and a sport shirt. Then you pass Rosalinda, wearing jeans and a sweater.

"Oh, this is fine," you think, "next we'll all be wearing cutoffs and halter tops!"

POSSIBLE CAUSES

Your employees believe that casual dress is appropriate in your work setting.

Maybe your company's policies allow occasional "dress-down" days and employees have taken liberties with the policy.

Your employees don't care how they look at work.

This is especially likely if you have a group of relatively inexperienced workers or workers who are new to your work environment. They may not have a clear understanding of acceptable norms.

> ***Hint:*** How employees dress isn't an issue at all in some work environments and only a minor one in some others. But if your workers deal with customers or members of the general public in a structured setting, their appearance matters—a lot! What outsiders see in their first encounter with your organization will color all their later interactions for a long time to come.

YOUR RESPONSE

If your employees believe that very casual dress is appropriate in your work setting:

What have you done to encourage that idea? Does your own choice of clothing encourage employees to dress a little too comfortably? Does the company have "dress-down" days often? Are they based on a formal company policy, or just whenever someone feels like dressing casually?

If the problem seems to be limited to just a few employees, you can deal with each person individually. But if the problem is widespread, you'll need to get the message out more formally.

That's not as easy as it sounds. Very few companies can get by these days with explicit dress codes. Certainly, you can't require suits and ties (or the equivalent) every day. You'll be deluged with grievances and complaints, or, perhaps worse, completely ignored.

Instead, you need to develop a policy that addresses the overall image you want your workgroup to present to customers and the public. That includes not only dress, but also the way visitors are greeted, the way you'll deal with complaints, and other customer-relations matters. The policy should link the specific behaviors you expect from your employees to the overall image that the company is trying to project. If at all possible, your policy should be coordinated with other groups in your company who have similar customer or public contacts, so your employees aren't singled out with special requirements. Better yet, try to get your company president, CEO, or even department head to sign a general policy statement that applies to all, or a large segment, of the company.

The next step, as always, is to follow through. Make sure that you model the behavior you want your employees to follow. If some employees seem to have trouble with the new policies, coach them so they understand exactly what's acceptable and what isn't. When you single out for recognition employees who have been outstanding in customer service, be sure that they're also models you want others to follow. If one of your workers did a terrific job in solving a customer's problem but comes to work inappropriately dressed, *and if that matters*, then that worker shouldn't be rewarded.

And, as a last resort, you can consider sending workers home who have real customer or public contact but who report to work too sloppily attired.

If your employees don't have enough experience in a work environment to know what's appropriate:

New employees, especially those fresh out of school, often have not learned basic workplace skills. These include not only how to dress appropriately, but also such essential rules as showing up for work (and on time), doing a full day's work for a full day's pay, or letting someone know when they're sick or have an emergency that keeps them from coming to work.

But these are *learned* skills. While many of us learned those skills from our parents or at school, and so seemed (at least in retrospect) to have learned them effortlessly, we also weren't born knowing that it was important to show up for work on time, or that slashed jeans aren't appropriate office attire.

So your task here is simply to teach the new or inexperienced employees what the expectations are for the kind of work your group does. If they appear to be acting from lack of knowledge rather than from lack of interest in the job, you'll need to approach the subject with sensitivity. Matters of dress and appearance are very personal; criticisms in these areas are often much more crushing than criticisms of the work itself.

Talk separately to each employee who's dressing inappropriately. Explain the image the company needs to project and how that image is made up of many components: the way customers are addressed (for example, "Ms. X" versus "Ann"), the way their questions and complaints are handled, whether they are approached in an outgoing or reserved manner,, as well as the way company representatives dress. For each of those components, describe your expectations and how those expectations contribute to the company's overall image.

In most cases, that simple explanation will be enough. If it's not, coaching and reminders should help. But if you encounter workers who take pride in not conforming and refuse, by words or actions, to dress appropriately, you should deal with them as you would with any other performance issue. The challenges in Chapters 5, 7, and 8 can give you some ideas.

SOMETHING TO THINK ABOUT

Because dress and appearance are so personal, be careful to limit your dress requirements to those situations where it really does matter. Some studies have shown that workers actually perform more productively when they can dress casually and comfortably, rather than in conformance with some standard. And if you limit your requirements to situations where there's a clear link between the company's image and its performance with customers or the public, you're more likely to get willing compliance rather than grumbles and workers testing the limits of what's appropriate—because the payoff will be much clearer for them and for the company.

No. 16 When Boredom Sets In

Your staff complains that work isn't fun

THE SCENE

"What?!" You spin your chair around and look at Kevin and Andrea.

"We thought we owed it to you to tell you," Kevin says. "Work here just isn't very much fun. Most of the time, it's a drag. And we really don't like that. I'm not sure yet, but a couple of us are seriously considering quitting—including her." He jerks his thumb at Andrea, who nods. "I don't know if you can do anything, but at least we told you."

You sit open-mouthed as he and Andrea walk out.

POSSIBLE CAUSES

Kevin and the others have unrealistic expectations for work.

Business magazines and books often quote managers, even CEOs, who say that work should be fun. So new workers expect that it will be.

They miss the socializing they've been used to on other jobs.

Many of the companies that offer temporary, low-skilled jobs to teenagers—fast-food chains pop to mind here—emphasize the social interactions on the job. When these teenagers move into permanent jobs, they often expect the same camaraderie there. Often, they don't find it.

Their jobs are truly boring.

The work may be repetitive and unchallenging—and demotivating as a result.

> *Hint:* As much as it may surprise (and perhaps even irritate) you, many workers today expect their jobs to be challenging. "Fun" may overstate their expectations, but work that doesn't offer challenges or rewards can result in excessive turnover just as surely as low-pay work. In fact, some employees will be willing to accept lower paying jobs if the work is sufficiently challenging and interesting.

Note also that none of the causes rules out any of the others.

YOUR RESPONSE

If Kevin and the others have unrealistic expectations for work:

We list this first because we expect that it is the conclusion you're most apt to jump to. And it may be right. But we hope you won't jump to it until you've at least considered the other two causes. You can perhaps do something about them. You can't do much about this one.

If their expectations really are unrealistic, the best you can do is to attempt to help the individuals become more realistic about what's available in the job market. If they're unskilled or semiskilled, most companies aren't going to worry about whether they're having fun or not. They're going to hire them, keep them as long as they want to work under the company's conditions, and then replace them when they leave in a few weeks or months.

As part of this, you can help them understand the real problems individuals with low skills have and that the most reliable way to avoid these problems is to learn marketable skills. Being a computer operator, a medical technician, or a legal assistant won't guarantee anyone a fun job. But it will increase their control over their work—because employers will *need* their skills—and let them have some meaningful choice in where they'll work and what they'll do.

If they miss the socializing they've been used to on other jobs:

Many companies with low-skilled jobs intentionally make up for low pay and even poor working conditions by not only permitting but encouraging workers to socialize on the job. Often, individuals form very close friendships on the job. Some companies sponsor bowling leagues and softball teams. Done right, this creates a work environment in which individuals with low skills, and compensated at comparably low levels, choose to remain on the job for years.

Listen carefully to Kevin, Andrea, and the others. Is this what they're really saying, or is it at least a big part of it? If so, what can you do about it? Is the group's work low-skilled? Then can you arrange it so individuals can have social contact with one another while they're doing it—without reducing productivity? If so, do it.

But you may not be able to permit much socialization. In this case, your basic strategy is to be very careful about the people you hire. Make sure they understand that they won't have much social contact on the job. If you communicate this clearly and they understand it clearly, you will at least have workers who will be willing to work without the chance to socialize. They will probably remain on the job longer and be at least somewhat more satisfied than Kevin and Andrea.

SOMETHING TO THINK ABOUT

Managers need to understand the work they supervise in depth, which includes understanding the kind of workers who will perform the work with the least strain. If your work is truly boring, hire people who're willing to do boring work for months or years. On the other hand, if your work can be made more challenging, reorganize it and find the people who want more of a challenge.

You probably know this by now, but just in case you don't, let us state it: People are very different from one another in what turns them on from nine to five. There are no universal motivators at work, no matter what the proponents of the current fad want you to believe. In general, you will come out best if you make your work and your work environment as interesting as possible. Do that to the extent you can, and be realistic about what you can do. Then hire people who want to do that kind of work and supervise them as well as you can.

If their jobs are truly boring:

Many jobs are simply boring in their current form, but what can you do about that? You can help workers develop more realistic expectations, hire workers who understand the work is boring and are willing to do it, and attempt to let workers socialize on the job as much as possible. Each of these will help, but all of them are relatively short-term solutions.

There are other solutions. Here are a few:

- When organizations understand and practice quality improvement, they normally make jobs more interesting for their workers, particularly if they're willing to let workers "own" (have full authority over) their work processes.

- Organizations that can effectively use self-directed work teams often make work far more interesting at the operating level. Team members often learn and use new skills and get the opportunity to work together to solve problems.

- When supervisors are willing to train workers fully and then delegate fully to them, they help make work more interesting for them.

None of these really make work "fun," but they do help to make it interesting and challenging, and for most people an interesting job is as good as a fun one. Check with your boss, the human resources department, or anyone else who might have some answers to see if your company uses quality improvement or self-directed teams. If so, you may be able to implement it in your workgroup. If not, see if you can make your employees jobs more interesting by using effective training and effective delegation.

CHAPTER THREE

Improving Your Employees' Approach to the Job

No. 17 RESISTANCE TO CHANGE

You keep hearing: "But we've always done it this way"

THE SCENE

You bite your tongue to keep from making a snide remark to Floyd and stalk back to your office. He's the third employee this week who's answered "We've always done it this way" when you suggested doing things a different way. You thought you were working with a conservative group of employees, and, boy, were you right!

POSSIBLE CAUSES

The employees really don't know any other way to do things.

The group may have been so stable and done things the same way for so long that no one has ever thought that there might be another way to do them.

The employees like the way they do things and are resisting change.

Employees often see a new management mandate as a way to force a lot of new ideas and more work on them, and they "dig in" to resist the changes.

The employees are actively fighting specific changes you want to make.

They may be fighting the changes not because they don't want to change, but because they don't like the changes you want to make.

> ***Hint:*** These three situations sound similar, but are actually different. You need to listen carefully and ask effective questions to find out what your problem is. Then you'll be able to solve it.

YOUR RESPONSE

No matter what the cause is:

It's not true that people don't want to change. Most people choose to change many times. But they do so only when they can answer "yes" to these three questions: (1) Will it pay off for me? (2) Can I do it successfully? and (3) Is it worth the effort it will take? And when someone else wants the change, it's necessary to have a "yes" answer to a fourth question: Do I trust the person who wants me to change?

These four criteria are what we all use to decide whether to change or not. When we can't answer "yes" to all four questions, we'll resist the change. On the other hand, when a proposed change meets all four criteria, we will change.

Your basic job, then, is to establish trust with your employees and show them "yes" answers to the first three questions.

Consider too that maybe your employees are right! Often the people who are involved in doing the work are the ones in the best position to determine whether a change (or the change you're proposing) will help or hurt. That's not always true; sometimes workers have a hard time seeing the big picture and get mired in the details of their specific jobs. But your employees' input is always valuable, even though you may not always adopt their suggestions.

If they really don't know any other way:

Find a change that you're sure meets the first three criteria and then explain to your employees what you're going to do and why. Give them a chance to ask questions. Be patient. No matter how good you think your idea is and how good they may later decide it is, making the change is going to make them uncomfortable.

If you can, wait to make more changes until the first change has "taken" and the group is comfortable with it. If it was an effective change, they'll be happy you did it. This will make the next change easier. If you string a succession of successful changes together, you'll probably get them to the point where change becomes natural to them. Then they'll begin suggesting changes, and you'll know that you've done your job.

If the employees are actively resisting change:

Don't get angry at their stubbornness. If you let the situation disintegrate into you versus them, you'll both lose.

Select a change that meets the three criteria. In this circumstance, it helps if the change is in response to a clear problem. ("We've got to do something to reduce the number of errors or we're going to be in big trouble.")

Here's a technique that often works. Start with the compelling reason to change. (Perhaps you've been directed to cut response time to customer phone calls by 10 percent by the end of the month or else.) Call the group together; tell them that it has to be done and how you propose to do it. Then tell them that if anyone has a better idea you'll be glad to consider it. If you don't get any ideas from them, go ahead and do what you said you'd do. If you do get ideas—and sooner or later you will—do your best to implement them (at least in part).

Remember, pick changes that clearly have to be made and make sure they're effective. This will start to build employee trust in you. Then you can start persuading employees to make changes that aren't required and may not be so obvious.

If the employees are actively fighting specific changes you want to make:

First, examine the changes you're trying to make. Are they really going to help? Are they what the work unit needs now? Will they make the group more effective or efficient, or are you just changing to make the situation more comfortable for you? In other words, do the changes meet the first three criteria from your employees' perspective?

If they do, try to persuade your employees that they do. If you can't, but try to force the change through, you'll create a situation where it's you versus your employees. Don't do this unless the change is absolutely essential (or absolutely required).

If your employees' opposition is really strong, you might agree to stop pushing the change if they'll come up with a better way to do it. That gives them an out and puts the ball in their court, without your backing down from the change.

SOMETHING TO THINK ABOUT

Sometimes incremental change is easier, and more effective, than a single dramatic change. If you can, structure a change in smaller bites, and begin by introducing the aspect you think will be most attractive to your employees. For example, you might decide to organize the work of your unit vertically (a whole process start-to-finish performed by each employee) rather than horizontally (each person doing a different step). If possible, begin by having all of your employees learn the last step first (the one that involves customer contact or the final touches on a finished piece of work). The sense of accomplishment that accompanies that last step will provide incentive for your workers to learn the earlier, and perhaps less satisfying, parts of the process as well.

No. 18 Quality Slips Off Target

Employees frequently produce unacceptable work

THE SCENE

Sunday morning finds you seated at the breakfast table with a cup of tea and Paul Strauss' latest work report. You eagerly begin to read, then note to your dismay that most of it doesn't make any sense. You can't follow his logic; sentences aren't clear; and you have no idea where his conclusions came from. You're especially disgusted because this is the third major product you'll have to return to one of your employees this month. Can't just one of them do something right?

POSSIBLE CAUSES

Your employees may not know what's expected of them.

This is most likely if you're newly managing the group or if requirements have recently changed in some way.

Your employees may not see any advantage to themselves in doing a better job.

Is there any reward to them for doing better work? What happens when the work is unacceptable? Do you rework the product for them, or are they required to fix the problem themselves?

The work environment may discourage good work.

Do your employees have access to all the materials they need to do their jobs well? How hard is it to get new tools or resources? Does your organizational structure facilitate the right people doing the right parts of a project?

> **Hint:** Poor performance by an entire organization requires different treatment from poor performance by an individual. You may have a situation where the poor performance is the result of a number of different individual performance problems. It's more likely, though, that your problem is systemic; something in the way your work is organized, or communicated, or reviewed as a whole is causing large numbers of your people to produce substandard work.
>
> If most of your people are producing poor quality work, don't be misled by the one or two who do well. They don't necessarily prove that you don't have a systemic problem. Some people will perform well in spite of almost any adversity.

YOUR RESPONSE

If your employees don't know what's expected of them:

Review the unit's work products again to see if there are aspects that are consistently being done poorly. Identify two or three changes in work procedures or processes that would correct the most common problems.

Find the training method that would best teach your employees how to do those two or three things better. Maybe a local training source for formal training? Or an employee who does one of those aspects well and could do some on-the-job training?

Tell your employees what you plan to do to help them learn the job better and that you intend to concentrate on specific items. Then provide regular feedback to them on how well they're doing and what *specific* areas they still need to work on.

If your employees don't see any advantage in doing a better job:

Set up an informal system of recognition for each job that's done well. This can be a public "pat on the back" or a more tangible form of recognition such as a certificate, a bonus, a gift certificate, or some other item that says "Good job!"

Ask your employees what motivates them. If they trust you, they'll probably tell you. As much as possible, try to devise rewards intrinsic to the job (better assignments) rather than extrinsic rewards like time off work.

While you may have limited authority to set up a recognition-and-reward system for your employees, you can see to it that they, not you, are the ones who suffer the consequences of their unacceptable work. Give your employees regular feedback on what they're doing well and not so well. When it's not done well, make sure *they* do the work over again until it's right. Devise other "natural consequences" for their poor quality, even if that means denying them a vacation day so they'll have time to rework an important assignment.

If the work environment is discouraging good work:

Review your work situation to see just what's getting in the way of doing a good job. Talk to your staff; they know better than you do what's getting in their way.

Examine the workflow and your organizational structure. Restructure the work if necessary to see that tasks are done in a logical sequence and that completed segments don't require rework by another person or function. Make sure that someone is ultimately responsible for the quality of every product and that that person sees the final result before it goes to you or to the next section for review.

If materials or equipment are getting in the way of quality work, make a friend of your local suppliers. Visit them to see what roadblocks stand in the way of their serving you. Offer to help, and follow through, in whatever way your position allows, to make their job easier.

SOMETHING TO THINK ABOUT

Most employees don't like to work in an organization that does poor work. If your employees do know what's expected of them and how to perform to those expectations, they'll probably be the best source of information on barriers to improved quality. Make a point of asking them, frequently, what you, or the company, can do to help them do a better job or produce a better product. Then follow through on as many of their suggestions as you can and keep them informed of what you've done to implement their recommendations.

No. 19 Short Attention Span

Your workgroup won't stick with new methods long enough to learn them

THE SCENE

"Well, that certainly was a fiasco," Stefan remarks. "One more 'quick fix' that broke more than it fixed. Now we'll spend even more time getting everybody back in sync with our old supply procedure when we could have just left it alone in the first place."

"Wait a minute," you reply. "That new process could have worked, and could have worked better than the old one if you'd just given it a fair trial. But you can't change a whole process one week and have it working smoothly the next. If we keep giving up on new ideas before we even give them a chance to work, we'll never be able to improve anything!"

POSSIBLE CAUSES

Your workgroup may resent having new ideas imposed on them.

They may believe that they are the people in the best position to come up with new work methods and resent outside intrusion.

The group may not be accustomed to trying new methods.

They may actively resist changes or they may just not know how to deal productively with them.

The group may not be comfortable with the decreased production that almost inevitably accompanies the first implementation of a process change.

Or they may think they'll be expected to produce at the same rate during the change period. That's a near-impossible task.

> *Hint:* Any change needs time to take root. First, people have to become comfortable with the *idea* of change, then they have to have time to implement the change itself. Whenever you introduce new methods or processes, you need to be sure your group understands that a reasonable "learning curve" is not only tolerated, but *expected*.

YOUR RESPONSE

If your workgroup resents having new ideas imposed on them:

Is the change one you've been *forced* to make because of a change in the company's policy or a decision that has been made somewhere above you in the hierarchy? If not, back up a little.

Explain to your workgroup what problems have been identified with the current process. What is it you're trying to correct? Get their ideas and suggestions. Make clear to them that this isn't just a perfunctory question and that you genuinely want their input and will evaluate their ideas along with the solution that's already been proposed.

If the new methods are entirely of your creation, it's especially important to include at least some of the group's ideas. Even better would be for the group to come up with an overall solution that's better than yours was. Demonstrating to them that you're not only interested in listening to their ideas, but that you'll implement them whenever you can, will improve the situation in two ways: Not only will you have a better solution, but you will also build trust with your employees, so when you *have* to impose new processes without their input, they'll probably be more understanding and accepting.

If this is a change you've been forced to make without input from your group, make sure you explain to them the situation and the reason for the change. Then brainstorm with them to see if together you can come up with ways to make the new methods work—to everyone's advantage.

If the group isn't accustomed to trying new methods:

Look back at Challenge 17 for some suggestions on introducing changes to the organization. Consider the three questions: (1) Will it pay off for me? (2) Can I do it successfully? and (3) Is it worth the effort it will take? If the change is going to work, you (and your group) must be able to answer "yes" to all three: Once you've figured out how to make all three answers "yes," you have the basic strategy for convincing your group to give the new methods a fair trial.

If the group isn't comfortable with the loss of production that accompanies the implementation of any new process:

What's the goal of the new process? Is it to increase the amount your unit can produce? Does it focus on improving quality? Does it implement some new technology or make your process more compatible with others inside or outside your organization?

Your primary focus, at least initially, needs to be on implementing the new methods in such a way that the goals of the new methods are met—or at least given a reasonable test. Be sure your employees know what they need to concentrate on and that other aspects of the work will be given less priority during this transition period.

Develop an estimated timetable by which you and your group think the new methods should be up and running smoothly. The length of time may be as short as a few days, but could run for several months if the process is a complex one or if it interfaces with many other processes. *Be conservative* in your estimates. Nothing *ever* goes as smoothly as planned, and it's better for morale and for your work statistics to implement earlier than expected, rather than later.

Do you know for sure that the new methods *will* be better than the old ones? Can you try implementing them in a small way at first, then going for full-scale implementation once all the bugs are worked out? This kind of "beta testing" is often used in introducing new technology and can help identify trouble spots before your entire operation comes to a grinding halt.

Finally, be encouraging during the entire process change. Expect foul-ups, roadblocks, frustrations, and occasional short tempers. Your continued calm encouragement will go a long way toward ensuring that your group sticks with the process changes long enough to see them through.

SOMETHING TO THINK ABOUT

Implementing a new work process is a lot like learning to ride a bike. When you first start out you fall down a lot and you can go only a few feet before you lose your balance and have to start all over. Your little brother or sister walking beside you seems to be moving a lot faster than you are. But once you get through the frustrating experience of mastering the new technique, you can speed along faster than you ever imagined. Patience is important for the person who's learning, but it's even more important for the coach on the sidelines. Practice it.

No. 20 CUSTOMER-AVERSE STAFF
Your team treats customers poorly

THE SCENE

"Why do you keep harping on dealing with the people in Julie's group-and why do you keep calling them 'customers'? They're employees just like we are, and their job is to take what we give them and use it the way they're sup-posed to. If they don't like it, they can tell us so and we can talk about it. In the meantime, we don't have time for all this 'customer' junk. Just let us do our job-and heaven knows we have enough to do!"

Ben looks around and most other members of the group nod. He turns back, a "See, I told you so!" look on his face.

POSSIBLE CAUSES

Your company has never stressed internal customers.

It uses a traditional model of internal interactions, where a workgroup pro-duces not what some "customer" wants but what the boss tells it to.

The workgroup is used to applying its own standards of what makes a good product.

Your employees believe they understand what makes their workgroup's prod-ucts successful and use that standard. They don't need any more information from other people in the company, even if you call them "customers."

The goals of the two units conflict, so your unit isn't willing to treat the other as a customer.

Your workgroup simply doesn't agree with what the other workgroup thinks is a successful product, and ignores the group's requests.

> ***Hint***: To many people, even those who are very much oriented toward satisfying external customers, the notion of an "internal customer" seems odd. They believe that the focus of the entire company should be on sat-isfying that external customer and that everyone within the company should be a part of the team effort. That's a legitimate stance, but it's only one way of looking at complex internal interactions.
>
> The notion of internal customers is useful for focusing the attention of your workgroup on what *someone else* needs from the products and services they produce. As we will discuss, it's easy for units to get caught up in their own definitions of "quality work" and "successful performance," while overlooking the real needs of the people who will use their work products. By thinking of other units in the company as "internal customers," you can refocus your workgroup's attention on what those other people need in a positive way, by using the "carrot" of customer satisfaction rather than the "stick" of performance complaints.

YOUR RESPONSE

If the organization has never stressed internal customers:

In this circumstance, you will get very little help from your boss or other managers if you try to get regular feedback from the people in the company who use your work products. In fact, your manager may think you're wasting time and tell you to get back to "real" work.

What do you do? Obviously, you can't start a big "customer" relations program with people in your own company. But you can attempt to find two or three workers who would be interested in dealing with the other units and work out a small program with them. For instance, you and this small group might schedule a brief visit with one of your internal customers. It doesn't have to be anything fancy to begin with, just a "How are you? How are things going? Anything we can do to help?" kind of visit.

You may find all kinds of dissatisfaction on the first visit, which certainly gives you the excuse you need to pay systematic attention to them. Or nothing may happen. If so, visit another unit your workgroup deals with. Be patient. The odds are very good that if your internal customers have no complaints it's because they don't really believe you'll pay attention to them. So, to test the way, a member of another unit may bring up a minor problem or two she's been having with your workgroup. That's your opportunity to demonstrate your responsiveness. Commit your workgroup to solving the problem, along with a date by which it will be solved—and keep your commitment.

You can be absolutely confident that if you demonstrate concern and responsiveness to the other units in the company who interact with yours, you will begin to find more than just a few opportunities to change your relationship with them. And when your boss asks you why you're going to all this trouble, explain that one of your goals is to cut out the unnecessary work you're sure your unit is performing.

If the workgroup is used to applying its own standards of what makes a good product:

Traditional organizations promoted this approach. So do the professions. Accountants know what makes a good report, programmers know what makes a good program, job recruiters know what makes a good hire, and human resources departments know the employment laws and regulations they have to adhere to. Increasingly, whether because they are professionals, want to be professionals, or are bound by an increasing volume of laws and regulations, workers and workgroups have and use their own definitions of successful results.

SOMETHING TO THINK ABOUT

Customers are very important, whether they're internal or external. If you and your workgroup believe this, here are two ideas that will make customer relations even more effective:

First, work at *being a good customer*. You have suppliers you depend on, perhaps both internal and external. You may not believe they treat you well, and they may not. But it's worth spending some time and effort to find out how to be good customers for them; it really will make your relationship with them both smoother and more effective. And when they see that you're willing to spend time and effort on being a better customer, they will probably begin asking what they need to do to be better suppliers.

Second, work at *educating your own customers*. There are certain things you just can't do, and if your customers understand what these are and don't expect them, you will be able to satisfy them better. There are other things that sound good at first but don't really work very well; you can see that your customers know what these are and why they don't work well. And there are some exceptions you can make occasionally that you can't even think of making routinely; it's important that your customers don't expect them routinely.

But internal standards are never enough, because they don't incorporate the legitimate needs of the people who will use your products and services. So what do you do? If you can find a few willing workers, follow the suggestions in the paragraph above. Now, though, add another level. If a "customer" is dissatisfied, your workgroup may be able to make a change and satisfy him or her, or it may not because the change would violate an internal standard. For instance, a manager might want accounting data stated in a way that the accounting unit believes distorts the real situation.

What you can do in each case, however, is discuss and try to negotiate the disagreements. The more the two units understand each other's work and each other's issues, the easier it will be for them to work together and the easier it will be for your unit to satisfy the other. In the long run, your unit will be more productive, will waste less time and effort, and will be more confident that it is satisfying real needs for its internal customers.

If the goals of the two units conflict, so your unit isn't willing to treat the other as a customer:

Now we add yet another dimension. Your workgroup believes that by giving its customers in other units what they want, they will want the wrong thing.

Managers will try to bypass the company's pre-hiring checks to get a job filled quickly. The manufacturing people will screw up the design so they can make the product more easily. So your workgroup's stance may be that "we" have to insist on our standards because "they" will screw things up if we don't.

That's a difficult attitude to change. It's even extremely difficult to get a workgroup to *consider* changing the attitude. If the organization strongly supports customer orientation and cross-functional teamwork, that will help. Make use of all the support the company can give you. Even then, expect to take a long time, do a lot of discussing, and endure a lot of emotional outbursts. These issues matter to many workers.

No. 21 Peer Rivalry

There's serious in-group fighting among your employees

THE SCENE

"I should have known I'd pay for this later," you remark wryly to no one in particular as Bill leaves your office. "I take one afternoon off and now half the staff's mad at me."

The senior employee you usually left in charge during your absences was out that day, so you left Pete in charge while you were gone, and now you've spent most of the morning hearing about "favoritism" and that it's not fair that you're "grooming Pete for the next promotion." With three hours of supervisory experience!

"But if it weren't this, it would just be something else," you muse. "Such a talented group of people, but they're always fighting about something!"

POSSIBLE CAUSES

Some occasional dissatisfaction among your employees is probably inevitable. If what you're faced with is this sort of "annoyance bickering," the best thing you can do is nothing. Any attempts on your part to make things better will probably make them worse by giving the behavior a prominence it doesn't deserve.

However, there are two cases where you can't afford to ignore infighting:

- When it's caused by real or perceived inequity in the way employees are treated
- When it's the result of serious dissatisfaction and employees' perception that they're trapped in meaningless work with no potential for advancement

In those cases, you must analyze the situation and take action. Otherwise, things will only get worse.

YOUR RESPONSE

If the infighting is caused by real or perceived inequity in the way employees are treated:

First determine the source of the apparent inequity. Is it the system itself (for example, the way work is assigned, the way raises and assignments are given)? Is it something you're doing? Or something someone else in the company is doing?

The next step is education. Often, employees don't even know that there is a system or a set of rules for making certain decisions. Let your employees know what the rules are and how you've applied them in the past. (In this case, perhaps you put Pete in charge because he had the next highest level of seniority with the company, though some of the others had more seniority in their positions.) If you explain how the decision was made and show that you'll be consistent in applying that rule, things will improve noticeably.

If there are no rules, consider drawing up a set of guidelines for your unit that covers the situations that most often cause contention. You can't make a rule for everything, and you shouldn't try. But you can identify for employees the criteria you use in making some decisions. Once they know what criteria you use and are convinced that you're following them, much of their dissatisfaction will cool.

And of course, if there are rules and they're not being followed, the solution is obvious: Follow them. If it's someone above you (like your boss) who's the source of the inequity, you can point out to that person the impact on morale and productivity. But if you can't change your boss' behavior, you may need to make some adjustments at your level to mitigate the damage.

If the infighting is the result of your employees' dissatisfaction with their jobs, the solution is not nearly so straightforward (and you may have less satisfactory results):

If you can change the way work is structured to make it more meaningful or increase advancement potential for even some of your employees, as long as you're not hurting the others, do it!

Manufacture opportunities for your employees to increase their direct contact with their customers. All work products should be of benefit to someone—either within the company or outside. (If they're not, you'll want to consider whether that work ought to be done at all.) As your employees have greater contact with the recipients of their efforts, the work will become more meaningful and the group can unite around the common purpose of serving the customer.

Let your employees know you're on their side. If the work truly is boring and dead-end, let your staff know you're aware of their dissatisfactions and that you'll do what you can to make things better. If your staff knows you as an empathetic boss, it will be harder for them to imagine you treating them unfairly.

SOMETHING TO THINK ABOUT

Don't confuse infighting with honest disagreement. In any group made up of strong, talented individuals, there is bound to be disagreement and conflict. In this situation, the proper cure is to manage the conflict creatively, not try to suppress it. How do you do this? Encourage your workers to come to you with their suggestions. Assign some of your more creative workers to look at the work your unit performs and figure out ways to do it better or more effectively. And always keep your employees focused on the end-users of their work. Have some members of the workgroup review your products from a customer's perspective to identify ways to be more responsive, and more indispensable.

No. 22 LOW MORALE

Your workgroup is demoralized and their work shows it

THE SCENE

Your new boss was right; the performance of this group of employees is mediocre. Their work always meets the minimum standard—just barely—but never gets much better. If you try to get them to improve, they ask you to tell them what to do in detail, or come up with a dozen reasons why it can't be improved. Worst of all, they don't seem to care.

POSSIBLE CAUSES

Their last manager was no better than marginal.

Managers who are barely competent don't take long to pass their shortcomings on to their employees.

Their last manager refused to support them.

This is another effective way to wreck a group of employees. If managers never stand up for their employees and always side with the people who criticize them, it doesn't take long for the employees to get the word and hunker down.

> *Hint*: Once in a rare while, you may find employees from whom even an effective supervisor can't get good performance. More often, however, ineffective supervision leads to an ineffective work unit.

YOUR RESPONSE

If their last manager was marginal:

Your number-one task is to prove your competence at the same time that you build up their self-confidence and willingness to produce.

Make it clear from the beginning that you know your job. This doesn't mean that you have to have all the answers; you don't. But you do need a clear sense of how to do the job, and you need to act on this sense.

Make it clear to the group what level of performance you expect from them. Do this at a group meeting and explain it carefully. Invite employees to ask questions (though they probably won't at this stage). If it's necessary, put your expectations in writing. The important point is for them to know what you want and that you're serious about it.

Insist on getting the performance you want. If a job isn't acceptable, explain what's wrong and have it redone until it's right. Depending on the group, this may be a long struggle, but for both your sake and your employees' it's a struggle you need to win.

Managers sometimes get into the habit of accepting substandard work and having someone else redo it (bad) or redoing it themselves (worse!). If you see signs that this was how the last manager did things, make it clear that you don't work this way, that you expect jobs to be done right the first time. Then follow through and make sure that all jobs are done right—by the employees responsible for them.

Another bad habit that sometimes becomes part of a work unit's culture is not getting things done on time. There is virtually no excuse for this, period. If your employees have too much work to do, it's your responsibility as their manager to adjust the workload. Except for that, your employees should expect to meet every deadline or to renegotiate the deadline in *advance* with you.

Are you doing all of this to be hard on your employees? Not at all. You're doing it because it's the only way they'll ever be able to take pride in what they do.

If their last manager refused to support them:

Normally, this is the only situation other than marginal management that can demoralize employees. Some otherwise competent managers always side with the people who complain about their employees.

The group is probably hoping that you'll be different, but afraid you won't be. In other words, they'll be cautious and wait for you to prove yourself.

Your basic tactics here are easy. When someone comes to you with a complaint about your employees, listen carefully, get all the facts that person sees them, and agree to look into the situation and get back to him. If the person is in a hurry, or very upset, promise to get back to him quickly, but don't make any commitments until you've talked with the employee(s) he's complaining about.

Talk to the employee or employees. Get their side of the situation. If you can back them, do it (always, not just in the beginning). If possible, let them take care of the problem with the individual who complained. If you have to come up with a different solution in order to satisfy a reasonable complaint, do it, but let your employees present the solution to the individual if you can.

In other words, see that the situation is resolved, but don't make your employees the bad guys. If they were careless or unresponsive or otherwise did a poor job, let them know it and let them know what you expect. But do it in private. And never correct them because someone complained; correct them because what they did was inadequate, whether anyone complained about it or not.

SOMETHING TO THINK ABOUT

If you want your employees to trust you and really produce for you, you need to protect them from outside harassment. This doesn't mean that you should overlook their mistakes; it does mean that you should deal with their mistakes in private and help them look good to the res t of the organization.

There's a related, but very important, point. To manage effectively, you have to delegate effectively, because when you delegate, you let the person act for you. Support the person you delegate to and support her actions (even if you have to undo her decision). This is the only way that your delegations can be successful.

No. 23 ARTIFICIALLY LOW STANDARDS

Your workgroup has set self-imposed production limits

THE SCENE

As you stroll quietly through the office, you notice the same lack of industry that you've observed before. No one is really "goofing off," but no one seems to be working very hard either. The whole atmosphere is laid back.

Back in your cubicle, you reflect on what it was like in the last office you worked in. It seemed like everyone was a lot more animated and got a lot more accomplished there. Of course, you recall a lot more grousing, too. "But maybe," you muse, "it was worth it. Here, my people do what they have to, but not one thing more."

POSSIBLE CAUSES

If employees are producing acceptable work at an acceptable rate, but nothing more, it's probably because they see no advantage in working harder. If it's important that they begin to produce at a higher rate, there are two areas you should examine as potential sources of improvement:

Employees may not see any benefit from increased production.

Some things in your operation may even *discourage* higher production. Are there rewards for doing more work?

There may not be any penalty for producing at the low level and there may be positive reasons for not doing more.

Employees may feel they'd be exploited if they did more work for what they're getting paid.

> **Hint:** Before you rush full tilt into a production improvement program, there's one other issue you should check—acceptance rate. If your group could be producing at higher rates, but it's likely that there'd be considerably more re-work of what's produced because of quality problems, then the company won't really gain from a higher production rate. First make sure your quality level is where it should be, then work on improving production.

YOUR RESPONSE

If employees see no benefit from enhanced production:

Look at your compensation and salary schedules to see if there's any way employees can share in the gains from increased production. Establish specific production goals at several levels and link some form of recognition to each level. This recognition, particularly for small production improvements, need not be monetary. However, an essential ingredient is that the recognition must be public; it should serve as a stimulant both to the recipient and to other employees who see how they can benefit from production improvements.

Discuss with your employees what you might do to help them increase production. Ask them what they see as benefits worth striving for and then implement as many of their suggestions as you can.

As you implement your new recognition systems, be sure that they're administered fairly and impartially. Let your employees know what the criteria are for recognition and don't change the rules without letting them know and telling them why you're making the changes.

If employees see some positive reason to continue their low level of production:

Identify what it is that's encouraging employees to produce at a low level and what's discouraging higher production. Review employee complaints over the past couple of years. Is there a common theme (or underlying message) in many of the complaints you've received?

Do what you can to remove the barriers to higher production and let your employees know what you can do and what you can't. If the disincentive is something as basic as the pay scales for their jobs (over which you may have little or no control), talk with employees about what you might be able to substitute for a change in pay rates.

Just as when your employees see no incentive to higher production, look at your compensation and recognition system to find ways to let employees share in the company's gains. If employees feel that the company's fortune is their own, they'll be much more interested in increasing its profitability.

SOMETHING TO THINK ABOUT

Employees have many different reasons for setting production bogeys lower than the level management believes is a "fair day's work," but they all boil down to one: This is what pays off best for them. To change the bogey, you have to change the payoff.

How do you identify what your employees will perceive as paying off for them? Ask them. You can either ask the open-ended question "What can we do to make it worth your while to produce more faster?" or—particularly if the options you can actually implement are limited—give them a choice among two or three incentives.

No. 24 Company Image Worries

Your company's poor reputation hurts your ability to get things done

THE SCENE

Angered and hurt, you slam down the phone. "That's totally unfair," you fume. "What does she mean she knew she'd have to approach this proposal conservatively as soon as she saw our company's name on it? I've worked hard with my group to make sure we put out only products we can all be proud of. It doesn't make any difference how good a job we do, my folks have had some bad press, and now nobody will give us a chance!"

POSSIBLE CAUSES

Your company may have produced substandard work in the past.

It may be that your poor reputation is at least partially deserved. Customers (both external and internal customers) will not be likely to take a risk with you again if they've been burnt in the past, unless you can convince them that they won't be disappointed again.

Your company may have produced technically adequate work that failed to satisfy your customers' expectations.

Customers don't necessarily know what's accurate or correct, but they do know what they want. Your job is to provide them with what they want or convince them that what you're offering them meets their needs even better.

Your company may truly have gotten unfair "bad press."

No one wants to admit error, and we're all falsely blamed at one time or another. An organization that really was at fault for poor products may have passed the blame on to you, or competitors may have made misleading comparisons between their offerings and yours.

> *Hint:* As your mother probably warned you, reputation is a fragile thing. That's true corporately as well as personally. Much of the business an organization gets is on the basis of reputation—for solid, accurate, reliable, responsive work. The best way to safeguard your reputation is never to allow it to be sullied in the first place. Corporate image is not just the concern of the Public Relations department; it must be a concern in every customer contact.

YOUR RESPONSE

No matter what the cause:

It should go without saying that you will never establish a reputation for high quality work if your work really isn't of high quality. Your first step in building a good reputation is to be scrupulous in ensuring that every product or service you offer is unassailable. Only then will any of the following steps be of any help.

If your company has produced substandard work in the past:

Be honest with potential customers and clients who are worried about your previous performance. Tell them what you've done to improve and show them examples of good work you've produced since the problems have been remedied. While you're in the process of reestablishing your good reputation, consider offering some services on a contingency basis: You'll get full payment only if the client accepts your work.

Try to expand your customer base. Approach people you haven't dealt with before, who may not have preconceived notions about the quality of your work.

Bite off only as much as you can chew. Start small. Be willing to spend a little extra effort at first producing a "perfect" product. You can use those first samples to show new customers (or to convince previous customers to give you another chance), and your "ultra-satisfied" customers can give good testimonials to your later prospects.

If your company has previously produced technically adequate work that failed to satisfy your customers' expectations:

Work out in advance with your customers exactly what you intend to do for them. Listen closely to their needs and wants and articulate back to them what you think you hear them saying. Tell them (in a formal contract, if it's appropriate) exactly what you're offering them and which of their concerns your offering will satisfy. Make sure you both agree on the product or service you'll supply and what it will do for them, before you provide the product or service itself.

If you're offering a product that will take some time to produce, set up a series of checkpoints along the way. These can be meetings with the customer or they can be sets of formal specifications. But whatever form they take, you'll need periodic points where you and the customer examine progress to be sure that he or she is satisfied. That way you can clear up any misunderstandings early, before they become major disconnects.

If your company received some unfair "bad press":

As closely as possible, identify the source of the erroneous information. It's tough to tackle an opponent you can't see. If the bad press appears to be the result of innocent misinformation or misunderstanding, consider confronting the person responsible for the misinformation directly to explain the true situation and try to enlist his or her aid in repairing the damage.

Consider an information campaign aimed at your most crucial customers. Through any of a variety of media and methods, public and individual, you can provide information to counter the "misinformation."

Contact some of your most loyal customers to explain the poor publicity you've received and to ask them for references or testimonials that you can use with prospective customers. Through special attention and high quality of delivery, develop a cadre of customers you can count on for support even if times get tough.

SOMETHING TO THINK ABOUT

When a company, or a particular work unit within the company, is accused of poor work, it attacks the reputation and self-esteem of each employee in it. If the accusation turns into a poor reputation, the employees' self-esteem may drop sharply. A major priority must be for you to help your workers increase their self-esteem by demonstrating your confidence in them and identifying and praising (on the spot) every improvement they make.

No. 25 UNWELCOME NEWCOMER

Everyone resents a newer employee you've promoted to a senior position

THE SCENE

"Does anyone here know anything about the problem we're having with Mason Brothers?" you ask in a staff meeting.

"Why don't you ask Petra?" is the sarcastic reply. "She obviously knows everything that goes on here."

You bite your tongue to keep from replying sharply, but this is just one comment of many. You promoted Petra to a senior job only a few weeks ago, even though she has been with the organization less than a year. The employees who've been there longer—and that's most of them—are openly resentful of her promotion. The resentment is so strong that it's beginning to affect productivity.

POSSIBLE CAUSES

You've violated the group's expectations for who should get promoted.

All groups have "norms" for who should get ahead. If there are few opportunities to get ahead in the unit, these norms become even more important.

Your employees may believe Petra doesn't know the job well enough.

In other employees' eyes, it often takes a long time for an individual to "prove" himself or herself on the job. Your workgroup may think Petra hasn't been there long enough to do so.

You may have promoted her for the wrong reasons.

These include a personal friendship with Petra or liking for her as a person without regard for how well she performs.

> *Hint:* Whenever you decide to take an action that isn't what your employees expect, be prepared for an adverse response. That doesn't mean you shouldn't take the action, it just means you must think about how you'll explain the action to your workgroup and be prepared to address their concerns.

YOUR RESPONSE

If the basic reason is your employees' expectations:

This is a common situation in all organizations. If promotions are few and far between, most employees expect them to go to the experienced, proven employees. There is a sense that employees have to "pay their dues" before they can get ahead.

If you made your choice carefully (and there's no excuse if you didn't), stick by it. Some of the resentment is meant as pressure to get you to change your decision. Make it clear that you won't, that you fully support Petra.

Make sure that you have clear performance-based reasons that you can explain to your workgroup for Petra's promotion. It's important to reward those employees who are able to learn new jobs quickly and take on additional tasks without detriment to the work they're already assigned. Let your workgroup know what makes Petra stand out from the others. Then, if your budget will allow, offer incentives for others who learn to perform to the same high standards. For example, a promotion to a more responsible, diverse position or an award for high-level work can serve as an incentive to others. Make Petra's achievements a model to which other employees can aspire rather than a prize that only one person can win.

Help Petra be successful quickly. If the position she's been promoted to is basically an extension of the work she was doing before, this may be easy. If there's a longer learning curve, you'll have more of a problem. Even in this situation, you can assign her projects that she can handle most effectively.

Make sure she's a success and that the other employees know it. However, let them see her *demonstrate* her successful performance; don't preach to them about how well she's doing. Petra's successful performance will be much more persuasive than your words of praise. Your workgroup will see for themselves that she was the right choice for the promotion, and you won't hear the griping about why you chose her for the position.

If they believe she doesn't know the job well enough:

As in the first situation, the keys here are making sure your workgroup knows why Petra was promoted and helping her become successful in the new job as quickly as possible.

For many jobs, especially in these days of frequent corporate restructuring, it's more important to be flexible, versatile, and a quick learner than it is to know the details of the work. General problem-solving abilities are often more critical than in-depth knowledge of a specific subject area. If that's true for your jobs, then Petra's selection wasn't based that heavily on how well she knew the job. Instead, it was based on how quickly she could master it and then move on to other assignments.

Reasonable as that approach may be, it's not what an employee wants to hear who's been in the same line of work for 5 or 10 or 15 years and was passed over for promotion in favor of a newcomer. But once this employee gets past the anger and resentment, he may actually learn more about how to operate in today's work environment than if you'd talked to him about it. And today's environment is definitely *not* the one he entered when he came to work a decade or more ago.

As before, help Petra be successful quickly to demonstrate to the workgroup that she was the right choice. This doesn't mean doing her work for her or giving her simpler jobs so she'll look good. You promoted her because she was good; now give her the support she needs and challenge her to perform.

If you did promote her because of favoritism or other nonperformance reasons:

It's probably too late to change the action, so you'd better do whatever you can to make Petra successful.

In addition, it would be a really good idea if you learned from the situation and never let it happen again.

SOMETHING TO THINK ABOUT

All work units develop their own "norms" about who should get promoted and why (and about who should get awards and why). If you're going to change them, lay the groundwork for your action in advance.

Whenever you're filling a job for which there are likely to be several internal contenders, you should identify the qualities you want in the senior position loud and clear *before* you fill the job. That way, all the employees who want a shot at the promotion will know what was expected of them, and you'll have a clear rationale for choosing the person who ultimately gets the promotion.

CHAPTER FOUR

Overcoming the Personal Problems of Your Employees

No. 26 ACCOMMODATING A SICK EMPLOYEE

A worker's serious health issues are a problem for you

THE SCENE

Gloria Singer, one of your most experienced employees, just confided to you that she has a serious illness. She's been absent for days at a time; even when she comes in she doesn't perform as well as she used to. Sometimes you wonder if there's a point in her being there at all, but she's not so sick you can justify sending her home. Your customers are pressing you for the work Gloria usually does, and other employees have begun to complain about having to cover for her.

POSSIBLE CAUSES

She may have a short-term serious illness from which she'll recover.

There are many illnesses that are very debilitating, but from which individuals do recover.

She may have a serious illness that won't get better.

This is a real possibility and a very different problem from a short-term illness.

She may be trying to hide other problems.

She may be covering up for serious family troubles, severe depression, or substance abuse. People are often embarrassed by situations such as these and find it easier to pretend they're physically sick.

> *Hint:* Be careful not to discuss her problem with other employees or to make a point of treating her "special." If she told you about her illness in confidence, respect that confidence.
>
> If you need to talk to someone, talk to a health professional or your organization's employee assistance program (EAP) counselor.

YOUR RESPONSE

If the illness is short-term:

Encourage her not to work unless her doctor clearly okays it. She should do whatever is necessary to help herself recover.
If your company is covered under the Family and Medical Leave Act (FMLA), make sure she knows her rights and how to apply for leave under the Act.

Without violating Gloria's privacy, explain the situation in very general terms to the rest of your employees and ask them to help carry her workload for a short while. For example, you could say something like, "Gloria's going to have to be off work for a while and we'll all need to pitch in and cover for her."

Follow up regularly—every week or so. Make sure that Gloria is recovering as expected. If she's not, look at the next response.

If the illness is a legitimate, long-term one:

Work out with Gloria how much work she can do and a reasonable reduced-hours schedule that you're both confident she can meet.

Identify the specific job tasks Gloria will keep and which ones she will give up (even if temporarily). Reassign the tasks she's giving up to other employees or hire a partial replacement (temporary help, part-time employees, and the like).

Establish a regular schedule (about once every month or two) for you and Gloria to discuss her condition again and make any adjustments (upward or downward) in her work schedule.

Help Gloria identify any sources available that might help her make up her lost income (disability benefits, EAP, and so forth).

As with the response to a short-term illness, make sure Gloria knows what her entitlements are under the FMLA and how to request FMLA leave.

If your company is subject to the Americans with Disabilities Act (ADA), find out what your obligations are to accommodate Gloria.

If the illness appears to be a cover-up for another problem:

Insist on medical documentation—preferably a release to talk personally with her doctor; don't accept a written statement unless there's no alternative.

If there really is another problem, insist that she get help for it. If your company has an EAP, make Gloria aware of it and recommend that she take advantage of it. Don't let her continue on as she is.

If she gets help, assist her in any reasonable way back to full performance. If she doesn't get help, insist that she perform fully or else you'll be forced to terminate her. Then follow through.

SOMETHING TO THINK ABOUT

If the employee has been a good, productive worker, you have an obligation to treat her as compassionately as possible. On the other hand, she has the obligation both to be completely honest with you and to take the responsibility for her recovery.

You should also look at other challenges in this book for more information on the FMLA and ADA and how they protect employees who have serious health issues to contend with.

No. 27 SUBSTANCE ABUSE

An employee appears under the influence of alcohol or drugs on the job

THE SCENE

Ben Morgan, your lead technician, pokes his head in your office door whispering, "Boss, can you come here a minute? There's something I want you to see." You follow Ben quietly, pausing at the corner of the open office area.

"Watch Leo," he says. "See how loud and talkative he's being on the phone? A few minutes ago he leaned over to say something to Krista and almost lost his balance. He's been acting strange for about an hour or so. Donna said his eyes are kind of glazed, and, look—he's drenched with sweat. I think he's on something, but I thought you'd want to handle this one!"

POSSIBLE CAUSES

There are a number of reasons why employees may appear to be under the influence of alcohol or drugs on the job, but regardless of the cause, there are certain steps that you need to take immediately. The cause *will* affect the way you follow up after this incident is over, but your first concern must be for the well-being and safety of the impaired employee as well as the rest of your employees.

The only piece of information you need immediately is whether this employee really is physically or mentally impaired, either by drugs, alcohol, or some other influencing factor. For the short term, it's the *impairment* that's important. You may know positively that it's caused by drugs or alcohol, but it could be caused by a lot of other things too, including several very dangerous medical conditions. Your first course of action is to decide whether there is an impairment, not its cause.

If you decide there is an impairment, and there seems to be no immediate danger to the employee, then you can take the time to figure out if drugs or alcohol are the cause. If they are, then it's also a good idea for you to find out, now or later, through discussions with the employee, *trusted* coworkers, and your own observations, whether the employee has a continuing pattern of substance abuse.

YOUR REPONSE

Whenever you suspect that an employee is impaired by drugs or alcohol on the job, there are two things you need to do immediately:

- First, get him out of any situation where there could be harm to the employee or to others. If the employee is working with a piece of equipment, get him off it. If he refuses, make it a firm order—with physical assistance from you or your company's security personnel if necessary. You already have an impaired employee; you don't need to compound the problem by having an injured employee.

- Second, observe the employee personally. Describe to him the signals that make you think he has a problem. For instance, say "Leo, you seem to be having trouble keeping your balance and I notice that you're pretty flushed, even though the rest of us think it's cool in here." Ask if he knows what's causing it. If it's a medical problem not related to drugs or alcohol, he may recognize the symptoms and be able to offer an explanation or a solution.

Important: If the employee is incoherent or displays any of the classic signs of physiological shock, get medical help right away. Even if he's drunk or stoned, he may be in physical trauma requiring immediate treatment. This is a situation where it's better to err on the side of caution.

Of course, all this should be done as quietly and with as little fanfare as possible. Although the employee may become confrontational, your calm, rational approach will help keep everyone from getting more upset. As you observe and talk to the employee, don't make accusations. Even if you're sure he's on drugs or alcohol, telling him, "I think you're drunk," is only likely to start an argument.

If you decide the employee is physically or mentally impaired:

Decide whether treatment is necessary immediately, and, if so, make arrangements for the employee to get treatment. In a large company, you probably have some medical staff, and you can escort the employee to them (or call them to your unit). In a smaller company, an urgent care facility or your local hospital is a good place to go if you can't arrange treatment through the employee's own doctor.

If medical care isn't immediately necessary, see that the employee gets home safely and explain to him why he's being sent home.

After the employee returns to work, follow up with him. Explain again what led you to deal with the situation as you did, and if you suspect repeated drug or alcohol abuse, refer the employee to your company's employee assistance program or to a rehabilitation specialist. Document the referral. If this problem persists and you have to fire the employee, the courts may want to know what you did to help him.

If you decide the employee is not impaired:

You need to decide next whether his behavior is unacceptable or just unusual. If it's within the bounds of acceptability, stop there. No further action is necessary. If it's not acceptable, explain to the employee what he's doing wrong, why it's wrong, and if it's not obvious, what he should do differently. Then follow up to see that the problem is corrected.

SOMETHING TO THINK ABOUT

As we say several times throughout the book, watch carefully for signs of alcohol or drug abuse in any performance or conduct problems you face. If you suspect that abuse is there, deal with it quickly. The longer you facilitate an employee's abuse of drugs or alcohol, the harder it will be for him or her to stop.

No. 28 Excessive Absenteeism

An employee takes a lot of time off from work because of serious problems in his personal life

THE SCENE

Your heart is breaking for Harley. He and his wife have always been very close, and now she has terminal cancer. You don't have the heart to refuse his requests for time off to be with her. Yet you also need him on the job. He's one of your most experienced employees, and the work is falling behind because of his absence. You don't know how much longer you can take not only his absences but his reduced efficiency when he is at work.

POSSIBLE CAUSES

It doesn't require much speculation to see what the cause is. Grief at the thought of losing a loved one is a universal human emotion. It's also one of the most powerful, and frequently disabling to those who experience it.

YOUR RESPONSE

For this situation:

It would be wonderful if we could give you an easy answer to the situation. We can't.

First, we can tell you what won't work: Becoming angry or impatient with Harley won't help the situation. He knows the problem he's causing you—he probably feels guilty about it. But none of that helps assuage his grief.

What can you do? Be as supportive as you can. Grief is emotionally very draining. Support from people who care eases the pain and helps an individual cope more effectively with the situation.

There are several actions you can take that may help both Harley and the work situation.

- First, very strong emotion—of any kind—is often very disorganizing. (Think, for instance, of how you responded to things the last time you were extremely happy or extremely sad.) Insist gently that Harley set a regular schedule, if possible, and follow it. This may help him be more available for work and to concentrate more effectively on work when he's there. It may also help him deal with his grief, by giving him some basic structure he can depend on.

- If the work situation and Harley's frame of mind permit, let him do some work at home. You have to be careful about this, of course—he may be even less able to concentrate at home than at work. But if he can concentrate and produce an adequate quantity of satisfactory work, it may help both of you to let him work some at home. If you try this, you should agree in advance on what he's to accomplish and how much time you expect him to spend in the office.
- If the illness is a lingering one and your company is covered under the Family and Medical Leave Act, review Harley's entitlements under the Act. If he's going to be off for an extended period of time, you may be able to replace him temporarily with someone who can produce the work you need, while preserving Harley's job for him when he's ready and able to return. Then arrange for a temporary replacement either by borrowing a worker from another section of the company or by using an outside placement firm.

For similar situations:

You have basically the same situation when an employee has to stay home often with a chronically ill child or parent, or otherwise keeps losing time from work because of a demanding personal situation.

- The "work-at-home" solution may be a good one in many of these situations. A mother who has to take care of a sick child, for instance, may still be able to put in almost a full eight hours of work a day.
- If the nature of the work requires that it be done at the worksite, explore the possibility of an alternative work schedule. One young mother we know worked an evening shift several days a week after her second child was born. She left her house when her husband came home, and worked until midnight.
- If the work involves customer contact, requires interaction with your other employees, or for other reasons must be done at the worksite during regular office hours, then you'll need to divide the work between the employee with the problem and one or more other employees. Another employee could share the work, and they could get together periodically to review their progress. (You can see how this could be combined with the work-at-home or flexible work schedule alternatives.)
- As we have suggested, the length of the situation is a critical factor. If it's going to be short, you can afford to make significant accommodations to the individual. If it's going to drag on, your alternatives will be fewer. No matter how long it will be, give the employee every consideration you can.

SOMETHING TO THINK ABOUT

When an employee has a serious personal problem, be available to listen to him. Don't begrudge him the time he needs to talk about it. But *don't* give him "pep talks" or try to talk him out of his emotional responses. He needs compassion, not advice.

No. 29 REPORTS OF DRUG ABUSE

You hear that one of your best workers is using cocaine on the job

THE SCENE

You sigh dejectedly. Tom Vasary has just told you that Jake Edwards is using cocaine on the job. You don't want to believe it, but Jake *has* been acting differently lately. Maybe he really is a user.

POSSIBLE CAUSES

Tom is trying to discredit Jake for some reason.

With today's emphasis on drugs, Tom may have decided to use the story to get rid of Jake or settle an old score with him or . . .

Tom is being honest but is mistaken about what he saw.

Again, with the emphasis on drugs, people may see abuse in innocent situations. Mistaken or not, their perceptions have to be dealt with.

Jake is using cocaine or some other illegal drug on the job.

Of course, this is the worst situation. It's hard to prove it, but absolutely essential to stop it.

> *Hint:* Your natural tendency may be to delay dealing with the situation. After all, you don't really know. *Don't* put it off. If Tom was mistaken, you need to get the situation cleared up as quickly as possible. If he wasn't mis-

taken, every day you put it off makes the habit more dangerous to Jake and increases the prospect that he will begin to exhibit performance problems.

YOUR RESPONSE

No matter what the cause is:

Question Tom in detail about just what he saw. If there's any doubt, ask why he thinks that Jake was using cocaine. Be careful; you need to communicate to Tom that you need these facts to act on the situation, and that you're not trying to put him on the spot.

Observe Jake's behavior yourself. Does he disappear for periods of time? Does he return from breaks exhibiting mood changes, agitation, or physical symptoms of drug use?

If possible, talk to one or two employees who you believe will level with you. Have they noticed anything unusual in Jake's behavior? Are they perhaps worried about him? This will be awkward. It will require great tact on your part. Your employees must trust you for this to work, and you must make it clear that you're doing this because of your concern for Jake.

If you're not absolutely sure that Tom wasn't distorting the situation, talk with Jake. You don't have to identify your source, but tell him what you've heard. Be prepared for him to react emotionally, no matter what the situation is. Stick with the discussion until you find out whether or not he has a fully believable explanation.

If Tom is apparently trying to discredit Jake:

You have a sticky situation on your hands. If you have clear evidence that Tom was lying, take corrective action against him for defaming an employee. (You can find detailed guidance for this situation in Chapter 7). If you don't have good evidence, follow the suggestions in the next response.

If Tom appears to have just been mistaken about what Jake was doing:

Call Tom in and tell him that you've concluded that Jake isn't using drugs on the job. Let him react to that.

If Tom reacts with relief (or another appropriate response), thank him for sharing his concern with you and counsel him gently on being careful about what he says, especially to other workers.

If Tom reacts defensively, try to find the reasons for his defensiveness. For instance, he may feel you're attacking him and trying to protect Jake. Or he may be reacting to your having caught him at trying to discredit Jake. Counsel him, strongly in this case, on being careful about what he says about others.

If it appears that Jake may be using cocaine or a similar illegal drug on the job:

Is Jake impaired now? If so, look at Challenge 27 for guidance on how to handle an impaired employee.

If Jake isn't impaired now, but you're convinced he's been using drugs on the job or has drugs at the worksite, confront him. If Jake's drug use on the job has been a problem before, you'll want to consider terminating his employment. If this appears to be an isolated incident, put Jake on notice that you'll be watching the situation carefully and that you will terminate him if you find that he's used drugs again while on the company's premises.

If you decide not to terminate Jake's employment, contact your company's employee assistance program (EAP) manager, or whoever is responsible for assisting with employees who have problems. Ask for his or her advice and follow it.

If you don't have anyone designated for employee assistance, demand that Jake take positive steps to deal with his drug use. Tell him that you'll be watching not only to see that he doesn't use drugs on the job, but also that his performance isn't impaired by drug use. Refer him to a professional for counseling. You can't force him to get help, but you can insist that his drug use not interfere with the job.

If you don't have enough evidence to confront Jake, make it a point to have contacts with him throughout the day. Does his mood change significantly? Does he sometimes act secretively?

If you believe that Jake is abusing an illegal drug, don't give up until he seeks help or you have to terminate him for using or for poor performance.

SOMETHING TO THINK ABOUT

In a situation such as this, you need to be sensitive, alert, and forceful. On the one hand, if Jake does have a problem the best thing you can do for him, yourself, and the company is to get him to seek help. On the other, you can't take formal action unless you get usable evidence that he's really using drugs on the job, or his performance becomes unacceptable.

Be patient but persistent. Drug addiction—whether cocaine or another substance—is a powerful, destructive force.

No. 30 Discrimination

An employee accuses another of racism or sexism

THE SCENE

"Mr. Fiorino, I know that you haven't had many women employees here, but that's no excuse. Conrad has been discriminating against me.

"How?" you ask.

"He always gives me the dirtiest assignments," Madeleine replies. "When I ask him for help, he tells me to get it on my own, but I hear him explaining to all the men just how to do things. He's written me up twice this month—for things I couldn't do anything about. If you don't get him to change, I'm going to file a complaint!"

POSSIBLE CAUSES

Madeleine is a poor or lazy employee who wants an excuse not to have to perform.

It's all too easy to settle for this kind of an explanation, and in most cases it would be the wrong one. But it does happen.

Madeleine is overly sensitive because she is the only woman in the unit right now.

When you're part of a minority, it's easy to interpret situations as discriminatory, even if no one intends them to be.

Conrad isn't used to having women employees and isn't treating Madeleine appropriately.

This may be happening even if Conrad has no intention to discriminate at all. He needs educating, and fast.

Conrad really is discriminating against Madeleine because she's a female.

Needless to say, this situation has to be resolved immediately.

> **Hint:** The days of *obvious* discrimination are almost over. Racism and sexism are more subtle these days. They're almost never overt and easy to spot. But that doesn't mean that racism and sexism have been eradicated,

and they're just as dangerous and as illegal as they were before. The moral? No matter how clear-cut things seem on the surface, don't throw discrimination out as an explanation until you've looked more deeply into the situation.

YOUR RESPONSE

No matter what the cause is:

You have a potentially serious situation on your hands. It's important to find out—quickly—all the facts you can.

Begin by having Madeleine tell you in detail what has happened that she believes is sexual discrimination. Be careful; don't give the appearance of putting her through the third degree. Make it clear that you want the facts so you can investigate what she's telling you.

If you can, try to observe Conrad for several days to see if he does seem to be treating Madeleine differently from the male employees. Also observe Madeleine herself to see if she's doing anything that might be causing Conrad's actions.

Early on, consult with your own supervisor, your personnel department, or legal counsel and follow whatever steps they prescribe.

If Madeleine appears to be a poor or lazy employee who wants an excuse not to have to perform:

Investigate and observe carefully before you reach this conclusion. Ask yourself if it's consistent with Madeleine's prior performance. If she's new, you may not know. If she's been an employee for long, though, has she always been like this? If not, avoiding work probably isn't the reason for her behavior.

If you're convinced she is trying to find an excuse not to perform as she should, tell her. Make your expectations clear, and then treat her as you would any other employee whose work and/or motivation were questionable. Be sure to document any discussions you have with Madeleine regarding the situation or her performance, and keep copies of her performance appraisals.

If Madeleine seems to be overly sensitive because she is the only woman in the unit right now:

This is another alternative that you should accept *only* when you've carefully checked out the possibility of genuine discrimination and ascertained that it is not the problem.

Talk with Conrad and, if appropriate, other men employees. Explain to them how Madeleine is feeling and ask for their help to make life in the unit easier for her.

Talk with Madeleine. Explain to her all you've done to check out what she said and the conclusions she's reached. Explain that you believe Conrad and others genuinely want to treat her as an equal and that you've asked them to be sensitive to her feelings. Ask her to reciprocate; after all, whenever there's a change in the workgroup it takes a while for everyone to adjust. Suggest that she come talk to you any time she believes she's being mistreated by anyone. (When she does talk to you, be just as thorough as you were this time in handling her concerns.)

Include Conrad in the conversation in the preceding paragraph. His assurances to Madeleine will probably mean more than yours.

If Conrad isn't used to having women employees and isn't treating Madeleine appropriately:

You have a serious situation on your hands, but at least it appears to be unintentional. Act quickly and decisively, but be tolerant and understanding of Conrad (and others, if they're also involved).

Talk clearly and firmly with Conrad. Point out what he's doing. Give him a chance to explain himself and expect that he may be defensive. But this isn't a discussion; your clear objective is to get him to change his behavior. See that he understands this and follow up to see that he has changed.

Tell Madeleine what you've done to investigate her complaint and the action you've taken. Be sure that she understands you believe Conrad didn't intentionally treat her differently, but that you've directed him to change. Ask her to tell you any time he repeats his sexist behavior, and if she does, follow up on it.

If Conrad really is discriminating against Madeleine because she's a female:

Act immediately. If the discrimination is clear and has harmed Madeleine's performance or advancement opportunities, discipline Conrad. If it's been a correctable irritant—and this is his first offense—counsel him pointedly and tell him exactly what changes you expect. He'll probably be defensive and may complain about reverse discrimination. Let him vent his feelings, but make it clear that he's to change, or else.

Follow up in a couple of weeks with both Conrad and Madeleine to see that the siuation is corrected. If Conrad hasn't changed, consult again with your boss, legal counsel or personnel office, and take whatever action is necessary.

SOMETHING TO THINK ABOUT

Before you respond to any allegation of discrimination, make sure you know what your jurisdiction's equal opportunity laws and your company's own policies require. Once you understand these, think about how you want your unit to operate within the framework they establish.

The analysis and actions we've described are equally valid whether the allegation is racism or sexism or any other illegal discrimination. In summary:

- Check to make sure you have the facts.
- If possible, observe.
- Then take the appropriate action quickly.

Even if you believe Conrad has discriminated, you may be tempted to treat him as though it was unintentional. This may work, but be careful. If you take this course of action, he may not realize the seriousness of the situation. And you may subject yourself to a complaint (or worse, a lawsuit) because you didn't act to resolve the problem effectively.

If there is discrimination, you need to deal with more than this specific occurrence. One solution is to arrange for an experienced facilitator to conduct workshops to help your employees understand the law, company policy, and (perhaps) their own prejudices. If there are pockets of resistance to cooperation and inclusion of all employees, schedule the workshops so that people who are resistant to changing their prejudices are separated from one another and intermingled with employees who are already moving in the right direction.

Above all, fight discrimination through your personal example. If you treat everyone evenhandedly and sensitively and expect each employee to do the same, most discrimination won't occur.

No. 31 Disabled Employee

A team member's car accident means he can no longer use the computer keyboard

THE SCENE

Your boss calls you, clearly in shock. "I just heard about Jeremy," he says, "such a good worker and such a terrible tragedy. He's lost his wife and his baby, and now I understand they've had to amputate one of his hands. All because of some stupid drunk driver!"

"I'm not sure what to do," you reply. "I certainly want to help him as much as I can, but I don't know what kind of work I can give him when he comes back that won't require him to use the computer. I don't want him to lose his job over this too."

POSSIBLE CAUSES

You know what the cause is: Jeremy's been in a terrible traffic accident and now he's going to have trouble performing any job in your unit. He's been a good worker and you want to help him, but you're not feeling very confident at this point.

YOUR RESPONSE

Even if Jeremy weren't such a good worker, you would still have obligations to try to accommodate him when he comes back to work. The Americans with Disabilities Act of 1991 (ADA) applies to many employers, and requires "reasonable accommodation" for certain individuals. Talk to your boss, your personnel department, or legal counsel about how the Act applies to your situation.

In this instance, you'll want to help Jeremy for humanitarian reasons as well as legal ones. Here some ways you might approach the situation:

• Identify the "essential functions" of Jeremy's position. These are aspects of the job that are so fundamental that they *must* be performed. Among the reasons a function can be classified as essential are that it's the reason the position exists, or because there's no one else (or a limited number of people) available to perform the function, or because it requires special experience or training. For example, if the purpose of a job is to check the identification cards of people entering the work area, a person who has a severe visual impairment will probably not be able to perform that essential job function. If the purpose of a job is to act as a receptionist, a person whose disability causes frequent absences from work may not be able to perform the essential function of the job. "Essential functions" are contrasted with those that are marginally related to the main purpose of the job. If, for example, a receptionist uses her extra time to do filing but there are other people who do the filing when she's too busy, the filing duty is clearly marginal and not an "essential function" of the position.

- If there are nonessential functions that Jeremy can't perform any more, assign that work to others in your unit. You may find that some of those tasks aren't critical to your workgroup's success and don't need to be performed by anyone in particular, or perhaps don't need to be performed at all.

- Identify any barriers to Jeremy's performance of the essential job functions. In this case, the loss of one of his hands will make inputting information to the computer difficult, if not impossible.

- Next, talk to Jeremy about what accommodations might be available that would allow him to perform the job. You might also talk to rehabilitation experts, perhaps ones Jeremy knows and has worked with or rehabilitation experts at state agencies whose job is to help people return to productive work.

- Be as creative as you can possibly be in devising accommodations. You can always reject those that prove unworkable. Look at changes in scheduling (e.g., if an employee's impairment causes him to tire easily, schedule difficult tasks earlier in the day), restructuring (e.g., restructure Jeremy's job and the jobs of others in the unit so that other workers do the computer input, while Jeremy fields phone calls), job aids (which can be either technological assistance or human assistance, as in a reader for a visually impaired employee or a TTY device for a hearing-impaired employee). Depending on a particular employee's disability, other possible accommodations might include establishing a part-time schedule for the employee, reassigning him to another position, providing job coaches to help with training, providing a reserved parking space, or providing equipment to help the employee. You might have to make just one accommodation or a combination.

- Examine the probable effectiveness of each possible accommodation you've identified. A "reasonable" accommodation will allow the employee to perform his essential job functions but won't overburden you as an employer. If, for example, the only accommodation you and Jeremy could identify is to hire someone to whom Jeremy can dictate his work and who then inputs it to the computer, the cost to the company might be prohibitive. In that case, the accommodation would not be "reasonable." So look for another accommodation.

- Develop a plan. In Jeremy's situation, you might decide to give him more phone duties but, because he can't avoid all computer work, purchase voice recognition software so he can "dictate" to his computer rather than input through the keyboard.
- Follow up. Talk to Jeremy about how the accommodation is working, more frequently at first, less so over time. Assess his performance using the accommodations you've agreed upon. There may well be some fine-tuning to be done as you and Jeremy adjust to his situation.

SOMETHING TO THINK ABOUT

Accommodating a worker's disability isn't just the right legal solution, it's the right business solution. Whenever you can salvage a good employee, it's a less expensive alternative than hiring a new employee and training him to perform your job. Turnover costs, not just in the direct expense of finding and training your new employee but also in the loss of productivity until your new worker learns the job.

Whenever you possibly can, make accommodations for your sick and injured employees. They'll be just as motivated to do a good job for you after their illness or injury as before, and they already know how to do the job.

No. 32 ALCOHOL USE

She comes to work frequently with alcohol on her breath

THE SCENE

"Whew! You don't want to get downwind of Carla," remarks Jane to Leila, one of her coworkers.

"Is this the first time you've noticed?" replies Leila. "For months, she's been coming back from lunch reeking like a brewery. Somebody ought to say something to her, but it's not going to be me!"

This isn't the first time you've heard this conversation; only the speakers have changed. Everybody seems to have noticed Carla's luncheon habits. But what can you do? Isn't it Carla's business what she does on her own time?

POSSIBLE CAUSES

Carla may just enjoy having a drink at lunchtime.

It may not affect her performance, and while her coworkers may discuss her habits among themselves, it may not impair her relationships with them.

Carla may enjoy having a drink, with no impairment of her performance, but the obvious odor of alcohol may put off some of the people she deals with at work.

Carla may come back from lunch under the influence of alcohol—to the point where it impairs her ability to concentrate and to handle her work assignments.

YOUR RESPONSE

If Carla is not impaired by her lunchtime drinking, and it seems to have no negative effect on her interactions with customers or coworkers:

It's best to leave it alone. Unless her off-the-job activities affect her on-the-job effectiveness, what Carla does on her own time *is* her business. If there is clearly no connection, then you have no basis for intervening.

If Carla is not impaired, but her interactions with others suffer:

Take her aside quietly and explain that her relations with customers, or others around her, are affected by her alcohol use. Emphasize that she can do what she wants at lunch—except when her activities interfere with her effectiveness later on. Explain that the odor of alcohol is offensive to some people and that diminished relationships with customers and coworkers harm her job performance.

Decide what action you'll take if Carla doesn't change. If it's possible to reassign her to work where she has little interaction with others, consider that solution first.

Make clear to Carla the possible consequences of not changing her luncheon behavior, whether that's a change of assignment or disciplinary action. Emphasize that an assignment to work that involves little interpersonal interaction is likely to hamper her career progress, but that the choice is hers. She can change the way she spends her lunch period, or she can incur the consequences.

Take this opportunity to make Carla aware that assistance is available if she needs it. Refer her to your employee assistance program or, if your company doesn't have one, an outside source of help for substance abuse problems. Remember: You can't force Carla to accept assistance, you can only enforce your own work performance standards.

If Carla's ability to do her work is impaired:

Deal with the issue immediately and firmly. See Challenge 27 for specific instructions for dealing with employees who are under the influence of alcohol or drugs on the job.

SOMETHING TO THINK ABOUT

Be sure you separate the problem of alcohol on an employee's breath from the completely separate problem of an employee whose level of performance is impaired by alcohol or another drug. While the former may be part of an abuse problem, it isn't always.

No. 33 OFFICE ROMANCE GOES AWRY

A messy breakup of two employees is creating problems in the office

THE SCENE

Julie is the last to arrive at a staff meeting, and all the places are taken except the one beside Don.

"Well," you say to yourself, "this should be interesting. The hot office romance decays to smoke and ashes. Let's see how uncomfortable it gets in here today."

A pleasant surprise—there are no sharp exchanges and no overt hostilities, but it's obvious that the rest of the staff is on edge, probably because of the blow-up the two of them had just a few days ago. The situation is awkward for everyone. So what happens now?

POSSIBLE CAUSES

As in a few of the other cases we've looked at, it's not necessary here to know what *caused* the problem, but it is necessary to have some information about the situation:

First, does the breakup seem to be affecting the performance of either of the two people involved?

Second, regardless of how well the principals themselves are handling the situation, is it having a negative effect on the rest of your staff?

> **Hint**: A cardinal rule of management is this: You're justified in involving yourself in your employees' personal lives only to the extent that what they're doing off the job affects what happens *on* the job. If these two former lovers hurl epithets at one another, slander each other, or worse when they're not at work, but are models of decorum on the job, then you have *no* basis for getting involved. But as soon as what's happening in their personal lives begins to affect their work, or that of others, you should step in firmly and swiftly.

YOUR RESPONSE

Regardless of the situation:

Do not, repeat *do not*, treat one of the members of this pair significantly differently from the other unless you have a clear work-related reason for doing so. We've seen situations in which one member of a couple was reassigned to a position generally perceived as less desirable while the other member stayed put, with no obvious reason for the disparate treatment. That almost invites a discrimination complaint.

If the breakup is affecting the performance of the people involved:

Have a talk with the affected employees individually, explaining in some detail to each one the deterioration you've noticed in his or her work performance. Let the employees know that you're aware of their personal situation and delicately inquire if that situation could be the cause of the performance problems.

Offer to refer the employee to a counselor or to provide other appropriate assistance to help him or her work through the situation. At the same time, make it clear that you expect the performance problems to be corrected. Emphasize that the situation you're concerned about is *not* the breakup, but the deteriorating performance.

If you can arrange it without causing the work of your unit to suffer, offer the employees a reassignment, permanent or temporary, to allow time for emotions to cool.

If the relationship is having a negative effect on the rest of your staff:

Observe carefully to see whether the actions of the two employees are the cause of the disturbances in your staff, or whether it's the staff's *anticipation* of trouble that's affecting them badly. If the problem isn't due to anything the two employees themselves are doing (or not doing), then you can't hold them responsible. In that case, time and continued civil relations between the parties will probably solve the problem.

If you can attribute the negative effects on the staff to either of the two employees involved in the breakup, then talk to the employee(s), explain what behaviors are causing strained relations among the staff and remind them of their responsibility to establish and maintain effective work relationships.

Then see that they take whatever steps are necessary to mend the relationships with their coworkers.

SOMETHING TO THINK ABOUT

Office romances can pose even greater challenges (whether during the romance or as a result of a breakup) if the romance is between a manager and a subordinate. Many companies have explicit policies against dating between managers and their employees—and for good reason. When the relationship is moving along smoothly, there's a perception among other employees (whether justified or not) that the manager is showing favoritism to his or her subordinate. And when the relationship falls apart, the situation described here is even more challenging. If your company doesn't already have a policy about managers dating their employees, establish one. . . and stick by it.

CHAPTER FIVE

Building Win-Win Relationships with Employees

No. 34 Rude Employee

A key supplier is angered over your employee's offensive manner

THE SCENE

"Charlie, I can't believe I have anyone who would pull a dumb stunt like that. I can absolutely, certainly promise you it won't happen again. My God, I'm mortified!"

And you are. You slam the receiver down and start for the door. You've known that Art Mayfield's people skills weren't the greatest, but yelling at the manager of Eastern Manufacturing and then hanging up on him is too much.

POSSIBLE CAUSES

Charlie (or someone else at Eastern) did something that provoked Art.

So far, you've heard only one side of the story.

Bad blood has been building between Art and Eastern.

It may be that this is a "last straw" encounter.

Art really did "blow his stack" without reason.

105

Hint: What Art did was wrong, regardless of its cause. The question isn't whether to take strong corrective action. The question is whether you can remedy the situation short of firing Art.

YOUR RESPONSE

No matter what the cause is:

Make sure that your own anger is under control. This is going to be a rough situation, and you need a clear head to deal with it. That doesn't mean you shouldn't be mad. You should, and Art should know it from the word go. But your anger should be controlled. If it isn't, take a walk, kick some file cabinets, do whatever you have to do to get back in control.

Then call Art in. Tell him exactly what you've heard. Don't exaggerate. Don't pull punches. Let him see how angry the call made you. He needs to know that he's in trouble.

Now, here comes the really hard part. Give him every chance to explain his side—and listen, listen, listen. This is hard to do, but in this serious a situation it's absolutely necessary. If the encounter gets too emotional, break it off and get back to Art later.

If someone at Eastern really did provoke Art:

In this situation, you must consider Art's record with the company. If he's been a good worker, and this is the first time something like this has happened, give him the benefit of the doubt.

If possible, have him get back to Charlie himself to mend the situation. You keep close tabs on it, though—both to support Art and to make sure that he's doing what needs to be done.

If Art can restore the relationship effectively, go lightly on him. Perhaps a short, unequivocal counseling session will be enough. But he needs to understand clearly that, regardless of what anyone at Eastern did, his conduct can't be tolerated. If he understands, let him continue working with Eastern.

If Art is too involved in the situation, or lacks the skills to handle it effectively, you get back to Eastern and Charlie, quickly. If you can do it in person, that's the first choice. If not, get on the phone. See if Charlie realizes and acknowledges the contribution he made to the problem. If he's calmed down and is willing to cooperate, see if you can get him to talk with Art. If Charlie and Art can smooth out their relationship, fine. If they can't, move Art and get someone else to work with Eastern.

SOMETHING TO THINK ABOUT

A great deal has been made—and justly so—about pleasing customers. Maintaining good relationships with suppliers is only slightly less important. You cannot tolerate having employees who do anything less than deal effectively with the companies you depend on for your raw materials.

But suppose you hadn't made this clear to Art? Suppose you didn't communicate effectively to your workers how critical the relationship is? Suppose you didn't take the relationship with Eastern seriously enough? In that case, slack off on Art, he's not the main culprit. Start remedying the situation by changing your own attitudes and actions toward Eastern and your other suppliers, and be sure you convey your change in perspective to your workers.

If Art won't face the problem or can't help you solve it, take strong action. Just what's best will depend on your company's policies. Admonishment, suspension, reassignment—any of these might be appropriate options.

If bad blood has been building between Art and Eastern:

Art has helped create an extremely serious situation. He should have informed you of what was happening long ago. His not doing so is just as critical as the incident.

Again, take prompt action with Eastern. Try to work with Charlie or anyone else at Eastern to find out what went wrong and remedy it. At this point, you must first do whatever is necessary to resolve the situation with Eastern. If Art can be of any help, use him, but carefully.

Evaluate your options with Art. Unless there were mitigating circumstances—very mitigating circumstances—it will be a long time before you can trust him to deal with suppliers again. If you can find a position where his skills can be used without the danger of alienating others, do so.

If not, supervise his contacts with suppliers and customers very carefully for the next few months to be sure there are no signs of new troubles brewing.

In either case, he should have the definite feeling that he just barely avoided disaster.

If Art lost his temper and alienated Eastern without reason:

Forget Art for the moment and get back to Charlie. Do *whatever* you must to reassure Eastern that this was an isolated incident, one that won't happen again. Assure them that they won't have to deal with Art again. If necessary, cry real tears and promise them your first-born.

Then take care of Art. The basic question is: Has he been a good employee in the past, and is he apt to be so valuable in the future that he shouldn't be fired?

If you can answer "yes," take forceful action short of firing Art. The action should definitely include moving him into another job, even one at lower pay.

If the answer isn't "yes," fire him. That may sound inhumane, but it's necessary.

No. 35 Flextime Abuse

An employee on a flexible work schedule has falsified his work hours

THE SCENE

"Betty, this is serious. Are you sure Arnie left at 3:30 last Wednesday?

"I promise you there was no mistake. He came out and checked to see if you were here. When he saw you weren't, he went back, turned off his computer, and left. I waited till today to tell you so he'd have turned in his time sheet—and I'll bet it shows he worked until 5:30 or 6:00."

"It does. I've been afraid this was happening, but this is the first concrete evidence I've had. Are you willing to put this in writing if necessary?"

"Sure, I don't want him or anyone else screwing up flexible scheduling—I need it too much."

Betty isn't your best worker or the easiest one to manage, but she's completely honest. If she said Arnie left early, Arnie left early.

POSSIBLE CAUSES

The workgroup is very sloppy about flexible work hours.

You haven't been paying much attention to how accurately workgroup members record their time. They have the impression that nobody really cares how accurately they track their hours.

Arnie has been abusing his flexible work schedule.

He's simply been using the freedom it provides to get paid for more work than he puts in.

Hint: Note that these causes may be interrelated.

YOUR RESPONSE

If the workgroup is very sloppy about flexible work hours:

Flexible work hours are a tremendous benefit for workers that costs the organization nothing and often enables it to retain workers it would otherwise lose. But the benefit doesn't police itself. Unless workers know that management is paying attention, someone is going to start taking advantage of the situation. If that person gets away with it, others will take advantage. Soon productivity will drop and the organization will have to decree an end to the flexibility.

Arnie may be abusing the flexible schedule because of your inattention. How do you correct the situation and correct it quickly? Start by talking about it at group meetings. Make it clear that workers can enjoy the benefit only as long as they use it responsibly. Review everyone's time sheets periodically and question any reported time that looks out of line.

Most important, though, be there at the beginning and the end of the workday. If you typically come in later but your earliest workers log in at 6:00 or 6:30, come in at that time occasionally. You might get a cup of coffee and wander around enough to chat briefly with everyone, to make it known that you're there, and that there's no telling how early you might show up at work. And if you don't usually stay until the end of the scheduled workday, adjust your schedule to remain until then. And make sure your workers know you're there.

If Arnie has been abusing his flexible work schedule:

Call Arnie in and tell him what you've learned. Don't start by lecturing him. Ask him what he has to say and listen carefully. Regardless of how certain you are he's falsified his time sheet, you should give him every opportunity to present his side of the matter.

What if he denies that he left? Now it's his word against Betty's, and if you believe she's telling the truth you take her word. (Be careful, though, that she doesn't have any reasons to lie or to "get" Arnie.) Let Arnie know that you don't accept his explanation and that you'll be watching him closely—both because you're concerned that he's not devoting as much time to the job as he's expected to and because you're concerned about his trustworthiness.

Suppose he admits it, but claims that everyone else is doing it? Ask him for evidence. If he has some, consider it. If it really is the case that large numbers of workers have been abusing the flexible schedule, you should just admonish Arnie briefly and then take all of the steps described in the first response to cure the systemic problem.

If Arnie can't produce real evidence that "everyone is doing it," proceed as though he were the only one abusing the system, because he's the only one you have concrete evidence on. And while you don't necessarily want to make an example of Arnie, he and others have to understand that taking advantage of the system simply isn't permitted.

A final comment. Anyone who consistently abuses flexible work hours should be removed from the flex schedule for a long enough period of time to get the point that you take this matter seriously. How long? Normally, at least a month and quite possibly longer. This is too important a benefit to treat lightly.

SOMETHING TO THINK ABOUT

It's unfortunate, but a supervisor's job always has something of the policeman in it. Most of the time, most workers abide by the rules and manage themselves. But there's always the one individual who believes the rules are for someone else, and tries to take advantage by shaving the work day here and there, taking extended breaks, getting and making private telephone calls—the list goes on and on.

It's important that you catch these abuses and stop them. The important point isn't punishment, though you may have to discipline individuals. The key is to communicate clearly that the rules are meant to be followed and that you won't tolerate individuals breaking them simply for their own benefit. In the long run, this keeps workers out of trouble. It may also persuade individuals who would have cheated on the system if they'd had the chance to remain productive and employed.

No. 36 Fails to Manage Priorities

She does what she likes, not what needs to be done

THE SCENE

When you passed Marybeth's desk, you couldn't help but look at what she was working on. Sure enough, it was the new office layout. She's doing it again! You've told her at least three times that the end-of-month reports need to be done before she works on office improvement. What do you have to do to get her to follow the right priorities?

POSSIBLE CAUSES

Marybeth honestly believes that the office layout is more important than the reports.

This doesn't make her right, but at least she's being conscientious.

Marybeth is getting burned out on her regular duties.

She'll turn to anything that will relieve the boredom.

She's undisciplined and sets her priorities by what interests her.

> **Hint:** One of the basic skills of a fully competent employee is the ability to set appropriate priorities. When an employee can't do this, you (the manager) can't fully delegate work to her.

YOUR RESPONSE

No matter what the situation is:

If you've lost your temper, wait until you cool down. Then call Marybeth in, and be straightforward. Tell her you saw what she's working on. Then give her the opportunity to explain her side of the situation. While it might not seem so, it's most important to listen carefully to an employee when you believe she's in the wrong.

If she honestly believes that the layout is more important than the reports:

This requires skillful listening. You told her to set other priorities, but she believes she should do the layout instead. Ask her why, and listen carefully as she tells you. Otherwise you may end up seeming arbitrary—which will probably make her angry and make the problem even harder to solve.

If she convinces you she's right, agree with her. Work out a satisfactory set of priorities for the reports and the layouts and agree that she is to follow them.

If she set her own priorities because you wouldn't listen to her, assure her that you'll listen next time—and do so. But counsel her that she's not to disregard your instructions in those cases where you've set clear priorities.

Suppose she had the chance to persuade you but couldn't, and then set her own priorities regardless of what you said? Tell her clearly and firmly that her behavior is not acceptable. Warn her that if it happens again you'll have to take away some of the more distracting (and obviously more interesting) work. Then, if it does happen again, be as good as your word.

There's one more possibility. Marybeth disagreed with you but didn't say anything. What now? Would you have listened if she had said something? Are you sure? If you're sure, see that Marybeth understands that, in those cases when you set the priorities, it's because they're important—and that you expect her to follow them. If you wouldn't have listened, or if you give people the impression that you wouldn't, that's something you need to work on.

If she's getting burned out on her regular duties:

Marybeth may want to do what you told her, she may even think the reports are more important, but they've gotten so boring and empty for her that she'll do almost anything else to avoid them. In Challenge 16, we discussed how to deal with an employee who finds his job boring. Look at it for some suggestions that might apply to Marybeth's situation.

There's one other point to consider. Is Marybeth a relatively new employee? If so, a basic problem may be that she isn't cut out for the job she's doing. Perhaps you can reassign her, or help her get reassigned to a job that fits better. At the least, you should show her how—if she does her current job well—she might get promoted to more interesting work.

If she sets priorities by what interests her:

This may be a good characteristic for an inventor or tinkerer, but it shows a lack of discipline in most other jobs.

It's not necessary to know why Marybeth is this way, but it may help to know. Is she just young and inexperienced? Has she been working for an ineffective supervisor who let her do what she wanted? Or is she simply so hard to deal with that no one has wanted to tangle with her?

Whatever the situation, you do need to exercise some care—especially if she's a good worker (or potentially so). Her preference for the layout work may indicate that she's in the wrong job or doesn't do well at some of her regular duties. When the immediate problem is solved, see if job changes are warranted (as in the preceding response).

Now that we've said all that, the problem is that Marybeth isn't doing what she should be doing and what you told her to do. You need to call her in and explain clearly that following the priorities you set is a basic requirement of the job and that you expect her to comply. If she complains about the work or disagrees with your priorities, offer to discuss that further with her—*after* she completes the reports.

After this situation is settled, you may need to have yet another talk with Marybeth. If you think she'd be receptive, you need to explain to her the problems she'll create for herself if she gets the reputation of wanting to work only on jobs she finds interesting. Show her that from a manager's point of view the best and most promotable employees are those who are willing to do whatever the organization needs done.

SOMETHING TO THINK ABOUT

In the long run, all workers (including you and us) are happiest and most productive doing duties they like. One of the fundamental tasks of management is to get the right people in the right jobs. But this has to be balanced against the immediate need to get the work done, whether it's interesting or not. A good manager needs to keep both short-run and long-run factors in mind in all dealings with employees.

Whenever you can, build into each job some work that's challenging and creative. Even one or two duties that require workers to do more than follow a dull routine can liven up the entire work experience.

No. 37 Flouts the Rules

An employee is a poor worker because she won't follow work procedures

THE SCENE

Carlotta did it again! She handled that problem with Mrs. Woods beautifully—tactful, conciliatory, just the right note of urgency. She can charm suppliers out of almost anything. But when it was all over and Carlotta hung up the phone, did she document the call and let the shop floor know when they could expect the next shipment of supplies? *No, she did not!* She went on to make another call, so now no one knows when the material is due. And when someone else calls the supplier, not knowing that Carlotta already has, they're likely to get angry and not send anything. She *could* be such a good worker, if only she'd follow procedures.

POSSIBLE CAUSES

Carlotta may not see any value in doing things your way.

Particularly if there's no negative consequence to her for not following instructions and plenty of positive consequences for *not* following them (like positive experiences with the suppliers), Carlotta may view the established procedures as a waste of her time.

Carlotta may not know how to perform the particular procedures you're concerned about.

She may know a lot about how to wheel and deal on the telephone, but may have problems with the paperwork. In that case, she's most likely to do the things she knows well and skip the tasks with which she's less comfortable.

Carlotta may see herself as a free spirit who can't be bothered with your petty requirements.

She may consider that her failure to follow procedures "makes a statement" and sets her apart from her fellow workers—and it certainly does, but probably not in the way Carlotta expects.

YOUR RESPONSE

If Carlotta doesn't see any value in doing things your way:

Explain to her the importance of the procedures you've established and how her failure to perform them affects the rest of the unit.

Walk Carlotta through the other parts of your operation so she can see for herself how her failure to follow procedures makes it harder for other people to produce.

Look at the way you've organized the work and the consequences to Carlotta of not following procedures. Wherever possible, arrange positive consequences for following the procedures and negative ones for not following them. At the very least, you can make sure that following procedures is an item that's specifically addressed in your performance reviews.

Make sure Carlotta knows the consequences to her personally of failing to follow proper procedures—for example, poor performance appraisals, low (or no) raises, possible reassignment (into something less interesting or challenging).

If Carlotta doesn't know how to perform the procedures:

Talk to Carlotta to try to find out what parts of the job she's having problems with. Keep in mind that she may not tell you. She may prefer to disguise her lack of knowledge as a *refusal* to follow instructions rather than an inability. In that case, treat the situation as if she didn't see the value in doing things your way (as described earlier). Let her know the serious consequences of her continued failure to follow procedures and encourage her to tell you about any parts of the job she's having trouble performing.

If through your discussions with Carlotta or through your own observations you're able to identify specific areas where she needs help, find the best way to teach her those skills. There may be formal courses that she can take (particularly for things like basic literacy skills or keyboard skills). Or it may be better for her to work with an experienced employee who can coach her through the process until she gets it right.

Follow up with Carlotta. Congratulate her on her successes, and continue to identify and help her overcome her difficulties. However, be sure she understands that the ultimate responsibility for doing a good job is hers.

If Carlotta sees herself as a free spirit who can't be bothered with following your bureaucratic requirements:

This cause is somewhat like the first one, but not exactly. In this case, Carlotta may objectively understand the value to the organization of following procedures, but may not see their applicability to her.

Review with her the reasons for establishing the procedures and their importance to her job and to the rest of the organization. Try as much as possible to describe the effect of her failure to perform on other *employees* rather than on the organization. Often, the object of a rebel's actions is the impersonal bureaucracy; pointing out the harm her actions do to *people* may help Carlotta see the procedural requirements in a new light.

Emphasize to Carlotta the personal consequences to her of her failure to perform, including poor performance reviews and possible termination. She may still see her "cause" as more important and make a conscious decision not to follow your instructions. In that case, be prepared to follow through with the consequences you've outlined. If the procedures and employees' willingness to be team players are important to your organization, then, for the sake of the organization, you will have to "make a statement" of your own—by dealing assertively with Carlotta.

SOMETHING TO THINK ABOUT

In many ways, intentional poor performance is harder to deal with than is poor performance that results from employees not knowing how to do the work or from their inability to do the work. If someone doesn't know how, you teach her. If, after training, this employee is still unable to do the work, you find something else for her to do or terminate her.

Intentional poor performance is particularly troublesome because employees may *sometimes* perform as you want them to, but you can't predict when. And because the problem is one of *unwillingness* to do the work, there's nothing you can do to make the employee get it done.

If all this sounds terribly discouraging, remember that ultimately you are not responsible for your employees' performance. They are. You can coach, encourage, exhort, praise, reward, and correct them. But eventually, your responsibility ends. Not every employee will work out. Congratulate yourself on the successes, but don't beat yourself up about the failures.

No. 38 Bends the Rules

A key staff member ignores company policy to get the work done

THE SCENE

Monday morning finds you on your way to an important meeting in the farthest section of the warehouse. As you stroll briskly through the busy sections, you see Tim whip around a corner on his forklift, narrowly missing the corner of the stacks and another worker.

Tim always gets the job done—often faster than others—and has never had an accident. But he's had several near misses. It doesn't seem to matter how many times you stress safety rules in your staff meetings; Tim just ignores them and does his work his way.

POSSIBLE CAUSES AND YOUR RESPONSE

This situation is a lot like the one described in Challenge 37 in this chapter. The main difference is that Carlotta is a poor worker *because* she won't follow the rules, while Tim is a good worker *in spite of* the fact that he won't follow the rules.

The causes and responses for the two situations are about the same, with these differences:

It is less likely in this case that Tim doesn't follow the procedures because he doesn't know how. If he's a good worker who ignores rules to get his work done, chances are that it's because he sees a positive benefit (reaching his production goals) in not meeting your requirements and sees no benefit in doing things your way.

In Carlotta's case, there is a clear consequence of her failure to follow the rules (her poor performance). In Tim's case, there is no demonstrable result. He gets his work done, and he hasn't had any accidents. So the sole issue here is the violation of company rules.

Decide how important it is that Tim follow the rules. While he may be able to ignore safety requirements without having an accident, does his behavior set a bad example for other workers who may not be as skilled as he is? Does the nature of the work itself require that employees follow rules without question, even ones they don't agree with (as for example, when you're dealing with hazardous materials, confidential information, or in other sensitive situations)?

If you decide that it is critical that Tim follow the rules, then first explain to him your rationale. Acknowledge his good performance, stressing that truly good performance requires not only that the end product be right, but also that the procedures be followed correctly. Invite him to tell you if following the rules prevents him from meeting his production requirements and to suggest ways to rearrange assignments so that the rules don't get in the way.

Explain also that, regardless of how well he's performing, following company rules is also a bottom-line issue. Remind him that violation of the rules, if serious enough, could result in disciplinary action. Express your confidence in his ability to get the work out *within* the rules, and point out examples of employees who manage to accomplish a lot without violations.

Then follow up. If Tim changes his behavior, congratulate him. If the rules really may interfere with production, then overlook for a time slight performance slippages that may occur as he readjusts his mode of operation. If he fails to conform to the rules, remind him again—then take whatever corrective action is warranted.

SOMETHING TO THINK ABOUT

You always have a problem when a worker—good or poor—refuses to follow work rules. If the rules are inefficient, change them. If they aren't, explain and enforce them. In short, have as few rules as possible, and then see that everyone follows them.

No. 39 UNMOTIVATED NEW EMPLOYEE

A new worker is properly qualified, but seems poorly motivated

THE SCENE

"I just don't understand about Janine," you remark to your friend Harry at lunch. "Loretta over in Stock Accounting said she was her top producer, and Ruben in Inventory Control thought she was great. But as soon as she was transferred over to my group, she just sat down on the job. She's developing an 'attitude' too. I don't need another problem like that, but I also don't know what I can do to get her motivated here."

"Sorry, I can't help you with this one," responds Harry. "But it sounds as if you'd better think of something or things will only get worse."

POSSIBLE CAUSES

Janine may not like the work in her new assignment.

She may have interests or aspirations in another direction and not be interested in the work she's doing now.

She may have been comfortable in her old job and be fearful that she won't perform well for you.

That kind of anxiety drives some people to work harder, but for some people (Janine may be one of them), the normal response is to admit defeat immediately and give up trying.

She may not know how to do the work.

Many people equate ignorance (which is simply not knowing something) with stupidity (or the inability to learn). Fearful that they will appear stupid if they admit they don't know how to do the work, they never tell you what the real problem is. So lack of knowledge *appears* to be lack of motivation.

> ***Hint:*** Whenever an employee is not fulfilling your expectations for performance in a job, it's very tempting to blame it on lack of motivation. But many times, apparent lack of motivation masks the real cause. Before you place all the blame for poor performance on the employee, consider what else could be contributing to the problem. Then do what you can to remove those impediments. Your efforts don't let the employee off the hook for improving her own work, but they will improve her chances of success. And it's much better to salvage a current employee than it is to start all over again with a new, and unknown, worker.

YOUR RESPONSE

If Janine doesn't like the work:

Talk to her to find out what kind of work she's most interested in and point out to her those parts of her new job that are most similar to the things she likes to do.

Let Janine know that if she does well in her current assignments, you'll try to arrange for more of the work she finds interesting or help her find a job that's closer to what she's looking for.

Make it clear to Janine that your offers to help her don't substitute for her hard work and diligence in her current job. Be sure she understands that the responsibility for good performance is hers and that she'll still be held accountable for what she does (or doesn't do) in the job she has now, whether she likes the job or not.

If Janine is afraid she won't do a good job in her new position:

Talk with her to let her know that you don't expect her to know how to do everything exactly right when she first walks into a new job. Express your confidence in her skills, pointing out that she wouldn't have been placed in the job if you didn't think she was qualified to perform the work—and perform it well.

Make sure Janine gets to know everyone in the new office and has a special introduction to people in other organizations with whom she may have to interact in the course of her assignments.

Encourage her to come to you if there are parts of her job she's not sure how to handle, or identify a coworker who can be a good resource person (especially if you think she feels threatened by having to admit her imperfections to her boss).

Try to structure the job so that Janine's first few assignments are fairly simple ones that will give her an idea of what her job is and how to get things done in your organization without overwhelming her.

Most important of all, give Janine some time to adjust. You've told her you don't expect her to know everything right away, so don't act as if every mistake is a major failing. Let her know when she could have done better, but be patient.

If Janine doesn't know how to do the work:

Find out from Janine's previous supervisors, from the personnel department's files, and from Janine herself what kind of work she's done in the past and any training she's had that would equip her to do your job.

Identify the skill deficiencies she has that interfere with her performance. To do that, you'll need to keep some records of the things she does right and the things she does wrong. Fairly soon a pattern should emerge that will point to specific areas where she needs improvement.

Check with your personnel department to see if there are any formal classes available that Janine can take to learn the skills she needs.Formal classroom training, if it's directly related to what happens back on the job, is frequently the fastest way to gain knowledge or skills.

Identify a mentor for Janine—someone to whom she can go when she has questions or problems and who can check her work and help her correct her errors. It's better if the mentor is someone in the organization other than her supervisor or leader so she can feel free to admit problems without feeling threatened.

If there are several parts of the job Janine needs to learn, parcel out some of the work to several other employees and give Janine the few things that are *essential* to the job. As she masters those, you can add in the rest.

Encourage Janine and give her all the positive feedback you can. At the same time, let her know that you expect her to pick up on the job and that doing well is ultimately her responsibility, regardless of the amount of assistance you're able to give her.

SOMETHING TO THINK ABOUT

Note that every response we've discussed begins with a direction such as "Talk with Janine. . . " *Whenever* you have a problem with an employee, performance or otherwise, one of your first actions should be to talk to the employee. You may find that the answer is simpler than you'd thought.

No. 40 A "Down" Attitude
He's a great worker but his negative attitude drags others down

THE SCENE

Paula isn't exaggerating when she tells you how frustrating Maury is. He's consistently one of your top two or three producers, but he's so full of negativity that no one wants to work with him or even be around him. He fights every change, he assures everyone constantly that the company is about to reorganize the workgroup out of existence, and he criticizes even the smallest mistake to death. He just plain brings everyone down, constantly.

POSSIBLE CAUSES

Maury doesn't realize he's being so negative.

Sounds too simple, but it may be true. He just thinks he's giving his honest opinions.

He simply doesn't care about the others.

If his pay is based on his individual production, he may not see any reason to worry about his impact on everyone else.

He has a serious emotional problem.

He's "trapped" in his negativity, and his griping provides him a way to escape it for a while.

YOUR RESPONSE

No matter what the cause is:

You know what the problem looks like from outside; now you need to talk with Maury. More accurately, you need to listen to Maury, as carefully as possible. Don't be judgmental, but describe how his negative attitude appears from the outside. Then listen to how he sees it. Ask helpful questions, but don't put him on the spot.

The following responses concentrate on dealing with the specific situation of a specific employee. Be sure to read "Something to Think About" at the end of this problem for a suggestion on how to turn negatives like this into positives.

If he doesn't realize he's being so negative:

If you think this is the situation, be as tactful as possible, but point out to Maury the effect he's having on others. This may be all you need to do to get his attention. He may be a little offended by what you say, but he'll probably understand. (This may take several talks.)

This may not significantly change his negativity, but he may not voice it as frequently at work. This may be all you need. Make sure that both you and the other employees notice any improvement and recognize him for it. If you don't, he may conclude no one really cares and go back to voicing his negative feelings.

If he doesn't care about his effect on others:

Most employees are sensitive to other employees' reactions and want their approval. But some employees just don't care. Some will do what rewards *them*, with little or no thought for others. This is particularly true if the individual is a "loner," or someone the group doesn't particularly like.

One approach is to assign Maury duties that don't bring him into contact with others, if the group's work permits that. Then he can continue to be as negative as he wants and still produce what he needs to. Everything considered, this may be the simplest and quickest solution. (This may also work if you try the response before this one and it fails.)

If you can't assign Maury duties separate from others, can you make at least part of his compensation dependent on working effectively with others? No matter how negative he is, if he and other workers see that they have to work together or else, everyone will find a way to deal with the negativity.

If he has a serious emotional problem:

Don't play amateur psychologist and don't let anyone else in the workgroup do so either. If this is an emotional problem, it's beyond your capabilities to correct. If an opportunity presents itself, you might suggest that he get professional help.

Then limit yourself and the group to being as supportive as possible. Don't let his negativity frustrate you and other workgroup members or make any of you angry. That just makes it harder for everyone and makes it harder for Maury to control his negative comments. On the other hand, don't agree with his negative statements. Accept what he says, explain how you see the same situation if you want, then drop the matter. Don't get into arguments or extended discussions.

Once again, any time you or a workgroup member see even a small improvement, be sure to notice it and recognize it. If he can change, that positive response will help him do so.

SOMETHING TO THINK ABOUT

You want a workgroup filled with "can do, will do" workers—individuals with a genuine positive attitude. But you also need individuals who will be honest about proposed changes and who are picky about the quality of their and others' work. Their approach may be labeled as negative when they're really trying hard to help.

How do you manage the situation? Let's take a product that one of your "negative" workers thinks isn't good enough. Can he identify why it isn't good enough? Can he communicate to the individual(s) who produced it how to fix the problem or how to avoid it the next time? Try to get your workers to link suggestions for improvement with any problem they identify.

Encourage this approach in general. Whenever someone sees a problem in a product or a proposed change, ask the person to identify the problem as specifically as possible and to propose one or more ways the problem could be overcome. If you have some really negative workers, they may resist this. Let them, but insist on it as the price of voicing their negativity. It could turn around even someone like Maury.

No. 41 TECHNOPHOBIA

An employee refuses to adapt to new procedures or technology

THE SCENE

"Mac, you don't seem to be using your new personal computer very much."

"Nah. It just doesn't do that much for me. I still get all my work done, just like always."

Mac does get his work done, but only because Dimitri, your office clerk, knows how to turn his sketchy handwritten notes into contracts. Mac is the only one left who Dimitri has to do this for, and before long she's not going to be available to help him. How do you get him to start using his computer so there won't be a blow-up when that happens?

POSSIBLE CAUSES

Mac thinks the new technology is demeaning.

For him, actually "typing" the contracts is clerical work that's beneath him.

He thinks that it will make his job less interesting.

Many people associate new technology, especially automation, with boring jobs.

He thinks it may make him unnecessary.

It's hard to get someone to be enthusiastic about new equipment that may replace him.

He may simply be afraid he can't learn it.

If he doesn't try, he doesn't have to face the embarrassment of failure.

> **Hint:** In Challenge 17 we dealt with the situation of a work unit that didn't want to change. What applies to groups of employees also applies to individuals: People will change only when they believe that (1) the change will help them; (2) they can successfully produce the change; and (3) the change is worth the effort it will take.

Whenever you want someone to change, you need to show him that the change will be beneficial to him, is practical, and is worth it. When you do that, the person will usually change.

YOUR RESPONSE

If Mac thinks the new technology is demeaning:

For many people, using computers or fax machines or other office technology means doing their own "clerical" work. This is particularly true when they have to use a keyboard. Many of us were brought up to believe that only clerks use typewriters. When someone puts a computer with a keyboard on our desk, it looks like they want to make clerks out of us.

If that's how Mac looks at the situation, your first objective is to see that he understands the difference between using a personal computer and doing typing. A personal computer lets him do more of his job; it really means that *no one* does the clerical work.

You may also have to see that he has the skills necessary to use the new technology. No matter how he feels about computers in general, Mac may be uncomfortable because he doesn't have good keyboarding skills. Getting him self-paced training in keyboarding, or sending him to a class (made up of other nonclerical employees) will help.

Depending on the kind of work he does on the computer, it may also be possible to find voice-recognition software that will allow Mac to give dictation through his computer rather than type on it. Then he won't need significant keyboarding skills at all.

If the problem is attitude, though, skills training alone won't solve it. You'll need to explain to Mac how personal computers can make it easier for others to do their job. Perhaps you need to have another employee, one whom Mac trusts, show him how useful it can be. If he understands that his using his computer will help Dimitri move up to a better job, that may help, too.

If he thinks it will make his job less interesting:

Unfortunately, organizations have often used computers in ways that *do* make jobs less interesting. There are still work sites with rooms full of data clerks who do nothing but input information to a computer screen hour after hour. It's easy for employees to believe that a computer on their desktop will make drones out of them.

What you have to do is show Mac that this isn't the case. If you have another employee who's using a computer effectively, have him or her show

Mac how helpful it is. Perhaps there's a training course available that shows how to use computers effectively.

In general, computers make jobs easier and, often, more interesting. You need to see that Mac understands this. Once you can get him actually using it, he'll probably find it out for himself.

SOMETHING TO THINK ABOUT

Whenever you can, design your jobs so that the outcome, not the method, is what counts. Allow your employees the freedom, or at least some degree of choice, in how they achieve that outcome.

Most of the time, it probably doesn't matter whether Mac enters his own information into the computer, dictates drafts, or writes on stone tablets. What matters is that he produces work of acceptable quality and at an acceptable rate.

If you focus on the outcome rather than the method, you can more easily hold employees accountable for what they produce or fail to produce. And employees resistant to change may well figure out for themselves that they needs to make a change if they're going to meet their performance goals.

If he thinks he may be replaced by the new technology:

This is a common reaction to new technology, because technology is so often justified as a way of reducing the workforce.

If your company is intending to reduce workers because of this new equipment, you need to be honest with your employees about it. See if the company has a program for retraining and reassignment inside for displaced workers. If not, see if the company at least has an effective outplacement program or if early retirement is an option for some of your staff. If there's nothing else, explain to Mac that learning to use the new technology will make him more employable elsewhere.

Normally, new office technology *won't* reduce workers. If this is the case, see that Mac—and every other employee—knows it. He may still think it's demeaning or will make his job less interesting, but this will relieve him enough to let you work through the other problems with him.

If he doesn't want to try because he's afraid he can't *learn it:*

Many people avoid new and challenging situations to avoid the possibility of failure. Perhaps that's what Mac is doing.

If his fear is relatively mild, the combination of a little pressure and a lot of reassurance may be enough to get him to try the new technology. Other workers might help him and apply a little bit of peer pressure, too.

If his fear is strong, his avoidance of new challenges is probably a deep-seated character trait by now. Offer him your support, and consider helping him find an assignment in his "comfort zone," but make it clear that you expect him to continue to do his best for you until a new job comes through.

No. 42 Not Up to Snuff

A worker continually passes substandard work on to others

THE SCENE

"I was very disappointed in the feedback I got on your design layout for Coultrey Systems," you respond to the project leader. "Their office manager told me that the public areas looked great, but the cubicles you designed for each of their workers were so small they couldn't back their chairs away from their desks without stretching out into the aisles. What kind of a design is that?"

"Well, boss, you know I'm not one to pass off blame on other people. But I only assembled the pieces into the overall design plan. Marge is the one who designed the individual work-stations, and she assured me that *this* time she got it right."

This same problem seems to crop up over and over again. Every time a design plan goes wrong, Marge's name comes up. Too small, not enough power, inadequate lighting. . . The list goes on and on. But you can't review every component as it's designed, so you don't know until the end of the project that Marge has messed up again.

POSSIBLE CAUSES

Marge may not know how to do the work correctly.

Because her work isn't always reviewed separately, she may not receive adequate feedback to know what her performance problems are.

Marge may think it doesn't matter what the quality of her work is, because it becomes part of a larger product.

She may figure that someone else along the line will catch (and correct) her mistakes, or she may have decided that her errors will be compensated for somewhere else in the design plan.

YOUR RESPONSE

If Marge doesn't know how to do the work correctly:

Often, the performance of even well trained workers can deteriorate over time because of lack of continuing feedback. If Marge works independently and her input is accepted without review for inclusion into an overall product, she may lose touch with what's expected of her. Lack of some exterior objective criterion against which she can measure her performance means she has only her own subjective impressions to fall back on. And, with changes in the products she's working with, changes in technology, and even changes in others' expectations of her, she may fall further and further out of step.

To handle this situation, first, establish some kind of immediate, ongoing review process for Marge's work. Explain to her that you've received a lot of complaints about her work from the people who use her work products, and that you'll need to check out for yourself to see how she's doing. (That doesn't mean that you need to do these reviews yourself, especially if Marge works in an area in which you're not technically skilled. You should ask a senior member of your staff to review Marge's work and provide you the results. You and your senior worker can then work together to mentor Marge.)

Be aware that Marge may get defensive when you tell her that you've received complaints from others. She may demand to know who said what and deny that there's any problem. She may even claim that they're "out to get her." It is *not* necessary to reveal the names of the people who've complained; in fact, it's probably a bad idea to reveal their names unless you let them know first that you intend to.

If Marge is in denial, it's often very effective to have one or two of the people who use Marge's products meet with her, and you, to discuss in detail their complaints. That will help convince Marge that there really is a problem and that the complaints are legitimate ones. If your other workers aren't comfortable participating in that kind of meeting, well intentioned as it is, it's probably useless to insist on their attendance. They won't be very helpful in explaining the problems to Marge, and they'll just resent your insistence.

After you've spent some time reviewing Marge's input to the larger product and given her feedback on her performance, you will have some idea what's causing any remaining performance problems. Chances are that they'll fall within the situations we'll describe in Chapter 6. Look there for help with solving any performance issues that aren't resolved with regular feedback.

If Marge believes that the quality of her work doesn't matter:

How have you handled other complaints about the substandard work Marge has completed? Have you fixed the problems yourself? Have you had the other workers in your group fix the problems for Marge? Or have you sent them back to Marge for correction?

If there are no consequences to Marge herself for poor performance, it's inevitable that she'll decide that it doesn't matter whether she does good work or not.

- Begin immediately to hold Marge, and every other contributor, accountable for the input they make to the final product. Send back work that isn't acceptable and reward work that is completed especially well or exceeds expectations in some other way.

- Consider establishing specific teams for each product your group prepares. Hold the entire team accountable for the results. They'll quickly adopt self-policing practices that will make it unnecessary for you to personally review each component of the final product.

- Remember that teams don't have to be full-time assignments. Marge and your other group members can work with two or three teams at one time in the same way they might have worked before on two or three independent assignments at once.

- Be sure, too, that Marge and other contributors have an understanding and appreciation of the entire production process. Each person doesn't need to know all the jobs that go into making the final product, but they should all understand where all the components come from, who does what, how the final product is put together, and what use it's put to. It's easy for people who work only part of a process or product to believe that their contribution doesn't matter when in fact *every* contribution is important to the success of the whole.

SOMETHING TO THINK ABOUT

It's not possible to design a perfectly seamless organization, one where every process is "owned" by a single person or group that isn't dependent on anyone else to get the work done. But as you design the jobs in your unit, take care to have as few critical interfaces between individuals and groups as possible. No matter how well people work together, every interface becomes a potential source of miscommunication and error.

No. 43 Badmouthing Competitors

An employee openly criticizes your competitors to win new business

THE SCENE

Mr. Samuelson, your boss, motions you to a chair. "Jamie Seguin just called from Progressive. Guess what she had to say about Ronnie Mitchell?"

"He's been badmouthing Progressive again."

"You better believe—and this time is the worst yet. Not only did he point out one or two of their genuine faults, but he made up several. You know as well as I do that we and Progressive have to depend on each other as well as compete with each other. I promised Ms. Seguin that we were going to shut Ronnie up one way or another—and that's your job. You either have him get off our competitors' backs or you get rid of him. Am I clear?"

POSSIBLE CAUSES

This is how Ronnie has always sold.

When he learned to sell, he learned to sell negatively. He thinks this is how it's done.

Ronnie is insecure as a salesperson.

He's afraid that if he doesn't sell negatively he won't be effective at selling.

Ronnie enjoys tearing down other firms and people.

He maintains his self-esteem by attacking others.

> **Hint:** The three causes don't exclude one another. Two, or even all three, of them may be at the root of the problem.

YOUR RESPONSE

No matter what the cause is:

Knowing something about the cause of Ronnie's behavior will help you devise the most effective solution. It doesn't change your goal—to get Ronnie to stop attacking competitors.

If this is how Ronnie has always sold:

Ronnie may believe that attacking competitors is the most effective way to sell. When you tell him he can't sell that way, he equates it with being told that he has to be less effective. That's a basic hurdle you must overcome.

What about your other salespeople? Are there several of them who are very effective but don't sell negatively? Use them to point out to Ronnie that it can be done. That in combination with a clear explanation of what will happen if he doesn't change (he'll be fired) may be enough to get him to start changing.

If Ronnie does change his approach, you need to stay on your toes. Schedule regular meetings with Ronnie to check on his progress and ensure that he keeps the goal clearly in mind. Otherwise, he'll probably slip back into his old ways and you'll be on the spot again.

It may not be that easy. He may not think that anyone else sells as well as he does (and he may have the figures to prove it), and he simply refuses to change. If that happens, the two of you have a very straightforward talk. The subject: Does he want to keep on selling negatively and work for someone else or does he want to keep his job by changing his approach? If he decides to leave, and he's been a generally good worker, give him time to find a new job and arrange an amicable parting.

That's probably not really what you want. Presumably, you want him to stay. Remind him of the many benefits of his current job (we hope there *are* a number) and promise him that you'll work with him to help him change the way he sells. Assure him that as long as he'll work sincerely to change you'll support him.

If Ronnie is insecure as a salesperson:

This may be driving his insistence on selling negatively: He simply believes that he's not good enough to sell otherwise. Your task is to demonstrate that he is good enough. How? You can use some of the ideas in the preceding response. Whatever you do, though, your goal is to get him into a situation where he sells positively and successfully and then make sure he understands that he did so and how he did so.

You may need to "play" customer with him. Have him make a presentation to you in his usual way, negativity and all. Then have him change it to leave out the attacks and emphasize the positive points of your company's products and give the presentation to you again. The two of you should continue to work on it until it's polished. Then he should use it with a customer and report back to you on the results. (If he won't get too nervous, accompany him on a few sales calls so you can observe his performance and give him feedback. For the first few times, though, this will probably be too stressful for him. Later it may be a possibility.)

Remember to notice and recognize Ronnie for each improvement he makes, no matter how small. This is especially important just when he's beginning to change and it's hard for him to see progress. If he knows that you see and appreciate his attempts, it will help him immensely.

If Ronnie enjoys tearing down other firms and people:

This may be the hardest cause to deal with because Ronnie has developed a strong habit of attacking others. From his point of view, the fact that Progressive is a competitor gives him every excuse he needs to do so. Subtlety will probably get you very little in this circumstance. The situation needs to be met head-on.

Tell Ronnie how you see things and give him every chance to answer. Listen carefully and ask leading questions. You want to understand as clearly as you can just how he sees the situation and why he sees it that way.

Then you make your point of view clear—he changes or else. He won't like that. He may accuse you of picking on him or trying to make him look bad. Let him. Your job here is to get him to stop attacking competitors. Make sure he understands this clearly. Then let him make the choice.

If he's a good salesperson, offer to support him and help him change, though the responsibility for change remains his. But the choice is his. If he decides he wants to change, use the ideas from the preceding responses, but use them firmly. (For instance, you may want to insist on going with him on calls.) Have regular follow-ups with him and accept nothing less than clear improvement.

SOMETHING TO THINK ABOUT

When a worker (or manager) needs to change a personal behavior, the situation is always stressful. Changing is hard work, particularly without an obvious payoff. However, if the individual can see a payoff that's worth the effort, the change will be easier to make.

How do you aid the process? Try not to let workers get into situations like the one in this case where they must make major changes or else. Don't try to threaten them into changing unless absolutely necessary. Threats are normally the least effective motivators for change. Give workers a positive reason for change, preferably a clear payoff for them. Above all, convince them you are serious about the change and that you expect it to happen.

No. 44
ABUSING WORK-AT-HOME PRIVILEGES
Her work-at-home habits create performance problems

THE SCENE

You try very hard to be a good manager. It's obvious that your work-at-home schedule is a real boon to many of your workers, and to the workgroup. People appreciate being able to work around other commitments, and the kind of document processing you do can be accomplished anywhere. It doesn't have to be in a particular office or a particular building.

But what about Christie? She's going to spoil this arrangement for everyone. You can tell she's not doing much during her work-at-home hours, but you're having a hard time proving it. When you ask her what's she's getting done, she just smiles and says everything is "on target." What's that supposed to mean?

POSSIBLE CAUSES

Christie may not know what your expectations are.

She may have the idea that work at home is a kind of bonus for which she's not really accountable.

Christie may see work at home as a means of taking advantage of the system.

She may think there's no way you can tell whether she's producing or not, so she's free to do as much (or as little) as she chooses.

> **Hint:** At least in most organizations, work-at-home arrangements (also known as flexiplace) are not a normal condition of employment to which workers have any entitlement. The ability to work at home is sometimes conditioned on special circumstances, such as physical disability or unusual dependent-care arrangements, or it's treated as a privilege that employees earn. If you find that your employees are abusing their work-at-home time, you can usually take strong and swift action. But check first to see just what your company's work-at-home policies cover—whether they're a privilege or an entitlement.

YOUR RESPONSE

If Christie doesn't know what your expectations are:

You, and she, may have assumed that work-at-home hours could be handled just like work hours in the office. She gets assignments, she completes assignments, she turns in assignments. And for some kinds of work, that's true.

If Christie is responsible for processing documents, or for preparing textual or graphical materials, or for making telephone contacts, or other work where there's a clear production standard, it's fairly easy to hold her to the same production level out of the office as in. And you can make it clear to her that if her overall level of production drops, you'll have to reduce or eliminate her work-at-home hours.

But what if Christie's work output is not so easily measured? You can still set performance goals, either for her work-at-home time specifically or for a particular period of time (maybe few weeks or so at a time). If Christie can tell you in advance what she intends to accomplish in her work-at-home hours, and you agree that it's a reasonable expectation, you can have her report her progress to you when she returns to work. In that way, you can keep a close watch on what's going on.

If she can't tell you what will be accomplished in each work-at-home period, you should at least be able to establish milestones and goals for her overall work, keeping in mind her full work schedule (not just the hours she spends in the office), and hold her accountable for producing work against those milestones. Milestones that aren't met then become the basis for changing her work-at-home flexibility.

If Christie sees her work-at-home time as an opportunity to take advantage of the system:

The preceding response will solve this problem also. Make clear to Christie what your expectations are and how you intend to ensure that she really does produce when she's working out of the office. If her work isn't easily quantified, you can at least compare her production to that of other workers in similar positions (with or without work-at-home privileges).

The reminder that her output is monitored may be sufficient to change Christie's attitude toward her work-at-home responsibilities. If not, by having a system in place to keep track of her production, you've laid the foundation for taking whatever corrective action is necessary to improve her production rate. Chapter 6 will give you some ideas for dealing with continuing performance problems.

SOMETHING TO THINK ABOUT

As you undoubtedly know already, some workers have better self-management skills than others. Arrangements such as flexible work schedules and work at home are great for employees whose self-management skills are well developed, but can cause real difficulties for employees who are either not conscientious or have trouble keeping themselves together in even a traditional work setting. Some workers *need* structure in order to operate most effectively; others work best when they can develop their own structure.

Whenever you introduce more flexibility in your work arrangements, you also need to build in sufficient controls to be able to rein in employees who have trouble with the lack of structure. Your monitoring of the transition from a more-structured to a less-structured environment will ensure that everyone starts off on the right foot.

CHAPTER SIX

Helping Your Employees Succeed

No. 45 Chaotic Work Style

A poorly organized employee consistently misses deadlines

THE SCENE

"Gladys, do you mean to tell me that you're going to be late with the newsletter again this month?!"

"I'm sorry, Alfred, I really am. I took the material home with me every night this week and worked on it, but I just can't seem to get it together. If you could just get someone to help me. . .

You sigh. Gladys doesn't need someone to help her. She needs to get herself organized and quit spinning her wheels. But how to do it. . . ?

POSSIBLE CAUSES

Gladys may not realize that she's not organized.

Perhaps she's never worked with anyone who was really well organized.

She may never have had to learn how to organize herself.

In her previous jobs she may never have had to do anything but get the work done as it came to her.

She may not believe that it's important to organize herself.

Getting organized may seem too trivial for her to spend time on.

> ***Hints***: As you've probably realized already, none of the causes excludes the others. Gladys may not believe it's important to organize herself because she's never had to *and* never worked around anyone who did it well. One of the critical steps here is knowing just where to start.
>
> Remember, organizing your time and your work is a learned skill. Because of their past history, and perhaps their personalities, some people are better at it than others will ever be. But everyone can learn to be organized well enough to do what has to be done.

YOUR RESPONSE

No matter what the cause is:

Spend some time observing Gladys and talking with her. Your goal is to find out *how* she's disorganized. Does she put things off until the last minute? Does she spend too much time on the unimportant parts of the job? Does she start on something, work on it for a little while, and then leave it unfinished while she goes on to something else? It's important to get a feel for Gladys's specific areas of inefficiency.

It's important in this case, and in so many others, for the employee to believe that there really is a better way. As long as Gladys thinks her problem is just overwork—or even lack of ability—she's stuck in it. Once she sees that she can get out of the situation by learning some new skills, the battle is almost won.

If she doesn't realize that she's not organized:

This is good news and it's bad news. The good news is that once Gladys realizes she's not organized, she'll probably want to learn how to get organized. The bad news is that it may be difficult for her to see that she's not organized.

The easiest, least-threatening way for Gladys to learn that she's not well organized is to work with someone who is. Can you arrange a joint task that she and one of your best-organized workers can do together? (The other worker also needs to be one who can be helpful and not get frustrated.)

If you're good at organization and there's no one else to work with her, you can do it. (You're the second choice because it's going to be harder for her to relax and learn from you, her supervisor.) You may just need to tell her what to do, but you'll be more effective if you can ask questions and make suggestions.

Once Gladys realizes that she doesn't have the self-organization skills she needs, she'll probably be happy to have you or someone else help her gain them. It may also be a good idea to send her to a formal course on work organization, too.

If she's never had to learn to organize herself:

She may have had jobs before where she wasn't required to do much organizing. Perhaps she did the work as it came to her. She didn't have to organize it, so she never learned how.

This may not be as difficult as the situation above. If you can explain the difference between the work she did and her current work, with some examples, she may see the difference quickly. Having her work jointly with a well-organized worker can also help her see the difference.

Once she sees the difference, having another worker help her and/or sending her to a formal course should get her going in the right direction.

If she doesn't think that organizing herself is important:

If this is the case, it's helpful to understand why Gladys thinks this way. Does she see herself as a "creative" person and believe that being organized would get in her way? Does she think that "organizing" is something only clerks and secretaries do? Or does she just not realize that she's disorganized (back to the first response)?

If she insists that she's as organized as she needs to be, deal with her performance. Instead of talking about being organized, insist that she get her work done on schedule. If she feels pushed enough, she may ask someone else to help her get organized.

Having another person who's well-organized work with her is also a good idea here, particularly if she begins to feel pressure to meet deadlines. Once she sees that someone else can handle the same kind of work more easily and skillfully, she'll probably want to learn the skills.

When she accepts the need to organize herself, see that she gets the on-the-job and/or formal training she needs.

What if she still refuses to learn how to get organized? Deal with the problem as a performance problem and take whatever steps are necessary. See Challenge 46 for suggestions.

SOMETHING TO THINK ABOUT

All the responses to this problem assume that *you* are organized. Be sure that's the case. If it's not, your disorganization may be affecting Gladys and other employees. You may actually be making it harder for them to organize themselves. You can figure out what the solution is to that, can't you?

Perhaps you aren't disorganized but have been too tolerant of employees who are, giving them little incentive to change. For example, have you been accepting it when employees are late with assignments? Do you fuss and fume a little, then give up and take the assignment when you can get it? If so, *you're* a major part of the problem. See Challenge 47 in this chapter for suggestions on how to handle this.

No. 46 GOOD ATTITUDE, POOR RESULTS

An enthusiastic approach doesn't translate into satisfactory output

THE SCENE

Once again, Noor has given you a report you couldn't use. You thought you had done everything right: You called her in to explain exactly what you wanted, where the numbers came from, how to compute the percentages, the way to format the columns. She nodded in all the right places and even asked a couple of insightful questions. "Right away, Terry," she assured you as she left your office.

But the report she gave you is nothing like what you had in mind. Noor tries so hard, but it's just not working out.

POSSIBLE CAUSES

Noor may not understand what you want.

If she is obviously trying very hard to do a good job, perhaps Noor simply doesn't know what it is you're looking for.

She may not know how to do the work.

Even if she understands what you want, she may not know how to get there. This is particularly likely if she's recently been assigned new duties or is new to the organization and if what she's doing now doesn't bear much resemblance to the work she's done in the past.

Noor may be the sort of person who starts out well, but then doesn't deliver.

You may think she has a great attitude because of her apparent enthusiasm when you give her assignments, but that enthusiasm may be feigned to get you off her back so she can go back to what-ever it is she really wants to be doing.

YOUR RESPONSE

If Noor doesn't understand what you want:

When you assign work to Noor, talk with her about your expectations. Her lack of understanding may stem from one of two causes: Either she's been misinterpreting your instructions *or* you've been unclear in explaining what you need. In either case, your first step should be to have Noor tell you what she *thinks* you told her to do.

Where Noor's interpretation and your expectations don't match, clarify your expectations. Show her some examples of work that's been completed to your expectations so she can model her own work on it.

When Noor submits unsatisfactory work, try to put it in context. Show her who the customer is for her products and how her work affects other people's performance. By learning how her work is used by others, she'll be better able to identify the tasks it's critical that she do well.

Review Noor's work closely for a while. Look at her work each time she turns in an assignment or sample her products every day or two if they're things that don't normally flow through you on their way to the customer. Identify the things she's doing correctly and the areas that still need work.

An even better idea is to have Noor work with another employee who can review her work and give her pointers on how to do things better. She may be more willing to go to a peer for advice than to you, since she may believe that you'll hold her lack of knowledge against her at appraisal time.

After you've given Noor what ought to be sufficient opportunity and assistance to improve her performance, review her progress to decide if she's showing satisfactory improvement. She probably won't get better all at once, but you should begin fairly soon to see signs that she's catching on to what you want. If not, you'll need to make some hard decisions. Not only is it not fair to the organization and your other workers to carry Noor in a job she can't perform; it's not fair to her either. Try to find her another position in which she can perform satisfactorily, but, failing that, you must be prepared to terminate her as tactfully and sensitively as you can. If your company has a personnel department, the people there should be available to help you and Noor get through both the paperwork and the emotional upheaval.

If Noor doesn't know how to do the work:

Identify the specific areas in which she makes mistakes to isolate the parts of the job where she needs help. Decide what kind of training is best to give her the knowledge or expertise she needs (for example, classroom training, on-the-job training) and arrange for her to get it.

Work with her closely for some time to review each product and to identify the tasks she's doing correctly and those that still need improvement.

Encourage Noor and let her know that you have confidence in her ability to learn the work. At the same time, make sure she understands that it's her responsibility to do well, regardless of the amount of assistance you're able to give her.

As before, be optimistic but realistic. If, after your best attempts to teach Noor the job, she still doesn't improve, be prepared to move her to another position in your organization or to terminate her. That doesn't mean you've failed. *No* worker is equally good at every job.

If Noor starts out enthusiastically, but then doesn't deliver:

See Challenge 47 in this chapter for help in dealing with an employee who makes promises but doesn't deliver on them.

SOMETHING TO THINK ABOUT

Whenever you have an employee who clearly wants to do a good job, but is still having trouble producing, then it's particularly important that you step in *quickly* to help solve the performance problem. One of the unfortunate consequences of repeated failure is that even employees who want to do a good job eventually get beaten down so badly that they give up, don't care anymore, or even become resentful and hard to manage. By stepping in as soon as you discover the difficulties, you may be able to help your employee overcome them in time to avoid the demoralizing effect of continued unsuccessful performance.

No. 47 Missed Deadlines

He does great work but it's never on time

THE SCENE

"R. B., this is just a summary of the overdue accounts. You told me you'd have an analysis of them for me by today."

"I really meant to, but you know how busy we've been lately. I'm sure I can do the analysis by Wednesday."

"I certainly hope so!" you fume as you walk off. Will R.B. *ever* come through on time?

POSSIBLE CAUSES

R.B. is disorganized.

He means well but can't produce.

You accept it when employees don't deliver what they promise.

If this is the case, you've got to change yourself before you can change them.

R.B. worked for another supervisor who accepted it.

You haven't caused the problem, you've inherited it.

R.B. makes promises to "get people off his back," whether he can deliver or not.

In this case, you'll have to show R.B. that you'll be following up to make sure he's as good as his word.

> *Hint*: Unless R.B.'s problem is lack of organization, you have a serious problem of lack of work discipline. Good disciplined workers *always* deliver what they promise, when they promise it—or they let you know in advance.

YOUR RESPONSE

If R.B. is disorganized:

Look back at the first challenge in this chapter for suggestions.

If you accept it when employees don't deliver:

First, accept something else: *You're* the cause of their failure to come through for you. If you don't care about promises and deadlines, why should they?

There's a simple way to deal with this: Stop! Now! Get your employees together, explain the change and then enforce it. You'll probably get a great deal of static at first. Employees will say that you're being unfair and expecting too much. Change is painful; you can accept that. But *don't* accept work that isn't done as promised, when promised. You may have to counsel them a little, perhaps even threaten a little. Do it. They'll get the word, and your unit will start to run considerably better.

Don't go to the other extreme and insist that employees deliver no matter what. Something that genuinely has a higher priority or that causes an unavoidable delay may interfere with a deadline. In such cases, your employees must let you know *as soon as issues affecting a deadline arise.* Then together you can work out a realistic new schedule.

If R.B. worked for another supervisor who accepted it when he didn't deliver:

First, make sure you aren't reinforcing habits tolerated by R.B.'s former supervisor. Then have a talk with R.B., making the points suggested in the response to the preceding situation. Make it clear to R.B. that your standards are different from those of his former supervisor.

R.B. may feel that you're being unfair to him. However, if you've set clear standards and enforced them, your other employees will set him straight quickly. They deliver, and they'll expect him to deliver too. (Yes, it usually is that simple.)

If R.B. makes promises to keep people from pressuring him:

Unfortunately, too many employees (and their managers) fall into this trap. Somebody pushes them, so they promise anything to get the pressure off. Then the day comes to deliver what was promised, and the individual who did the promising is in trouble.

If the cause of R.B.'s lack of concern for meeting his obligations seems to be one of the preceding ones, keep your eyes open to see if this is also the case. Employees who'll promise anything to get out of a tight spot feel right at home with supervisors who don't insist that commitments be kept.

This situation will probably take a bit more time and attention. Start by making your position clear to R.B. Then be equally clear that you won't force unrealistic commitments on him and that you don't want him to let others do it, either. (There's a good chance that he won't believe this, so be prepared to have him test you on it.)

Follow up to ensure that he stops making unrealistic commitments and that he keeps those he makes. When he makes a commitment and delivers, praise him for it. If he doesn't deliver, counsel him. Be patient, but be firm. It may take a few times, but he'll get the message.

SOMETHING TO THINK ABOUT

It's worth repeating: if your employees don't deliver what's promised, when it's promised, there's a good chance that *you're* the culprit. Be realistic about what you expect from them and insist that they're realistic about it, too. Then expect that they deliver or tell you in advance why they can't—with no exceptions.

There's a very simple truth at work here. Most employees will produce what their supervisor will settle for. Even good employees will get sloppy if the supervisor has sloppy standards or (just as bad) has high standards but doesn't enforce them.

No. 48 Gnashing of Teeth

You see that a good performer is going to pieces under pressure

THE SCENE

"What's wrong with Brendan?" asks Sally. "He's normally so calm and easygoing. But today we've had complaints from three different people who said he gave them bad information and didn't seem to know what he was talking about. I know the line out at the reception desk is getting longer by the minute, and Keith said he'd help out as soon as he finishes with this client. But Brendan's just going to have to hold on until we can get somebody else out there!"

"I guess this isn't really a new problem," you reply ruefully. "Brendan falls apart whenever the going gets rough. He's such a good worker most of the time, I hate to get on his back about something that doesn't come up that often. But, unfortunately, when it does, he makes a bad situation even worse."

POSSIBLE CAUSES

Brendan may not have the skills to deal with stress and pressure.

He may know the job itself well enough, but may not have learned coping strategies to keep from panicking when the pressure's on.

Brendan may not be that good at the work he's assigned.

He may be able to get along okay when he has plenty of time to figure out what to do, but when things move along too quickly, he gets lost.

Brendan may have learned to fall apart under pressure to get himself out of an unpleasant situation.

If falling apart under stress in the past has resulted in people feeling sorry for him and bailing him out, he's likely to repeat the behavior in similar situations. Your job is to help him unlearn that behavior.

> *Hint:* There are very few jobs that don't require the ability to work under pressure at least some of the time. Brendan may be a good worker when he has little stress to contend with. You can try to structure his environment so that the pressures are reduced or so that they occur infrequently, but it's almost inevitable that sooner or later he'll be asked to perform under some kind of pressure—whether from deadlines, an angry client or coworker, or the boss looking over his shoulder on an important project. So regardless of how infrequently the situation occurs, it's in both his and your best interests to help him prepare ahead of time, not in the middle of the crisis.

YOUR RESPONSE

If Brendan hasn't developed his own mechanisms for coping with stress:

Start by talking to Brendan and explaining why it's important that he not let the pressure get to him. Make sure he understands the impact on other people when he falls to pieces—that he's not getting just himself worked up but others too and that his lack of coping skills only makes tense situations worse.

Find a good commercially available course on stress reduction that includes not only relaxation techniques but also specific tactics for planning around stressful situations. Send Brendan, then ask for his feedback both on the content of the course and what he plans to do to put the things he learned into practice.

Take some time to work out scenarios with Brendan in which you describe some of the kinds of pressure he's likely to encounter in his job (such as having 16 people lined up at the reception desk, all of whom want answers *now*). If you're both comfortable with the technique, role play the situations with him until he's had enough practice in dealing constructively with the pressure. If you're not comfortable with role playing, at least have him describe to you how he would handle the situation. Go over similar situations in several different sessions until you're confident that his appropriate response has become well ingrained.

If Brendan's work skills aren't strong enough for him to operate effectively under pressure:

Talk with Brendan to find out what skills or tasks generally cause him the most stress. Then have him practice those skills over and over until he can perform them to mastery. Note: Mastery requires that he be able to perform the task both *accurately* and *quickly*. If he has learned the tasks to mastery, he is less likely to fall apart under pressure since mastery is reached only when the responses become semi-automatic.

If it's appropriate, you may want Brendan to get some remedial training or you may want to review, step-by-step, what's involved in his assignments. Perhaps he knows how to perform each individual task, but gets muddled when he has to sequence steps rapidly.

If falling to pieces is a learned response to get him out of stressful situations:

Explain to Brendan, tactfully but firmly, why you have to count on him when the pressure's on and how his inability to cope hurts others in the organization. Let him know that you'll do whatever you can to help him develop coping strategies (including the actions we've discussed), but that you need his cooperation.

Give Brendan some time to come to terms with your requirements. Send him to stress-reduction courses and work out ways of coping with the stresses he's likely to encounter, as we mentioned before.

The next time a stressful situation occurs, don't rush in to help Brendan out. Give him a chance to use the techniques he's learned. Once he sees how you're counting on him, he may do fine. If not, and you have to step in, be sure to do a "post-mortem" with him to review how he handled the situation and what he could have done differently.

If Brendan improves his ability to perform under pressure, no matter how slowly, congratulate him on his improvement and stick with him. If he seems not to be improving, you can try a referral to your employee assistance program or another counseling service for more individual professional attention. You may be able to restructure the job to minimize the pressure, or you may want to help him find another job where ability to deal with pressure isn't so critical.

While termination is always a possibility when employees don't perform to your expectations, it's less likely to be necessary in this situation. If the ability to work under pressure is a real necessity in Brendan's position, and if he continues not to cope well, chances are good that he himself will be uncomfortable enough that he'll look for another job.

SOMETHING TO THINK ABOUT

All jobs have some stress associated with them—even those that appear routine and repetitive. When the stress affects your good workers to the point where their performance deteriorates, or where you see higher rates of illness or absenteeism or higher turnover, it's time (or past time) to take management action to reduce the levels of stress.

One effective way to reduce stress associated with a particular position is to isolate the stressful parts and divide them among several employees. For example, if the reception counter is always busy with demanding and unreasonable customers, rather than having an employee serve as full-time receptionist, assign reception counter duties to the rest of your clerical staff, perhaps in two- or three-hour increments. (But don't make the mistake of eliminating the receptionist position and dividing the stressful work among the rest of your staff without hiring another employee to relieve the extra workload among the clerical staff. That will only aggravate an already difficult situation.)

No. 49 High Volume, Low Quality

A team member pumps out a lot of work, but it's below par

THE SCENE

"Sarah, I see that Emile is our top producer again this month. Is he still making bunches of mistakes?"

" 'Barrels of mistakes' is more like it! I've spoken to him about it several times, but he just points out how much he produces. He won't listen to me, because I'm not his supervisor. I need you to take care of it."

POSSIBLE CAUSES

You set low standards.

Alternatively, you set high standards but don't insist that people meet them.

Emile learned how to work fast but not accurately.

He's continuing to do what he knows how to do best.

The real rewards are for quantity, not quality.

In many organizations, quantity is what's tracked and paid for.

> **Hint:** On the surface, this is an individual problem. However, if you let Emile get away with fast, sloppy work, others may start copying him. (This is particularly apt to happen if the compensation system stresses quantity at the expense of quality.) This gives you an additional reason to act quickly and effectively.

YOUR RESPONSE

If you set low standards (or high ones you don't enforce):

Let's be realistic here. What really counts in your company? In your unit? Is quality critical, or important, or an also-ran to quantity? Yes, "quality" is still a buzzword, but that doesn't mean that it's what's wanted, fought for, and rewarded.

If quality is a low priority for your company, your problem is much bigger than Emile. He may be producing exactly what the organization rewards. See the last response to this challenge to get some ideas on this.

Suppose the company wants quality, but you concentrate on quantity instead? The first question, of course, is why your boss lets *you* get away with sloppy work. Perhaps we'd better talk with him.

Since we can't, we'll just have to suggest that you get your act together. There's not room to talk about it in this book, but we can give you this: In a well-run organization, everything is done right the first time—*everything*. If you believe, live, support, and reward this, most of the sloppy work will vanish. Then it will be easy to deal with the occasional employee who hasn't gotten the word.

If Emile learned how to work fast but not accurately:

He's doing what most of us do—what we know how to do. In fact, even if he slows to half speed he may still make just as many errors.

What sounds like the sensible thing to do? Retrain him. Retraining is always harder than training, but it can be done. If Emile doesn't see the need for it, refuse to accept sloppy work and make him redo all of it. Make it crystal clear that you expect the work done right the first time.

That should get him in the right frame of mind to do some relearning. This is when you need to be patient, because he may have to begin over almost from the beginning. He'll have to establish new work habits, and they'll be difficult at first. Keep insisting, keep encouraging, and keep persisting.

One other thing: Make sure Emile understands that he can work just as fast without errors. Sound too good to be true? It's not. If he's trained properly, that's what will happen.

If the real rewards are for quantity, not quality:

Anyone who's worked for long in an average American organization has run into the dilemma. The company advocates quality and encourages its employees to produce quality. Then, when bonuses or awards are handed out, the people who get them are those who meet or exceed their quantity targets, without regard for quality. (Just in case you haven't noticed, the time it takes to produce something is out in the open and measured; the time it takes to *redo* it is usually hidden.)

If this is your situation, you're caught in a real bind. Unlike the first cause above, you're not the reason for the sloppy work. If the firm pays for quantity at the expense of quality, you probably can't change that. Does this mean there's nothing you can do? No. You can encourage Emile and others to produce quality work, which may help a little. If you have some discretion over bonuses or the amount of pay increases, announce that you'll base them on quality of result, not quantity. Then do it.

Make sure your boss knows how the company's preference for quantity over quality is affecting your unit. Perhaps you can enlist his or her help. Sooner or later, maybe managers like you and your boss can change the company's compensation policies.

SOMETHING TO THINK ABOUT

In some organizations, inspectors, senior workers, or leaders review everyone's work and redo any of the work that's substandard. Don't, DON'T, *DON'T* ever fall into this trap. Every employee should be responsible for his own work. If it wasn't done right, he redoes it. If the person has to do the rework and it detracts from the bonus he or the group gets, watch how quickly the rework will drop off.

Some companies still think productivity can be improved by emphasizing quantity at the expense of quality, if necessary. That's been proven wrong. The way to get productivity is by organizing for quality. When your people and your processes get it right the first time, then you'll get quality *and* quantity.

No. 50 HIGH QUALITY, LOW VOLUME
A perfectionist produces fine work, but too little of it

THE SCENE

Camille is one worker you can always depend on—slow and steady. Very, very steady, and *very, very* slow. In the three years she's been packing here, she's never had a package returned for breakage, or incorrect address, or falling apart in shipping. *But* as slowly as she goes, she might as well be wrapping fancy Christmas presents. The wrapping has to be just so, as does the tape, and the filler, and the label, and everything else. You admire her meticulousness, but Camille takes twice as long as she should. How can you hurry her up?

POSSIBLE CAUSES

Camille may lack confidence in her abilities.

She may fear that if she goes any faster, she'll begin to make mistakes (whether that's true or not).

Camille's skills may not be well developed enough to allow her to go faster without making errors.

She may do fine as long as she goes slowly, but may begin to make mistakes once she speeds up.

Camille may have a mental or physical disability that makes it impossible for her to go any faster.

> **Hint:** If you're not sure whether Camille will begin to make mistakes when she speeds up or just *thinks* she'll make mistakes, the only way to find out for sure is to test her. Tell her exactly what you're doing (finding out how fast she can go without increasing her error rate) and why (because her current production isn't satisfactory). Then instruct her to pack as many boxes, start to finish, as she can in a given amount of time (half an hour, an hour, two or three hours—whatever seems reasonable in your situation). Stand nearby during the test, giving her encouragement (and checking to make sure she really is increasing her speed). Then measure her production and error rates at the end of the specified period.

YOUR RESPONSE

If Camille lacks confidence:

Encourage her as much as you can. Let her know that you appreciate her attention to the quality of the product, but stress that quality also means on-time production, and the company won't be on time if everyone works at her rate.

Help Camille set goals for incrementally increasing her rate. If you want her eventually to pack eight boxes an hour and she's now at four or five, begin by increasing her requirement to six, then seven, and finally eight. Congratulate her on each success and reassure her of your confidence that she can make the next increment at the same high-quality rate.

Make sure your incentive system rewards production rate as well as quality, if that's what's really important in this job. Camille may not lack confidence as much as she lacks incentive to go any faster. If pay and rewards are based only on error rates, then there's no good reason, from Camille's standpoint, to go any faster, especially if her errors are likely to increase.

If Camille lacks the skills to go any faster:

Observe her as she packs several different kinds of items. Are there particular areas where she seems to have some trouble, where she hesitates or seems to have to think about each step as she completes it?

Wherever you find those hesitations or problem areas, isolate those tasks and teach them specifically. This is an area where you can probably delegate the teaching and practice-monitoring to one of your better workers. Have Camille practice the tasks to mastery, that is, until she can complete them both *accurately* and *rapidly*. Once she's mastered those isolated tasks, then she can begin to combine them with the other steps in the process to speed up her overall rate.

Don't stop when Camille's mastered the individual steps, however. She may still have problems when she tries to put them together. In that case, you can combine the individual tasks into larger and larger units, until she has the whole process down. You may find, as you observe her combining the individual steps into a whole process, that there are parts of the job that aren't organized as well as they could be. Are all the steps in the most logical sequence? Does she have to "undo" things she's already completed to complete another step? Are the materials she needs organized so she can get to them when she needs them, or are they in the way of something else? As you observe Camille, you may find that her production problems are simply an exaggeration of difficulties everybody's having.

If Camille has a mental or physical condition that prevents her from working faster:

Decide how important speed is to the success of the operation. Can you afford to let Camille continue at her slower pace? Does her lack of errors compensate for her lower production level?

If the organization will suffer by allowing Camille to continue at her current production rate, look at alternatives. Can she be assigned to some other work where speed isn't as important, or where her condition won't interfere with her production? Does your company have an employment program for handicapped employees that would allow Camille to remain in your unit, working at her own speed, but that would give you some relief from work-year quotas?

If you cannot accommodate Camille within the company, be as tactful and sensitive as you can in terminating her. Explain exactly why you're taking the action and offer her as much assistance as possible in outplacement efforts.

SOMETHING TO THINK ABOUT

Before you begin trying to solve a problem with the rate at which work gets done in your unit, look first to be sure that the rate really is a problem. Are your workers working at a slower rate because they're not experienced or not well trained? Or are they working at a slower rate because it's how they avoid having to do work two or three times over?

Slower work that results in less re-work is probably faster, in the long run, than faster work that later has to be corrected. Make sure you really have a problem before you begin to solve it!

No. 51
POOR PERFORMANCE BY AN INFLUENTIAL EMPLOYEE
A marginal performer is admired by others

THE SCENE

Gretchen is a real challenge. She's hardly one of your best workers—in fact, she's marginal at best. But people listen to her. She's never admitted to you that she's unhappy about anything, but the rest of the staff have certainly heard enough about it. And, unfortunately, they listen to her. She's stirred up resentment about your overtime schedule and your project assignments and your travel procedures—and probably a lot of other things you haven't even heard about yet. Not everyone pays attention when she complains, but enough do to cause you trouble. So how can you deal with her marginal performance without her causing more discontent in the ranks?

POSSIBLE CAUSES

Neither the cause of Gretchen's marginal performance nor the source of her influence with the workgroup is of particular concern here. We've discussed ways for improving poor performance, intentional and unintentional, in this chapter and elsewhere in this book. And it doesn't matter *why* the rest of your staff is willing to listen to Gretchen's complaints; the fact is that they do, and that's causing you problems.

Your intention here is twofold: You want to help Gretchen improve her performance and you want to stop her negative influence with your staff. This is *not* a situation where you can take the justified, but entirely ineffective, step of dealing with the performance difficulties while ignoring Gretchen's leadership role in the workgroup. That approach will just result in Gretchen's complaining more to her peers about your "unreasonable" demands and will do nothing to improve her performance or the group's morale. You *must* deal with both the performance and the influence at the same time.

This is a tough situation, and it's not one in which we can give you a neat set of steps to follow that, if performed correctly, will solve the problem successfully. What we *can* do is offer a number of suggestions, some of which will apply to your problem, some of which won't. Consider them in light of the specific characteristics of your "Gretchen" and your workforce, use the ones that you think will work, disregard the ones you think won't—and good luck!

YOUR RESPONSE

If your other workers are not aware of the quality of Gretchen's work:

They may accept her leadership more readily than they would if they had little respect for her technical competence. In that case, it may be effective to let your other employees see for themselves the kind of work Gretchen does. It's unlikely that they will have much faith in her critical remarks if they perceive them as a cover for her own lack of production. Of course, the way to make others aware of Gretchen's poor work is not by badmouthing, but by structuring opportunities for your staff to work with Gretchen and make their own informed decisions about her. Your intention here is not to discredit Gretchen; that's underhanded, unworthy of you as a manager, and likely to backfire. Your goal is simply to give other workers the chance to see that perhaps Gretchen's opinions about you and your management of the office are not as weighty as they once thought.

To the degree it's possible, given the kind of work your unit performs, assign some work to teams rather than to individuals. Make sure Gretchen is a part of the team and that one or two of your best workers are too. Make your expectations clear to the team members, both in terms of the product you expect at the completion of the assignment and in terms of the level of participation you expect from each of the team members. If Gretchen isn't carrying her fair share, the team will discover that quickly.

Again to the degree possible in your particular work situation, let some decisions be made by teams rather than by individuals or by you. If your unit is supposed to develop schedules (for example, for inventorying, for review of other work, for customer visits), assign a team to develop those schedules and make sure Gretchen is part of it. The degree of cooperation she exhibits in her dealings with you will probably also be reflected in her interactions with the team members.

Establish a peer review system. Instead of checking all your employees' work yourself, set up a system in which workers review each others' products. Include Gretchen as part of the peer review group. When you set up the system, establish regular rotation dates so that employees do not become so accustomed to reviewing the work of specific individuals that they lose their objectivity. Rotating review assignments also ensures that every employee gets the chance to review and evaluate the worth of every other employee's contributions (including Gretchen's).

If Gretchen is a marginal employee in a group made up largely of marginal workers:

In this case your challenge is a different one. The group itself will probably not be able to see that Gretchen's contributions aren't all that great, because they're all performing at about the same level. Challenges 18 and 23 discuss variations on the basic theme of *organizational* productivity problems. In correcting the organization's performance deficiencies and improving their overall morale, you may solve your specific problem with Gretchen. If the rest of the group responds to your efforts, but Gretchen does not, then the steps outlined in the preceding response may help after you've improved the productivity of the majority of your staff.

If Gretchen's performance and attitude problems stem from a dislike of the job:

Her perception of your management style and decisions will be distorted by her own unhappiness. That doesn't mean that other employees are less likely to listen to her. On the contrary, she is more likely to be listened to if she's bright and articulate and talented but simply misplaced in her current assignment. Challenge 53 in this chapter discusses steps you can take when an employee clearly isn't suited to the job.

SOMETHING TO THINK ABOUT

Moving to a new job, especially if it's with a new company, is a traumatic experience for most people. All the security and comfort of the old environment is gone, and an employee who's used to feeling competent and knowledgeable suddenly becomes a novice all over again. We can't stress too often that the most effective cure for many early apparent performance problems is *time*. Time to learn the work, time to learn the organization and how to work with the people in it, and time to adjust and become more comfortable in the new environment. Encouragement from you is important—frequently, that's all that's needed.

Don't respond to learning difficulties your new employees have in the same way you would respond to performance problems your experienced staff exhibit. With an established employee, you'll want to intervene as soon as you suspect there's a problem. But with a *new* employee, allow time for adjusting to the new environment and all the other changes that come with a new job. Then if things don't improve within a reasonable amount of time, you still have an opportunity to intervene.

No. 52 Underperforming New Hire

Something is keeping your new employee from catching on

THE SCENE

"You know, Barb," reports Kit, "Marta just isn't working out the way I hoped she would. Somehow she's managed to scramble up mail Zena's already sorted—and she lost an order from one of our best customers in the process. I don't know *how* many times I've gone over the steps with her—one, two, three. But the next time I look, she's screwed something else up. It's not *that* tough a job. I guess I shouldn't complain about Marta especially, though. She's no worse than the rest of the employees we've hired lately."

POSSIBLE CAUSES

Marta may not have the basic skills she needs to do the job.

She may lack such essential skills as basic literacy, or ability to alphabetize, or basic math skills. More and more of our entry-level workforce does.

Marta may not like the work.

She may have interests or aspirations in another direction and not be interested in the assignments you've given her.

Marta may be poorly motivated.

She may just be filling in the time until something better comes along, or she may not see any value in the work she's doing. But for whatever reason, she's really not motivated to do a good job.

> **Hint:** If you're not sure whether the problems you're having with your employees are due to lack of skills or lack of interest, you can answer that question by asking yourself another. "If this employee's life depended on performing this job adequately, could she do it?" If the answer is "yes," then you have a motivation problem. But if the answer is "no"—if the employee couldn't perform, even if her life depended on it, then you have a problem with her skills or abilities.

YOUR RESPONSE

If Marta lacks basic skills to do the job:

Talk with Marta and review her job application and the other items in your personnel file to find out as much as you can about what skills Marta does have and the kind of work she's done in the past. If your company has a training department, the training personnel may also be qualified to give basic literacy and computational literacy tests to find out what skills Marta has. If not, you might try the testing services of your state's employment services department.

Check to see whether your company offers any formal classes where Marta can learn the skills she needs. If not, and if the skills deficiencies Marta has seem to be shared by a lot of your new workers, look into contracting with local schools or training vendors to develop specialized training for your workers.

Identify a mentor for Marta to whom she can go when she has questions and who can check her work and help her correct her errors. She's more likely to consult an employee other than a manager because she won't feel her job's being threatened when she admits problems.

If there are several parts of the job Marta needs to learn or isn't doing well in, parcel out some of the work to other employees. Then start teaching Marta the parts that are essential to the job. As she masters those, you can add in the rest later. Encourage Marta whenever you can.

By dealing with Marta's skills problem early, you give her a much better chance of improving before she develops negative attitudes about the work or about working for you.

If Marta isn't interested in the job:

Talk to Marta to find out what kind of work she'd rather be doing. Then point out to her those parts of the job that are most similar to the kind of work she likes.

Let Marta know that if she does well in the job she's on now, you'll try to arrange for more of the work she finds interesting or help her find a job that's closer to what she's looking for.

At the same time, make it clear that Marta can't expect you to help her if she doesn't help herself. She's got to show you that she can do good work before you give her something more responsible to do or recommend her to another manager.

Also make sure that Marta is aware of the consequences of continuing to do poorly in this job. Regardless of how uninteresting she may find the work, she needs either to find herself a new job or face termination from this one for failure to perform.

If Marta is poorly motivated:

Different people are motivated by different things, but if Marta's level of motivation is typical of the new employees you're getting, you need to ask yourself some questions: Is the job set up to reward employees for doing the right things? Or are there rewards to employees for doing the wrong things (or for not doing the right things)? For instance, does your company reward quantity production exclusively without consideration of the quality of work? Do your employees understand how their jobs fit into the "big picture"? Do they see the unit or company's work as worthwhile? Are there obstacles to doing good work here that discourage employees from even trying (like insufficient work space or resources)? Answering these questions and resolving any problems you uncover won't benefit just Marta—they'll benefit the whole workgroup.

If employees don't see any benefit in doing a better job, consider setting up an informal system of recognition for each job that's done well. This can be a public "pat on the back" or a more tangible form of recognition such as an achievement certificate, a bonus, or a gift certificate. In addition, set up systems that make the employees themselves the ones who suffer the consequences of their poor work. Give your employees regular feedback on what they're doing well and not so well. When the work is not done well, make sure *they* do it over again until it's right. When new employees like Marta come on board, review with them your reward systems, so it's clear from the start why they should do good work.

If workers don't see the "big picture," put together an orientation program for your new employees that describes what each kind of job does, who the customers are (internal or external), and what impact the job has on other people or operations. Describe the company itself in some detail, identifying the services it provides or the products it makes. If it's not obvious, explain what value these products or services have. Then make sure everyone receives the orientation as soon as possible after joining your unit, along with current members of your unit, such as Marta.

You might also consider revising your recruiting literature or your interviewing techniques to emphasize the contributions the company and your unit make. If employees are excited about the kind of work you do before they even start work, they'll be much more likely to perform enthusiastically (and well).

Review your work situation to see just what's getting in the way of doing a good job. Talk to your current staff. Examine the work flow and your organizational structure. Make any changes you need to see that tasks are done in a logical sequence and that completed segments don't require rework farther down the line. Make sure someone is ultimately responsible for the quality of every product and that this person sees the final result before passing it on. Finally, do whatever you need to do to get your workers the supplies and equipment they need. Workers who don't have the necessary equipment or supplies can't do a good job, no matter how well motivated they are.

SOMETHING TO THINK ABOUT

When we've talked about some of the basic skills Marta may need to acquire to do her job, it's been in terms of skills that make up the content of the work (such as reading, writing, and similar skills). But there is another whole class of skills that Marta may not have—basic work discipline skills. These include things such as knowing that it's important to arrive at work each morning—on time; knowing that it's not acceptable to spend the workday on personal telephone calls or out in the hall chatting with friends; or knowing that when you make a commitment to do something you're expected to follow through.

Many of the newest entrants to the workforce lack even these basic skills. They didn't learn them in school, and they haven't picked them up anywhere else. Appalling as that may seem, it's a workplace problem that will only become more common in the years ahead.

The most effective way to teach these skills to a new employee is to have her work with a mentor for several months—someone who can coach her not only in the technical skills required for doing the job, but who can also gently nudge her in the right direction when she begins to take extra-long lunches or spends an inordinate amount of time talking to her friends on the telephone.

No. 53 New Hire Misses the Mark

You find that a staff member clearly isn't suited to the job

THE SCENE

It doesn't seem to matter what you do. Chuck has managed, one way or another, to mishandle every single assignment you've given him in the past six months. Even when his work seems to be acceptable, almost invariably you find out later that something was missing or just slightly off course. And although he's not rude to your customers, somehow he always manages to irritate them. He doesn't fit in with the rest of the group, but his problem isn't something you can get a handle on. You're not sure whether he doesn't like the job or can't handle the work; either way, this clearly isn't the job for him.

POSSIBLE CAUSES

Chuck may not feel comfortable with the assignment he has.

Perhaps Chuck got in over his head accepting the job. Conversely, he may be accustomed to being the "star" in the office—either because he's the best at what he does or because he has a unique role—and this job doesn't offer that opportunity. Chuck will either have to adjust to this new role or be miserable until he can find something else.

Chuck may not find the work interesting.

It may just not be in a field that he has any interest in. It may be an administrative position—when Chuck's really a "people person." It may involve a lot of travel—when Chuck would rather be at home. Or it may just involve a subject area that Chuck doesn't care about—and so he's bored.

Chuck may not feel that he fits in with the rest of the staff

They may have different interests or styles of interaction than he's comfortable with. As a result, he separates himself from the group and tries to think of ways to get out of joining their activities.

> *Hint*: Often it's hard to tell whether a person is going to be suited to a job when you hire him for the position. He may come in with excellent credentials and appear to be just who you're looking for, but end up not working out. Over time, the employee will become discouraged and stop trying. He'll decide the fault is yours or the company's. ("This is a dumb job, anyway. Who cares whether it's done well or not?" he may tell himself.) While you may believe that employees are responsible for their own happiness or unhappiness (and they are), it is still in your best interest to help them adjust to the situation or find another job. An employee who doesn't like what he's doing 8 hours a day, 250 or more days a year isn't likely to be very productive and may develop more serious performance or conduct problems over time.

YOUR RESPONSE:

If Chuck doesn't feel comfortable with his assignment:

Make sure he knows how to do the work. Challenge 57 in this chapter provides some tips on working with employees to be sure they learn what they need to know to do the job. If Chuck has been a "star" in the past and has the opportunity to learn the new assignment, he's got a good chance of being a star again.

Talk to Chuck about the aspects of the assignment he's not comfortable with. Think about how you can change the emphasis of the job a little to accommodate his specific goals. If it's not possible to restructure the position, let Chuck know up front and help him in his efforts to find a more satisfactory assignment.

If Chuck isn't interested in the work:

See Challenge 39 for steps to take when an employee is assigned work in which he's not interested. Offer your support to Chuck in finding an assignment that more closely matches his interests, but make it clear that you expect him to continue to do his best for you until a new job comes through.

If Chuck doesn't feel that he fits in with the rest of the staff:

See Challenge 5, which offers advice on an employee who doesn't relate to the group. You'll be working with the rest of your unit as well as Chuck to try to help him become more a part of things.

SOMETHING TO THINK ABOUT

An individual may not fit a job for three reasons:

- He may not have the ability to do it.
- He may not want to do it.
- He may not have an affinity for that kind of work—that is, no matter how good he is or how hard he tries, the work just isn't satisfying to him.

When you have a real mismatch between a person and his job, your best bet is to help the person get a more suitable one as soon as possible. Don't waste your time verbally beating on or otherwise trying to "motivate" the individual. That will only frustrate you—and won't do anything to improve the employee's performance.

No. 54 Unacceptable Performance Level

An average performer slips even lower on the performance scale

THE SCENE

"Boss, I hate to complain—but I just can't live with this!"

Ellen Wegner has just dumped Ollie Berlin's latest run on your desk. Once again, a high percentage of the sheets are smeared or out of register. Once again, Ollie is going to have to do a job over.

In the last couple of months, Ollie's work has clearly slipped from average to unacceptable. You've been living with it and hoping it would improve. But now you've run out of hope; it's time to do something.

POSSIBLE CAUSES

Ollie has a personal problem that's distracting him from his work.

Some painful situation outside work may be worrying him to the point that he can't concentrate on work.

Ollie may have a physical problem that is preventing him from doing work correctly.

Ollie may be abusing alcohol or another drug, and it's gotten bad enough that he can no longer perform effectively.

Ollie may be "burned out" on his job.

He just doesn't care anymore.

> ***Hint:*** While the cause of Ollie's poor performance is important, you need to focus your action on the performance itself.

YOUR RESPONSE

No matter what the cause is:

You're going to have to talk with Ollie, of course. First, though, you might want to talk with Ellen and other employees who work with him. Anything you can learn from them about Ollie's performance and its deterioration will help.

Then talk with Ollie. Deal with the performance, and be very straightforward with him. You can't accept this level of performance, and he needs to know it. But don't attack or threaten him, or be angry with him for it. Just start with the bare fact that his performance isn't satisfactory.

Give him every chance to reply and listen carefully. The more he can tell you about why he's slipping, the better. The reverse is also true: if he evades the problem or can't come up with any reason for it, or if he just makes promises to do better without explaining the performance slide, the situation's going to be harder to deal with.

If Ollie seems to have a distracting personal problem:

We deal with these problems in several places, especially in Challenge 28. Turn to it for suggestions on how to helpfully deal with Ollie.

If Ollie seems to have a physical problem that's interfering with his performance:

We also deal with physical problems in a number of other challenges, particularly in Challenge 26. This should give you the information you need to deal with Ollie's situation.

If Ollie appears to be abusing alcohol or another drug:

Whether Ollie drinks or uses drugs on the job or on his own time, his performance is suffering. You have the right to require him to do whatever is necessary to improve his performance.

If Ollie owns up to his drug-abuse problem, work through your employee assistance program coordinator or another rehabilitation professional to develop a plan for Ollie. Put together a plan that's tailored to where he is in the rehabilitation process—but resolve that you'll no longer facilitate his addiction by overlooking his performance issues.

Suppose your company doesn't have a formal program, and there's no one to help you? Many hospitals have rehabilitation units, and someone there will probably be happy to work with you. If the problem is drinking, talk to someone in a local chapter of Alcoholics Anonymous. Somewhere in the community there will be people who can help.

Wherever help comes from, remember this: Insist that Ollie perform satisfactorily—starting now, and without relapse. If he doesn't, "keep book" on him. Document his poor performance. Keep putting pressure on him. The worst thing you can do with an addict of any kind is to make his addiction less painful for him. Keep the pressure up without relief. It's the kindest action you can take.

Take a look at Challenges 27 and 29 for additional guidance with this situation.

If Ollie is burned out on the job:

This may be the hardest situation of all to deal with effectively. Job burnout probably happens to most of us at some time or another. But you can't accept it as a continuing reason for poor performance.

Don't deal with job burnout by blaming Ollie or by trying to "motivate" him out of it. Neither will work very well. You might see some improvement for a little while, and then things will be back just as they were.

One of the first solutions to think of, if it's available, is finding another job that Ollie could be reassigned to. Of course, it would have to be a job that he'd be interested in; reassigning him to another job that's equally as boring to him won't help for long.

Another solution might be to add extra duties—more interesting ones—to Ollie's job. This should be done as a reward; he gets to do them *only* if he performs his basic duties well. The result might be both that Ollie performs acceptably and that he produces more work.

Another solution is more demanding, but might be the best one. Do your employees often burn out on their jobs? Are several of the jobs the kind of boring, dead-end ones that produce burnout? If so, can you reorganize your work so that each employee does a greater variety of the duties? If the work is done piecemeal, can you rearrange it so that each employee does all, or most, of the steps necessary to produce a final product?

This last approach is called "job enrichment." We don't have room to go into it in greater detail here, but it has produced excellent results in some companies. If it sounds as if it might work for you, find out more about it.

SOMETHING TO THINK ABOUT

It's easy to react emotionally to the *causes* of poor performance, to get angry at an employee who drinks too much or feel sad for one with serious problems at home. As a manager, though, you need to objectively focus on the poor performance itself, and to deal with it—primarily as a performance issue, not as a personal issue. In the long run, that's the way you're most helpful to the company *and to the employee.*

Keep talking to your employee about your expectations for his performance, where he meets those expectations and where he fails to meet them. Let him know that you're supportive of his personal life, but that you still expect him to perform when he's on the job. Often the structure of the work environment is what keeps people going when things are falling apart at home.

No. 55 Surprise:
Substandard Work from a High Performer

An outstanding worker fouls up an important job

THE SCENE

"I can't believe this!" you exclaim with dismay. "Clark usually does such a great job on everything I give him. He's the one person I can count on to do things right when no one else knows how. And now this, this, this. . ."

Words fail you. You've got a report due to your boss tomorrow, and what Clark has given you is *useless*. Well, the immediate problem is to get this fixed so you can present it on time. But next—what to do about Clark?

POSSIBLE CAUSES

Clark may not have understood what you wanted in the assignment.

Especially if Clark is usually a good worker whom you can rely on, you need at least to consider that part of the problem was a failure to communicate.

Clark may not have set his priorities effectively.

He may have had a number of tasks and didn't give this one enough priority to get it done well on schedule.

Clark may have had personal issues that distracted him from performing this assignment as well as the others he's done in the past.

He may have a sick child, marital problems, worries about finances. He may be getting ready to leave for a long-awaited vacation. Good employees may be able to put those distractions out of mind to concentrate on the job at hand. But not everyone can, and no one can *all* the time.

Clark's performance in general may be slipping, with this foul-up just the first sign you've noticed.

Think about the other things he's done recently. They may not have been this dramatically awful, but have they been up to Clark's usual standard? If not, consider that this may not be a single incident of poor performance, but may be the start of a trend.

Hint: This list doesn't even begin to cover all that could be wrong. Clark could have had too little time to devote to this assignment; he may not have understood what the purpose of the assignment was; he may not have wanted the assignment and saw this as a way to "get back" at you; or there could be even more causes. One thing you can be sure of, though— when an otherwise good employee delivers a substandard product, you need to get to the bottom of the situation fast.

In each case, you have two distinct, and distinctly different, concerns. The first is the substandard report. The second is the conditions that led Clark to produce it. Each needs to be dealt with, but the underlying conditions are almost certainly more important and more serious than the report itself.

YOUR RESPONSE

If Clark misunderstood what you wanted in the assignment:

Ask Clark to tell you what he thought he was assigned to do in this project. Note the areas that differ between his ideas of what the assignment encompassed and what you intended.

For each area of misunderstanding, identify for Clark how the overall assignment would have come out differently if he had done things the way you intended.

Then, for each area of misunderstanding, try to find out from Clark what he thinks you said to him. If you can figure out what you said (or what he thought he heard) that caused the misunderstanding, you'll be better able to avoid a repetition.

If Clark didn't set his priorities effectively:

There are actually two problems here. First, he didn't set the right priorities. Second, he didn't tell you he couldn't produce a quality report by the deadline you set. You have to deal with both issues.

Deal with his failure to set priorities right by reviewing his work with him regularly and helping him readjust his priorities as necessary. Don't redo the priorities for him. Help him go through them and develop the judgment necessary to set them effectively for himself. (If you set them for him, you may have found yourself a job for life.) These sessions should be fairly frequent at first, then further and further apart until they become unnecessary.

Clark's failure to tell you he couldn't produce a quality report on time is a separate problem, and one that's just as serious. Every employee should know that he or she has to let you know *in advance* if a deadline can't be met.

No exceptions! Enforce this. But also make sure you listen when an employee tells you he can't meet a deadline and help him readjust the deadline (or his other priorities). It takes *both* a firm requirement and a willingness to listen.

Give him back his work product and make sure he gives it the priority it should have. Meet with him as frequently as necessary to see that he gets it done.

If Clark had personal problems that detracted from his performance:

Discuss with Clark his *performance* deficiencies. If he offers the personal problems as a reason for his failure on this assignment, offer him your understanding and your help in getting outside counseling or assistance (if he needs it).

Let Clark know that because he's been such a good employee in the past you'll stick with him through the tough times too. But also let him know that there are limits to how much the organization can handle and that you expect him to take responsibility for working his personal problems out so that he can resume his productive role in the company.

Then follow up. If things get better, let Clark know that you've noticed and give him a pat on the back. If things don't get better, make sure Clark knows the consequences of continued poor performance, continue to counsel him, and take action if necessary.

If Clark's overall performance is slipping:

There are a lot of reasons why Clark's overall performance could be deteriorating. See Challenges 46, 47, 50, and 54 for possible solutions.

SOMETHING TO THINK ABOUT

Performance problems can have many causes. This scenario and discussion illustrate several of the most common ones: misunderstanding requirements, lack of knowledge, and personal problems. But regardless of the cause, anytime a good worker begins to have problems, it's important to step in as soon as you see that there is a problem. The more times an employee fails, particularly if he doesn't know *why* the failure occurred, the more likely he is to become frustrated and give up.

No. 56 Refusing Assistance

An employee isn't doing well, but won't accept help from others

THE SCENE

Abel came to your outfit right out of technical college. He has a two-year degree in drafting, and he seems plenty sharp enough to do the job. He's been with you for almost four months now, though, and he hasn't learned as much about the job as he should. The big problem is that he insists on learning it on his own; he won't let anyone else help him.

POSSIBLE CAUSES

Abel is trying to establish himself in the unit.

New employees often feel they have to prove themselves. Sometimes they do this by refusing to admit they have to learn.

Abel has always had to learn on his own and doesn't know how to accept help gracefully.

The way that the others are trying to help him isn't effective.

They may (or may not) mean to be helpful, but don't do it very well.

> *Hint*: There's one other possibility you need to consider. Abel may not *know* he's not doing well. Sometimes, employees are so engrossed in trying to learn everything at once and are so overwhelmed that they don't know what it is they don't know. So Abel, with his still very superficial understanding of the work, may believe everything is just fine. In that case, your first task is to explain to Abel just what the problems are and that he *does* need help. Maybe then he'll accept the assistance that's been offered and your problem will be resolved.

YOUR RESPONSE

No matter what the cause is:

As in so many of the situations a supervisor encounters, you need to talk with Abel and try to find out how he sees the situation. But because he's a new employee, he may be very defensive about his behavior. If he is, don't respond emotionally; just deal with him calmly and learn all you can about the situation. You may also want to talk with some of your other employees. What do they perceive to be the problem? Just as important, how do they feel about it?

One other point: In each of the following situations, *you* can always take responsibility for helping Abel. Abel may be willing to accept help from you because you're the supervisor. He may feel less threatened by getting assistance from you, or he may feel that he can't refuse it. However, this isn't normally an acceptable solution for very long, because Abel should get used to working with other employees to solve his problems. But it may help him and the group get over an initial impasse.

If Abel is evidently just trying to establish himself in the unit:

Help your other employees understand what's happening. They may feel that Abel "ought" to want help from them. If they do, explain how hard it is for him to ask for it and accept it and why.

Help them become more skilled at offering help in a way he might accept. Offering effective assistance requires interpersonal skills as well as technical ones. They may be doing fine on the technical level but need some coaching to develop their own coaching skills. (The last response in this section has more ideas on this.)

At the same time, try to build up Abel's self-confidence. Assure him that he will be accepted by the group. Gently suggest to him that it's all right to admit he needs help while he's learning the work of the unit.

If Abel has evidently had to learn on his own and doesn't know how to accept help gracefully:

This may seem strange, but it happens. His parents may have felt that he would learn best on his own, or may not have been available to help him. He's always learned by himself. He may even feel that it's wrong or a sign of weakness to have to accept help.

You probably can't change Abel's long-held approach quickly. He's had a long time to develop this trait, and it will change slowly—but it will change if you and your unit have the skills to help him.

Start by focusing on the group. Help Abel's coworkers develop a very "low-pressure" approach to helping him. If one of your employees is particularly good at this, you might want to let him or her offer most of the help. Remind the workgroup that it will take time for Able to change, but that they probably will see results.

If the group is trying to help him in ineffective ways:

The group members may not have the interpersonal or communication skills they need. They may feel that it's Abel's "place" to let them help him, or expect him to ask them. Then, when he won't accept help, they get angry. They may even feel that their own expertise is being challenged.

Obviously, you need to help them deal with these feelings. If coworkers are upset with Abel, they'll play a part in creating a vicious circle that has nowhere to go but down. You need to work with both Abel and the rest of the workgroup to reverse this vicious circle.

All of the ideas in the preceding responses may be useful here, as well; however, you may still need some others. Here are a few possibilities:

- Get training for some or all of your employees in how to do on-the-job training. (Get it for yourself, too, if you need it.)
- Help employees remember how it was when they were new. If they really understand Abel's anxieties, it will help them be more patient.
- Provide your workgroup with training in communications skills. Maintaining effective communication in a stressful situation is difficult for everyone. Training can help.

SOMETHING TO THINK ABOUT

All the preceding suggestions assume that Abel shows the basic skills and attitudes he needs to be a good employee. If that's the case, it's best to be patient and help him develop. However, if Abel seems to lack even the most basic skills and attitudes, much less patience is called for. Try to understand him, try to help him, but insist that he put forth the effort to become a good employee. If he doesn't, take action to reassign him to a more suitable job or help him find a job elsewhere in the company, or consider terminating him if necessary.

No. 57 Inability to Master Key Tasks

A new hire can't seem to learn the harder parts of the job

THE SCENE

Rosemarie came to work for you about six months ago. She's a good worker, dependable, friendly, and cooperative, but she consistently messes up your unit's time and attendance records. It shouldn't be that hard—just a few simple arithmetic computations and entries in an automated system—but for some reason Rosemarie just can't get it right. You don't want to have to fire her, but things can't go on like this much longer. Last week two employees were short on pay because of her mistakes.

POSSIBLE CAUSES

Rosemarie may lack basic skills she needs to learn the job.

She may not know basic arithmetic or may lack keyboard skills or knowledge of the software program she has to use. These skills are prerequisite to learning the more complicated time and attendance system, and she'll need the basic skills first.

The tools you're using to teach Rosemarie may not be appropriate for her learning style.

If you're using a manual or written instructions, they may be hard for her to understand. If another employee is teaching her, that employee's explanations may not be meaningful to Rosemarie. You may need to find another way to get the message across.

Rosemarie may not be able to learn this particular task.

She may have a learning problem that interferes with her ability to learn the arithmetic skills or other parts of the job.

YOUR RESPONSE

If Rosemarie lacks basic skills she needs to learn the job:

Identify what the skills are that she's lacking. What does she consistently do wrong? For a while, check each step in the process as she completes it. Does she do the arithmetic right? Does she make mistakes using the spreadsheet program?

Once you've identified Rosemarie's specific skill deficiencies, decide the best way to train her in those areas. Your company may have classes in basic arithmetic and keyboard skills or you may be able to make arrangements with a local school for remedial training. Software vendors often provide training on the systems they sell. Or you may decide that the knowledge Rosemarie lacks is so specific that you can best train her right on the job.

After you've completed the basic skills training, review how the whole job assignment is to be performed so she can see how her new skills fit in.

Follow up. Continue to check Rosemarie's work to see if she still has problems. If the work is not performed very often, she may lose the skills for lack of practice. Consider a job aid she can use to walk her through the process each time she performs. If training and job aids don't help, then look at some of the other possible causes.

If the training method you're using doesn't work with Rosemarie:

Consider some alternative ways of presenting the information. If she's been reading a manual, then do some one-on-one tutoring. If she's been working with another employee, have that employee explain the process to you so you can determine whether someone not already familiar with the work can understand the explanation. Put together a step-by-step instruction sheet. Some people learn better by *seeing* what they're learning; others learn better by *hearing* it. Try to match the learning method to Rosemarie's learning style.

If your company has a training department, ask the professionals there to help you figure out the best way to organize and present the material Rosemarie has to learn.

If Rosemarie is simply unable to learn this part of her job:

Decide how important this task is to successful performance in the job as a whole. Is this something you could assign elsewhere without detriment to the job or the efficiency of the organization? If so, consider giving the work to someone else and assigning Rosemarie work where she can make valuable contributions.

If the task is integral to Rosemarie's position, then decide how important Rosemarie is to the company. Is there another job she could be assigned where she could work productively (even at a lower pay rate)? If so, and Rosemarie is someone who's valuable to the company, offer her the other assignment. If she refuses, or if she's not that valuable, then her poor performance warrants termination.

As tactfully and sensitively as you can, explain to Rosemarie why she's being fired. Let her know that you appreciate the good work she's done for the organization and explain why her performance deficiencies require that you terminate her. If she really has been a good, hard-working employee who just couldn't learn the job, offer her the opportunity to resign and work out with her what you'll tell any prospective employers who contact you for a reference.

SOMETHING TO THINK ABOUT

If some of your employees have to perform complicated procedures or perform some critical tasks only infrequently, create a *job aid* for the work. A job aid is like an abbreviated version of an instruction manual; it's a "cheat sheet" that lists the steps of the process in summary form to help employees who already know the job remember what to do and in what sequence.

Job aids won't teach inexperienced employees how to do the work, but they're invaluable for reminding knowledgeable employees how it's to be done.

No. 58 SLOPPY WORK

To meet a deadline, an employee turns in a substandard report

THE SCENE

You told Edwina you wanted the report today, and you got it today. Lot of good that did you—it's going to have to be redone. Superficially it looks good, but its poorly organized and the conclusions aren't well supported. Edwina isn't your strongest employee, but she usually does better than this. So what do you do now?

POSSIBLE CAUSES

Edwina is beginning to slip from acceptable performance to substandard performance.

This may be a result of personal problems, health problems, substance abuse, job burnout—any of a wide variety of conditions.

The deadline didn't give her enough time.

She did her best, but it wasn't possible to get out a quality product in the time she had.

She's angry at you about the deadline, and this is her way of showing you.

She's just waiting for you to complain so she can tell you how unfair (or dumb, or rigid) you were when you forced the deadline on her.

You weren't clear about what you wanted.

All too often, employees produce the wrong product because they didn't understand clearly what was wanted.

YOUR RESPONSE

No matter what the cause is:

If you're angry, get over it. Then call Edwina in, tell her how dissatisfied you are, and ask for an explanation. *Don't* be judgmental or accusing.

If she feels she has an explanation, listen carefully to it. If she doesn't have a ready explanation, probe a little bit. If the explanation is too glib, probe a little bit more. Keep digging, if necessary, until you have a "feel" for the situation.

If she may be beginning to slip into substandard performance:

Look back at Challenge 55 in this chapter; it will give you the information you need to deal with this situation.

If the deadline didn't give her enough time:

Here the underlying problem is lack of communication, lack of trust, or both. The first question to be answered is *why* she didn't have enough time. Did you impose the deadline without listening to her objections? Were you afraid she was "padding" her estimate? Did she know she didn't have enough time, but was afraid to say so? It's critical to find the answer.

Once you find the answer, there's much work to be done. First, you both need to agree that you won't repeat the actions that led to the bad deadline. Then you need to stick to your agreement. The next time you assign work with a deadline, you need to help each other live up to the agreement.

Give her the report back, set a mutually acceptable deadline, and expect a fully acceptable product by the deadline.

If she's angry at you about the deadline:

Edwina may be angry with you for any of a number of reasons. Realistically, she may not have had enough time. Or she may not have handled her priorities well. Deal with that situation. But that's not enough.

The question that most needs answering is: *Why* was she so angry that she chose to set both you and herself up for failure this way? Is she so frustrated because you won't listen to her that she's decided to do this in hopes it will get your attention? Is it because of a completely unrelated grudge she has with you? Is she reacting in this manner because she didn't get her way with the deadline in the first place?

Spend the time you need to figure out why Edwina was angry and what the two of you need to do about it.

If this action got her anger off her chest, give her back the report and agree on a time when she'll finish it. If she's still angry, you may want to give the report to someone else to finish. If so, make it clear to Edwina that, regardless of the cause, this was a performance failure on her part. If it seems appropriate, reflect this incident on her next performance appraisal (and in her next compensation review).

If you weren't clear about what you wanted:

Perhaps you're the cause of the problem. Review the following descriptions and see if one or more of them apply to you. If so, then listen to Edwina's reasons for the poor report, and be willing to accept responsibility for her inability to produce the report you really wanted.

- You don't explain projects carefully to employees. If you get back many projects that aren't done as you want, this is probably one of the major causes.

- You don't ask effective questions to see if the employee understands what you want.

- The employee doesn't know to ask for clarification, or is afraid to do so. She may think that you view questions as a sign of ineptitude. Don't just tell Edwina that you want her to ask questions; communicate in your response that you welcome her questions and want her to ask as many as she needs to be sure she understands what has to be done.

- You don't trust the employee, so you discourage her from asking questions. Or perhaps she doesn't trust you, and is reluctant to come to you with questions. (This is very much like the preceding problem of anger—but when lack of trust is a cause, the problem is more serious.)

Spend however much time you need to understand what's happening and start to correct it. If you and the employee can't agree at the beginning on what's wanted, you will both lose at the end.

SOMETHING TO THINK ABOUT

When a good employee stumbles on one product, it's easy to overlook the stumble. That's a judgment call. But it's also easy to convince yourself that *each* incident of poor performance is an isolated one—and that way you don't have to deal with it. But every performance problem is easier to solve if it's caught quickly and dealt with quickly—if not the first time you're dissatisfied with an employee's work products, then at most by the second time. Let your employee know her work isn't up to par and that you want to help her improve her performance.

No. 59 DETERIORATING WORK HABITS

A new employee started out well, but performance quickly slips

THE SCENE

"Did I make a mistake, or what?" you ask one of the other section supervisors in bewilderment. "Pete Yokohama seemed like such a good candidate when I interviewed him, and his first few weeks on the job he was like a house afire. But in the last several weeks, it's as if he's run out of steam. He's slower, he's making more mistakes, and he's not learning the new stuff nearly as well anymore. I just can't figure out what's going on."

POSSIBLE CAUSES

Pete could be in over his head.

Assuming that you structured his learning the new job so that he learned the simpler parts first, he may have reached his learning saturation point. He may never get much better at the work than he is right now.

Pete could have run into a particular part of the work that he can't get a handle on.

It may have him stymied so that it's interfering with the parts of the job he's already mastered.

Pete might be disillusioned with the work.

He may be having second thoughts about having accepted your job offer, and his performance is beginning to reflect his disillusionment.

> **_Hint:_** Whatever the cause of the problem, don't give up on Pete too soon. Learning is *not* a continuous upward curve. People learn incrementally—in fits and starts. Figure out what the cause is and deal with it. But maintain your faith in Pete. Chances are that this is just a temporary roadblock, and he'll still live up to your expectations. But if you begin to treat him like a loser already, he'll give up on himself too. And then you'll both lose.

YOUR RESPONSE

If Pete is in over his head:

What kind of recommendations did you get about Pete when you checked his references? (You *did* check his references, didn't you?)

Did his former supervisors say he was a quick learner? That he was slow but once he learned something he knew it backwards and forwards? That he learned enough to get by but didn't stick with the details?

What kinds of jobs did Pete hold before yours? Were they equally demanding or complex? Or is this a significant step up for him?

If Pete's former supervisors tell you that he's had learning difficulties in the past, or if this is a major job change for him, you should talk to Pete to probe more deeply into his skills and aptitudes. You might want to consider arranging for him to take a battery of aptitude and interest tests to see if he's suited for the kind of job he's been placed in.

If Pete really has reached the limits of his abilities and you are convinced that he won't be able to learn parts of the job that are critical to his successful performance, you must take action to move him out of the position. If he has other skills that you want to retain, try to find another position for Pete, where he can make a contribution, in your group or elsewhere in the company. But if you decide that Pete's not going to work out anywhere, then it's best to let him go now. Once you've decided that his skills and aptitudes aren't sufficient for your organization, you shouldn't spend your time (and his) needlessly delaying the inevitable.

If Pete has met a temporary roadblock:

First, don't panic. And don't let Pete panic. Let him know that you expect there to be some areas he'll have more trouble learning than others.

Especially if your reference checks revealed that Pete has had some initial problems grasping new tasks in the past, you need to reinforce your faith in his ability eventually to learn the work.

Try to figure out what he's having problems with. Is it the volume of work (does he need help in organization skills)? Is it the complexity of the work (can you break the work down into smaller segments that he can master one by one)? Is the problem in specific subject areas (can you provide some on-the-job mentoring or some formal training to help him)?

Take a look at Challenge 57 in this chapter. Temporary roadblocks often occur only in those harder-to-perform parts of the job.

Work with Pete to develop a specific improvement plan. If necessary, give him some slack on the parts of the job he's already mastered so he can concentrate on the areas in which he's having problems.

But, above all, keep reassuring Pete, over and over, of your continued confidence in his ability to learn the job. We know from personal experience that it can sometimes take months for employees to learn specific tasks, even tasks you think they should be able to master in days or weeks. Every employee learns at a different pace. And, in most cases, it's more important to learn to do the job well than to learn it quickly.

If Pete's become disillusioned with the job:

This will be most obvious from the attitude and enthusiasm (or lack) he shows toward the work. But be careful! Some people also show frustration (like from not being able to learn) by "tuning out." While you may be more accustomed to seeing frustrated employees react with anger or impatience, apparent indifference is not an uncommon response either.

But if your observations and your discussions with Pete reveal that he's not happy with the way the job is turning out, it's time to have a frank discussion with him about your expectations for his performance and the consequences of poor performance. Explain that if he's really unhappy in his work it's better for him to leave of his own volition (or to decide to put up with his disillusionment and perform anyway) than to be taken out of the job. Offer him whatever help he needs to learn the job and to be successful. Describe the *realistic* opportunities available for recognition and for advancement. But be clear that the choice is his. Your job is to see that his job gets done and gets done well. Ultimately, Pete needs to understand that your overriding concern is for the health of the company.

And if he neither "shapes up" nor "ships out"? Treat his performance problems as you would any other in your workgroup. Other challenges in this chapter illustrate a number of approaches.

SOMETHING TO THINK ABOUT

Moving to a new job, especially if it's with a new company, is a traumatic experience for most people. All the security and comfort of the old environment is gone, and an employee who's used to feeling competent and knowledgeable suddenly becomes a novice all over again. We can't stress too often that the most effective cure for many early apparent performance problems is *time*. Time to learn the work, time to learn the organization and how to work with the people in it, and time to adjust and become more comfortable in the new environment. Encouragement from you is important—frequently, that's all that's needed.

Don't respond to learning difficulties your new employees have in the same way you would respond to performance problems your experienced staff exhibit. With an established employee, you'll want to intervene as soon as you suspect there's a problem. But with a *new* employee, allow time for adjusting to the new environment and all the other changes that come with a new job. Then if things don't improve within a reasonable amount of time, you still have an opportunity to intervene.

No. 60
POOR PERFORMANCE FROM A MINORITY EMPLOYEE

You hire a minority with high ratings who doesn't live up to expectations

THE SCENE

You shake your head in dismay, disappointed and feeling let down. Your newest employee, a minority group member who got excellent ratings from his last two supervisors, is a nonperformer. Here you are, in the middle of a production crunch—and now you have to deal with this mess with Rick!

POSSIBLE CAUSES

Rick may really want to do well and have ability.

But he may be lacking in self-confidence or may never have gotten the proper training. (Individuals in minority groups usually get the same formal training everyone else does but may be missing informal "This is how you really do it" training from other employees.)

He may really want to do well but lacks the ability.

He may lack one or more key abilities for this kind of work. Or he may not be temperamentally suited to it.

He may be a poor performer because that's what he wants to be.

He may be content to "get by" with as little work as possible. (Remember, though, this could be a symptom of lack of self-confidence, lack of training, or lack of a key ability.)

> **Hints:** Listen carefully and ask probing questions. An employee's first answers in any confrontation are likely to be very different from his real thoughts and feelings.

If you settle for the surface answers, you won't find the real cause, and that means you won't be able to meet the challenge.

YOUR RESPONSE

If Rick really wants to do well and seems to have ability:

Give him routine but meaningful work to do. You might want to assign another employee to help him. See that help is available to him, but also make sure that no one else will do his work for him. If necessary, provide formal or on-the-job training.

Follow up regularly and frequently, anywhere from every day to once or twice a week. Praise his progress and use his mistakes to help him learn.

Gradually increase the variety and difficulty of what he's assigned until he's performing the full scope of his job. This may take weeks or months. It will be easier and faster if the rest of your employees are willing to work with him.

If he really wants to do well but doesn't seem to have the ability:

Make sure that this really is the case. It's painful to admit that you harbor lingering stereotypes, but it's a fact of life. If Rick really wants to do well, don't decide he can't until he's had a real chance.

Give him routine tasks with plenty of help (as in the response above), until you have a clear idea of what he can do. This may take several weeks or months if you have the time.

If after giving Rick sufficient time and support to learn you're convinced that he can't do the job, discuss the situation realistically with him. Try to arrange a change to a less demanding job in your unit or elsewhere. As long as he's conscientious, support him in every way you can.

Don't "carry" him, or overrate him in hopes you can pass the problem on. It may solve this particular problem in the short run, but you may not want to live with the long-range consequences.

You can find more guidance for this situation in Challenge 57 in this chapter.

If Rick's a poor performer because that's what he wants to be:

Again, make sure this is really the case and not just a cover-up for lack of self confidence, and so on. Remember to be careful about the stereotypes you may have about Rick's minority group.

Assign him a regular, routine workload, the kind of work someone in his position is expected to perform. Give him assistance when appropriate (but make sure no one else does the work for him).

If he gives in and performs, so much the better. If not, look at Challenge 39 for ideas on how to deal with poorly motivated employees. But deal with him.

If you push Rick and he threatens to file a discrimination complaint:

Double-check your expectations. Make sure you're *not* treating him differently from non-minority workers.

From a purely practical standpoint, some battles just aren't worth fighting. You may be convinced that what you're doing is right and nondiscriminatory. If you think you're likely to lose in a discrimination complaint or that the fight will tear apart your work unit, you need to think hard about the situation. Will the benefits of success outweigh the negative consequences?

If the benefits outweigh the dangers, confront the equal employment opportunity issue head-on. Tell Rick that although he has the right to file a complaint, and that you're convinced that what you're doing is best for him and for the company. Then document every action or discussion with him and start building your own case.

And what if you think the outcome isn't worth the effort? You have a serious problem on your hands. You can't let him just "slide by" because of his threat. Our best advice is to keep constant pressure on him to perform at the same level as the others. If that's not practical, see if you can assign him mean-ingful, useful duties that he can perform. The critical point is to somehow see that Rick becomes a productive member of your work unit.

SOMETHING TO THINK ABOUT

No matter how tempting it is to concentrate on the fact that Rick is a member of a minority group, don't forget that this is first of all a *performance* problem. The situation will never be completely resolved unless and until the performance issue is resolved. The issue of minority group status is a distraction, but it's not the real issue.

Deal with the performance issue as you would with any other employee. Keep the minority group issue where it belongs—as a secondary, low-level concern.

CHAPTER SEVEN

Encouraging Good Workplace Ethics

No. 61 STRETCHING THE TRUTH

One of your best workers lied in an investigation

THE SCENE

You stare sadly at the report lying open on your desk. It's all too clear that Jeremy Cook lied in the investigation. The report says that on at least two occasions Mike Murgaty, one of your team leaders, approached Jeremy to try to talk him into participating in his land development scheme. But Jeremy denied to the investigators that Mike had ever discussed the subject with him. Jeremy's one of your best workers—reliable, hard-working, and trustworthy—or so you thought. But a lie is a lie, isn't it?

POSSIBLE CAUSES

A lie is a lie, right? Well, yes—and no. Anytime an employee lies, it chips away at the bond of trust that is the basis of all of the relationships we form, at work and elsewhere. And the answer to that breach of trust is usually fairly automatic: An employee who lies is fired, because from that point on, you never know when you can believe him and when you can't.

But there are some extenuating circumstances that require that you at least *consider* an exception to that rule. You may still decide that you can't afford to keep the employee on the payroll any longer, either because you can't trust him or because you have to make a clear statement to the rest of the staff. But in certain situations, you owe it to the employee to at least consider some alternatives.

Jeremy may have believed he was expected to lie in the investigation.

Particularly if the employee being investigated is in a sensitive or highly visible position, or if he's one of the company favorites, Jeremy may have thought that he was supposed to protect the employee and the organization. His dishonesty may actually have been misguided loyalty to the company.

Jeremy may have been pressured to lie.

He may not have decided on his own that he was expected to lie; others in positions of influence over him may have fostered that impression. He may even have been threatened with loss of pay or stature or position—or with physical harm.

Jeremy may have lied to protect himself.

This is the most likely situation, and the least forgivable. Jeremy may have been implicated in the wrongdoing being investigated, or in some other wrongdoing that is likely to be revealed in the course of the investigation. He may have lied simply to keep his own transgressions from being discovered.

> **Hint:** In deciding on the appropriate action to take, consider not only the employee's motivation, but also the effect of your decision on the company (including the rest of the staff). Your bottom-line position must be that lying, or any action that undermines your trust in an employee, is intolerable. If it's well known in the company that the employee lied, then you have no choice but to take some corrective action. Regardless of the employee's misguided loyalty or perception of outside pressure, you must make it clear to the staff that you expect them to be honest, and trustworthy.

YOUR RESPONSE

If Jeremy believed he was expected to lie:

First, be sure that Jeremy really did believe he was expected to lie and that this isn't an excuse for his unacceptable actions. Even if Jeremy has been entirely trustworthy in the past, remember that he has broken that trust, so anything he says is suspect until he has proven himself again.

If you're convinced that Jeremy is being honest with you about his reasons, explain to him what you would have expected of him in this situation and why his attempts to be a loyal employee were misguided. Make sure he knows that he can come to you if a similar situation arises again—both for clarification of your expectations and for support for his honest testimony.

Decide what corrective action is appropriate. If Jeremy lied about something relatively minor that had no material effect on the outcome of the investigation, if his false testimony is not a matter of public knowledge, and if it's clear that he gained *in no way* from his lie, you may be able to let him off with a warning. If any of those conditions are not met, take corrective action in accordance with your company's policies. Your human resources department will be able to help you decide on an appropriate action and work through the required procedures.

If Jeremy was pressured to lie:

You will need to do an investigation of your own here. Find out who Jeremy felt was pressuring him. Get names, dates, places, records of conversations. Have Jeremy document his contacts in writing. Talk to other witnesses in the original investigation who may have been pressured by the same person(s) to see if they were approached. If your company has an investigations or security division, ask for their help in following up. Your human resources department may also be able to help you investigate Jeremy's allegations. If, at any point, it looks as if there is possible criminal activity involved, go immediately to your company's legal counsel to determine what your next step should be.

After you've collected all the information you can, make a decision about whether Jeremy had good reason to believe that he was being pressured to lie in the investigation. Remember, there are many kinds of pressure, some more subtle than others. It doesn't take a direct threat to convince an employee that he needs to listen, but you do need some reasonable basis for Jeremy's perception of outside pressure.

If it appears that Jeremy really was pressured and reasonably expected some harm to come to him if he didn't lie, explain to him how you would have wanted him to handle the situation. Make it clear to him that he could have come to you, that you would have supported him and taken action against those who were pressuring him. Some minor corrective action may still be appropriate (for example, an oral admonishment), but it could also be appropriate to let Jeremy off with a warning.

If Jeremy misperceived pressure where none existed, you will have to take stronger measures. Explain clearly and firmly the standards of honesty to which you expect your employees to adhere. Make sure Jeremy understands what he did that was wrong and why it was wrong. To make sure other employees get the message, you may still need to take some corrective action. Decide what corrective action is appropriate. If Jeremy has been a good employee and trustworthy until now, it may not be necessary to fire him. A suspension or a demotion to a position of lesser trust may be sufficient. But if there's any doubt about your ability to trust him in a similar situation again, terminating his employment is the most appropriate action.

If Jeremy lied to protect himself:

The appropriate course here is clear. Make sure Jeremy knows what he did that was wrong and why it was wrong. Then separate him from your organization.

Let him know that his dishonesty is a matter of record and, subject to your company's policies, that you'll let his prospective employers know the reasons for his termination when they do reference checks.

Particularly if you work for a large company with multiple offices, make sure your human resources department has documentation to support the termination and a recommendation that Jeremy not be rehired within the company. Ask them to keep the records on file so that he isn't inadvertently rehired by another division that doesn't know his history with the organization.

SOMETHING TO THINK ABOUT

While it should go without saying that employees are expected to be honest and trustworthy, this might be a good time to write a policy letter on the subject. Have it signed at as high a level in the company as you can, then present it to your employees with your own personal endorsement.

No. 62 Public Criticism

He embarrassed you in front of your boss

THE SCENE

You can't believe it! You assure your boss that everything is on track for the Smithson job, then call Joe Esch in to confirm it. Instead, Joe tells you pointedly that he isn't doing anything on it because you haven't gotten him the spec sheets you promised. You ease Joe out the office door, mumble the best excuse you can think of to your boss, and try to look calm as you follow Joe back to your work area. Now it's time to deal with Joe.

POSSIBLE CAUSES

Joe was just giving you an answer.

For some reason, he didn't understand what its consequences would be.

Joe is angry because you're holding up a project you assigned him.

Maybe he really has to have the spec sheets before he can go on.

Joe's been holding a grudge against you and this was his chance to make you look bad.

Sometimes employees have long memories.

Joe wants to get you replaced as his boss.

> ***Hint:*** Watch your anger! This kind of situation really gets under the skin of most managers. That's okay, but don't take any action to resolve it until you've cooled down.

YOUR RESPONSE

No matter what the cause is:

You guessed it, you begin by talking with Joe—after you've calmed down. Give him every chance to tell you why he did it.

Then, no matter why Joe criticized you in your boss' presence, make it clear that he's not to do it again. How clear you have to be depends on the situation, but don't leave any question in his mind about what will happen if he repeats the behavior.

If Joe was just giving you an answer:

As painful as your embarrassment might be, this is the easiest situation to deal with. Explain to Joe just what his response caused and how he should have handled it. Then make sure he knows not to do it again. Finally, explain that you're not angry with him because you realize he acted out of ignorance.

If Joe is angry because you're holding up his project:

Perhaps Joe is a conscientious worker. Perhaps you really emphasized the due date when you assigned it to him, and he wants to get the project done on schedule, but he feels that you're holding up his work.

You have two issues to deal with here. First, face up to your failure to give him the materials he needed. Perhaps he could have reminded you that you promised them, but if you made the commitment he has no responsibility to serve as your memory. You blew it. Give him the spec sheets, or tell him exactly when you'll have them for him.

Second, tell Joe clearly that he's not to criticize you in front of your boss again. This may make him upset, but stick to it. Explain how he's hurt himself as well as you—and remind him that you would never criticize him in front of your boss either.

If Joe's been holding a grudge against you:

You may have to probe a bit to find this out. But it's important that you do.

When you find out what caused the grudge, try to work it through. Is Joe unhappy over work assignments, because you asked him to work overtime on an evening when he had big plans, or because he had to change his vacation schedule to meet a major deadline? This can be an opportunity to get the issue out in the open and lay it to rest.

While you may not be able to deal with it now, there's another question you need to ask: Does this point to a continuing problem in your relationship with Joe and perhaps with others in your unit? If it does, take this incident as the occasion to deal with the underlying problem.

If Joe wants to get you replaced:

In that case, this specific incident is probably the least of your worries, but you have to deal with it. If what Joe did was really blatant, you may want to take some corrective action.

The deeper issue is Joe's wish to get rid of you. Is there something specific you did that offended him and that you might be able to settle now? Sounds as if you need to do it. Any manager who has employees working to get him removed has a serious problem, one worth every reasonable effort to resolve.

What if no resolution is possible? You'll hope Joe is the only one who really wants you out of your job. If that's the case, you might want to see about getting him reassigned. (His behavior in front of your boss may help you get your boss's support for this.) If there's no realistic step you can take, just stay aware of the situation and be prepared. Joe may go too far, and then he may be the one who leaves, whether he wants to or not.

Suppose most of your employees would like to see you taken out of the job. Why do they? If it's because you're carrying out your boss's direction to "shape up" the unit, make sure they know that you have a mandate to follow, with full support. If it's because your supervisory style creates unnecessary friction, then perhaps you should work on changing it.

SOMETHING TO THINK ABOUT

We've been concentrating on how you handle Joe, but there are two other issues you can't overlook. First, it's important to handle your boss. You can't undo the damage that Joe's comments did. You can make sure that your boss knows that you have the situation in hand that that everything is okay. (By the way, if Joe is behind so that the project due date will have to slip, don't let it. Do whatever you have to do get it done on time. Remember, you said it was on track. Your credibility is at stake here.)

The other problem is you. *Why* didn't you get the spec sheets to Joe? You intended to but it just slipped your mind? Remember what good intentions pave the way to. Do what you have to do to see that this kind of thing doesn't happen again. From now on, when you make a commitment, keep it—period.

No. 63 Covering Up

He may have lied about completing an assignment

THE SCENE

"Charlene, are you sure you don't have the production report?"

"I know what a production report looks like, and I can promise you it never got to us."

"I specifically asked Vic if he'd finished it before he left yesterday and he told me he had. I'd never have let him take the day off today if I'd known it wasn't done. I'll grab him as soon as he walks in tomorrow and get him to finish it."

POSSIBLE CAUSES

There's been a mistake somewhere.

Vic finished the production report, but it didn't get to Charlene.

There was no mistake—Vic lied.

Vic may have lied.

The situation looks suspicious, but. . .

> ***Hint:*** This may seem like a small thing. After all, it was only one report, and it was only one day late. That's almost beside the point. Employees need to live up to their commitments, or you won't be able to rely on them. You also don't want employees you can't trust—whether it's because they're unreliable or dishonest. This is serious, and Vic needs to understand how serious it is.

YOUR RESPONSE

No matter what the cause is:

Once again, begin by calming down, then call Vic in and confront him with the situation. Give him every chance to explain, but ask the hard questions if you have to.

If there's been a mistake somewhere:

Find out what happened to the production report and get it to Charlene. Do whatever you have to do to see that the problem isn't repeated. (This could mean revising an office procedure.)

If the mistake happened because Vic was sloppy or didn't follow through, counsel him. The problem was embarrassing to you and the unit—as well as to him—and he needs to make sure it never happens again.

If Vic lied:

The only serious question you're facing is whether to keep Vic or fire him. This may seem like a harsh approach to one small lie, but now you don't know how many times in the past Vic lied and you didn't catch it.

If Vic is a good employee and this is the first time anything like this ever happened, it may be enough to give him a stern admonishment. It's also possible—though not likely—that there were extenuating circumstances that might mitigate what he did. Be understanding, but don't forget how serious the offense was.

In this circumstance, you also have to remember the effect of your action on others. If you merely "sweep the incident under the rug," it will communicate to the rest of your employees that you think lying is no big deal, and they may decide to try it, or they may think that Vic is unfairly getting away with something. Either way, you're inviting trouble.

If Vic may have lied:

Suppose this is what happened. You're deeply suspicious of Vic, and no one can find the report. Then, three hours after he returns to work, he "discovers" the report in a desk drawer and immediately carries it to Charlene's unit. He apologizes, explaining that he thought he'd put it in the office mail but that it got stuck in some other material. Did he really misplace it, or did he rush and get it done as soon as he got back?

There's no way you can find out for sure. . . this time. You can talk with Vic, and you can make two points loudly and clearly:

- The situation looks extremely suspicious. Even if he did misplace the report, he's raised a question in everyone's mind. It will be that much harder for you and others to trust him the next time.
- Even if he's being completely honest, he dropped the ball. He knew finishing the report before he left was a condition of taking the day off. He should have made absolutely sure that either Charlene's unit or you had the report.

Whichever is the situation, he's put a question mark by his performance. Now it's up to him to perform so well that the question mark gets removed.

SOMETHING TO THINK ABOUT

Lying is an extremely serious offense. It not only destroys the trust between employee and manager, but it calls into question the whole past performance of the individual. Its effects go far beyond the immediate incident.

Just as it's important for you to be able to trust your employees, it's at least as important for them to trust you. If you lie to your employees and get found out—and sooner or later you will get found out—it will destroy your credibility and any trust they have in you. There's virtually nothing you can accomplish by lying that's worth that. So resolve that you'll never tell your employees anything other than the truth. That may sometimes mean that you're not in a position to tell them anything—but no information is better than misinformation.

No. 64 Trash Talk

An employee tries to discredit a coworker

THE SCENE

"You'll never believe what Vivian just did," Ross confides at lunch. "She told the people on the Willenbacher account that she could get them a 20 percent price break if they signed a contract in 15 days! Can you believe it? That's the only reason she got that contract in so fast. She thinks she's 'Queen of the Hill' right now, but I'd never stoop to a trick like that!"

Oh, no? *You* know why Vivian closed that deal so quickly; you've been working with her on it since the beginning. And there was nothing underhanded about it. So who does Ross think he's fooling? And why is he out to get Vivian?

POSSIBLE CAUSES

Ross may be jealous of the attention Vivian is getting.

He may crave the same attention and think it's easier for him to shoot down someone else than to prove himself.

Ross may be trying to sabotage Vivian's chances for advancement—whether a promotion or a reward such as a bonus or public recognition. This cause is related to the first, but the intent to harm is greater.

Ross may have misunderstood the facts.

He may be repeating a version of the story he heard from someone else. That version may have been distorted either intentionally or unintentionally farther up the line.

> ***Hint:*** Unless Ross genuinely misunderstood the situation and is inadvertently passing on bad information, it doesn't make a lot of difference what his true intentions are. Just as the trust between supervisors and subordinates is critical to the operation of any group, the trust among the members of the group is also critical. Whenever you have a situation in which one of your employees is trying to discredit another, there are two things you need to accomplish: (1) You must make it clear to the employee at fault that you will not tolerate that behavior, and (2) you must do all you can to repair the damage to the offended worker's reputation.

YOUR RESPONSE

If Ross intended to discredit Vivian, whether because he's jealous of the attention or because he wants to keep her from getting some benefit:

Let him know *immediately* that you're aware of what he's doing and order him to stop spreading the falsehoods.

If this is the first time he's engaged in this behavior and if the damage to Vivian is minimal, you may let him off with just a warning, preferably a documented one. Make sure he understands that you consider his conduct unacceptable and that you will deal harshly with any repetition of this behavior.

If he has a history of similar conduct, or if Vivian has really been hurt by his rumors, you'll need to take much more severe action. Termination wouldn't be out of line, especially if yours is a business where cooperation and teamwork are essential. If competition among employees is encouraged in your line of work, lesser measures are appropriate. But even then, it's important that Ross learn from this experience the limits of acceptable behavior—that he can compete just as well, if not better in the long run, by improving himself rather than by discrediting others.

If Ross was inadvertently passing on bad information:

Let Ross know that his information is incorrect, tell him the real story of how Vivian pulled off this brilliant feat, and enlist his help in undoing the damage he's done. Require that he talk again to people to whom he repeated the wrong story and give them the right version.

Give Ross a warning about trusting everything he hears "on the street." Especially if he's new or if yours is a competitive business, make sure he knows the dangers of turning into a dupe for someone else's plans to discredit others. Express your confidence in his own good intentions and his ability to learn to distinguish those sources he can trust from those he can't.

In either case:
You need to take some positive steps to restore Vivian's good reputation. You can begin by spreading the word among your staff of Vivian's exemplary work, perhaps offering it as an example of a strategy others might want to copy.

You might also consider some public recognition of Vivian's achievement. If the circumstances are appropriate, your repetition of the true story and stated approval of Vivian's actions will go far in overcoming the negative effects of another's gossip.

SOMETHING TO THINK ABOUT

The fact that Ross spread false information about Vivian may be symptomatic of a greater problem in your unit—namely, excessive competition among your employees. Look at how employees are recognized and rewarded. Is the competition for recognition a "zero sum game"? In other words, does everyone else lose when one person wins?

As much as you possibly can, develop your reward structures so that everyone can be a winner. That may mean lavishing praise and non-monetary rewards on your good performers rather than allocating a pot of money of finite proportions. But however you decide to structure the rewards themselves, make sure that it's possible for everyone in the organization to achieve them.

No. 65 Chronic Lateness

A staff member keeps "banker's hours" at your expense

THE SCENE

As you walk through the work area, you notice that Yoshi's desk is empty. You glance at your watch; it's already 15 minutes past starting time. He didn't ask for any time off, so there's only one likely conclusion you can draw: he's late again. Sure enough, as you finish your errand and walk back, there's Yoshi rushing in. This has got to stop.

POSSIBLE CAUSES

Yoshi has family responsibilities that take time in the morning.

You've been letting him and others get away with being late and not saying anything.

He's concluded it doesn't matter to you if he gets in late.

He's beginning to develop a bad habit.

This is the first sign of a serious personal problem.

He may be indulging in too many late nights, either drinking to excess or abusing other drugs.

> **Hint:** Just one employee coming in "a little late" may not seem like much. But when this happens and you don't seem to mind, it sends a message to other employees. The message may be that you don't care, or that you're a "weak" supervisor, or that you play favorites, among other possibilities—all of them negative.

YOUR RESPONSE

No matter what the cause is:

Need we say it yet again? Begin by talking with Yoshi—and don't put it off. The rest of the office is probably already watching to see whether you're going to deal with the problem.

If you're really irked, though, put off talking with Yoshi long enough to cool down. Although it wouldn't hurt for Yoshi to know you're unhappy with him, you need to be able to listen objectively to what he has to say for himself.

If Yoshi has family responsibilities:

It wasn't too long ago that mothers were the ones who were late because they had to get kids off to school. Not any longer. Many fathers now take on these responsibilities. And it's not just taking care of the kids anymore; increasing numbers of working people have to take care of aging parents.

If that's the situation, and Yoshi is otherwise a good worker, make whatever accommodations you can to his situation. Will it help if he starts his workday later and stays a little later to put in a full day? Can he start a little late and make up the difference by taking a short lunch? Could you even consider "flex-time" for the entire unit?

The important point is that if Yoshi has honest reasons for not getting to work at the normal time, it's proper to try to fit his work schedule to his personal schedule. If you can't, of course, then you have to deal with his tardiness as a performance problem. But try very hard to avoid that.

There's one other important aspect of the problem. Why hasn't Yoshi told you he has personal matters that prevent him from getting to work on time? He's been late several times; he should have taken the initiative to explain this to you. Even if his reasons for tardiness are the best and you do accommodate his situation, you need to counsel him on this point.

If you've been letting him (and perhaps others) get away with being late:

You've been sending them the message that it's okay to be a little late—whatever "a little late" is. Yoshi figures that if you don't care, why should he?

It's time to stop that foolishness—your foolishness—right away. That doesn't mean chew out Yoshi and then ignore the problem again until it hits you in the face. It means having an honest talk with him, admitting that you've been getting lax, and then making it clear that you won't overlook tardiness in the future. If you've been letting others get away with the same thing, talk with them also, either singly or in a group.

Yoshi or one of the others will probably test you on this, quite possibly the next morning. Be ready for it. There's no point in letting your frustration show; after all, you helped cause the problem. But confront the situation and be firm about it. That will probably end the testing. If it doesn't, do some serious counseling, maybe even writing up the offenders.

If Yoshi is beginning to develop a bad habit:

He may have been a good worker, so you didn't want to push him the first time or two. But now his tardiness is turning into a habit, and it's time to stop it.

Talk to Yoshi, make it clear what your standards are. If he makes excuses, brand them as excuses and reject them. If he has poor work habits, he may not think that tardiness is that important. Make it clear to him that it is.

Don't be surprised if he resents this and gets angry. Just accept it, but repeat that you won't tolerate the tardiness. Then, if he's tardy again, counsel him immediately. You'll probably want to write him up this time.

Keep the pressure on. If Yoshi likes his job, he'll start getting there on time. If he doesn't, treat it as a performance problem and deal with it that way.

If this is the first sign of a serious personal problem:

Yoshi may be drinking too much, so it's hard for him to get going in the morning. He might be producing the same result by abusing other drugs. Perhaps his home life is bad, so that it's emotionally difficult for him to start the day.

There are dozens of possible causes. If Yoshi is a normally good worker who's suddenly starting to have bad work habits, or if the excuses he gives you don't hold up at all, he may well have this kind of problem.

Look at the challenges in Chapter 4 for suggestions on how to deal with a worker who has a serious personal problem.

SOMETHING TO THINK ABOUT

It's only natural to give a good worker some slack. If Yoshi is a good worker, you may not want to hassle him just because he's late a time or two. Although this seems reasonable, you don't want to let him set a pattern, either. It's possible to talk about his tardiness without being harsh or authoritarian—and that's what you need to do, as soon as you see the tardiness isn't an isolated event.

No. 66 A Thief in Your Midst

Your unit's supplies are being pilfered, but you don't know who's doing it

THE SCENE

Tina brings you this month's third loss report on a missing calculator. Then there's the power stapler that no one can find. And the boxes of disks and ink cartridges that can't be accounted for. Nothing big is missing (yet), but you're getting concerned. How can you stop all this before it gets really out of hand?

POSSIBLE CAUSES

Your employees think it's okay to take small equipment and supplies to use at home.

Over the years, this has become an informal "fringe benefit" for them, one they count on.

Someone in the unit is stealing to support a substance abuse problem.

Much of the theft in this country is committed to support drug habits. That may be happening in your unit.

You have a thief in your unit.

Security in your office is too lax.

Someone who doesn't work for you is stealing from you, because you don't have control of visitors in the work area.

> **Hint**: This is a good time to be careful, systematic, and rational. Don't jump to conclusions or take rash steps without getting the facts. See if there's any office gossip about the thefts, but don't act on it until you've verified it for yourself.

YOUR RESPONSE

If your employees think it's okay to take small equipment and supplies for personal use:

This may seem strange, particularly if you're used to an office where supplies are strictly controlled or where the culture just doesn't tolerate personal use of company property. It does happen. It may be a long-standing practice that started and escalated simply because no one ever told employees they couldn't help themselves to company supplies.

You might start by talking with your boss or other managers and see what the firm's practices are. One or two of your senior workers might be willing to talk with you about it.

If the company doesn't intend for employees to take equipment and supplies, you need to stop your employees from doing it. *Don't* start by being judgmental and demanding. Explain how the situation developed and that you expect it to stop. If you know what the cost is to your unit and/or the company, tell your workers that. Most employees will understand. If one or two of them don't, and you've made what you expect clear, treat the incidents as thefts. The next three "responses" will help you with this.

If someone in the unit is stealing supplies to support a drug abuse problem:

If the supplies and equipment are being stolen by one person and if they're items that could be resold, there's a chance that person (or someone close to him or her) has a drug abuse problem.

Talk to some of the employees you trust the most. Have they noticed that someone is behaving differently or showing other symptoms of an abuse problem? Combine this with your own observations. Someone who's abusing drugs enough to start stealing to support the habit is probably showing his habit in other ways, too (late for work, increased errors, and so forth).

If it appears that an employee is abusing drugs, deal with the situation promptly. You can find suggestions on how to do this in Challenges 27, 29, and 54.

If you have a thief in your unit:

If one of your employees is a thief, catching her may be very difficult. First of all, she's probably had experience at it. Second, she can pick her times and places; if necessary, she can hold off for a few weeks until you and everyone else relaxes. Finally, she knows that you have to be very careful about accusing anyone, to keep from offending innocent employees.

If there are several employees in whom you have complete confidence, solicit their help. If two or three people are watching constantly, it's much harder to pilfer. But remember not to let up just because a week or so goes by without a theft.

If your situation permits, you may want to lock up the items that could be stolen. Then they can be checked out to employees when they're needed and checked back in at the end of the workday.

If security is too lax:

Perhaps the problem isn't with your unit at all. It may be easy for someone from another work area, or even from outside the company, to slip in and walk off with small items.

This is often the easiest situation to deal with successfully. There's almost always something you can do to protect the company's interests. At the least, you can have your people keep their eyes open and notice anyone from outside the unit immediately.

This need not be perceived negatively by the people who visit your unit. It's courteous to greet individuals from outside the work unit and ask if you can help them with something. If they have business with your unit, they'll appreciate the attention. If they don't belong there, this will help them decide to leave.

Even if one of the other causes seems to be the right one, you should check out the security of your work area. Is it easy for outsiders to get in without being noticed? If it is, change your procedures. You don't need to keep people out, just to make sure that you know when and why they're there.

SOMETHING TO THINK ABOUT

When all of your employees feel that they share in the success or failure of the company, they'll be less likely to undermine it by stealing its supplies, or equipment, or reputation, or time. To accomplish that buy-in, it's not necessary to implement profit-sharing or stock-options or other actual ownership programs. What's necessary is that you make each employee feel that the company depends on him or her, that each individual has a valuable and unique contribution to make to the company's future.

How do you do that? Very simply. You recognize good performance and employees' contributions. Monetary rewards are nice; public recognition can help; but most of all, you need to say a personal "thank you" whenever an employee goes out of his or her way to give the company a boost. It's not just good etiquette; it's good business.

CHAPTER EIGHT

Corralling the Free Spirits in Your Company

No.67 Open Insubordination

A worker publicly refuses to follow your request

THE SCENE

"I don't care what you do, I *will not* touch that mess in the storage room. You get somebody else to do it, or you do it yourself." With that, Jolene stalks out of your office.

POSSIBLE CAUSES

Jolene may believe you've asked her to do something that's unsafe.

Jolene may believe you're picking on her. As she sees it, you've unfairly singled her out for the job.

She may believe that what you want her to do is "beneath" her.

She may see that as menial, humiliating work.

She may not like the work and isn't going to do it.

Sometimes, people's reasons are no more complicated than that.

203

> *Hint:* There are two distinct problems here. The first is Jolene and her motives. The second is the impact of her action on other employees. You have to consider both.

YOUR RESPONSE

No matter what the cause is:

You may have a good idea of the cause, or you may not. Either way, at least initially, give Jolene the benefit of the doubt. Don't jump to the conclusion that she's wrong. Listen with an open mind and give her every chance to explain her actions.

If Jolene honestly believes you asked her to do something unsafe:

This can be a little sticky, but there's broad agreement in our society that an employee may refuse to carry out a direction that she believes endangers her health or that of others, is illegal, or violates common moral standards. An employee is at risk whenever she refuses to follow a management request, but if it's for one of these reasons the refusal may be justified.

It may be difficult to tell whether Jolene means this or is just using it to get off the hook. This is where skillful listening comes in handy.

If she genuinely believes what you told her to do was unsafe, then accept that as a sufficient reason for not doing it. But it doesn't answer everything. You still have to address questions such as:

- Did she tell you she thought it was unsafe at the time you asked her, or is she using that as an excuse after the fact? (If she did tell you, why didn't you pay attention?)
- Did she ask you to let her explain? (And, if she did, did you refuse to let her?)
- Did she tell you *why* she thought it was unsafe? (Again, if she did, did you listen?)

If you were ready to listen to her, but she didn't give you a reason for her refusal, she didn't do what a conscientious employee should. Talk to her about that. Then make sure the two of you agree on how you'll handle the situation in the future (if it may reasonably come up again).

If Jolene believes that you're picking on her:

This can also be a little sticky, but for different reasons. How do you tell if this is the case, or just a convenient excuse?

Here's where you have to be really honest with yourself. What is your relationship with Jolene? Were you trying to "show her who's boss" or force her to change a "poor attitude"? Were you angry with her before the situation came up? Or—we hate to ask, but we have to—were you influenced by the fact that Jolene is a woman or (perhaps) a minority?

If you're convinced you treated Jolene as you would have anyone else, you still have to deal with her feelings that you were picking on her. And you should deal with them, regardless of what else you do. As long as she feels that way, situations like this are likely to occur over and over again.

What if you may have picked on her? Discuss it openly. If it was based on her personal characteristics or traits, such as a negative attitude or a lack of team spirit, discuss these with her. Give her plenty of room to express herself. See if you can get the situation behind both of you.

If she honestly believed you were picking on her, it's not really appropriate to take corrective action this time. Agree that if a similar situation comes up again, instead of Jolene storming out, you'll both call a "time out" and talk it over.

Nevertheless, make it clear that if she refuses to follow a work request again, you'll need to take some corrective action. Her honest feelings buy her one pardon, but only one. Make sure she understands the options open to her the next time such a situation occurs. (See the last part of the preceding response.)

If she believes the work is "beneath" her:

Golly—another sticky one! This dances right on the border between excusability and lame excuse.

Here past practice may help you decide. If there's a clear practice that employees in Jolene's job do that kind of work, *and if she knows it*, she has no excuse. If they don't usually do it, or if she's never been told, her refusal may be understandable (although you still need to address her unprofessional way of dealing with it). If there is no consistent practice—well, back to square one! If employees in her job don't normally do this kind of work, both of you need to understand why you expected her to do it. If you've decided to change how things are done and just didn't tell anyone, you shouldn't be surprised when she reacted as she did.

Now, suppose employees in that job regularly do what you directed Jolene to do. Would she reasonably have known that? If she wouldn't have, make sure she knows now. If she should have, use the suggestions in the next response.

Again, no matter the situation, use the suggestions at the end of the first response to make sure the situation never happens again.

If she doesn't like the work and isn't going to do it:

She picked the wrong place and time to make her point. This is where you and Jolene have a heart-to-heart talk about how much she wants to continue to have a job. It should be a *serious* talk; clear insubordination is one of the reasons for discipline—including termination—accepted by almost everyone.

If she's an otherwise good worker and appears to have learned, you may want to close off the situation by admonishing her and perhaps putting an annotation in her personnel file. If she's marginal, or she clearly has learned nothing, look into more severe corrective action—perhaps even terminating her. (Sound cruel? Remember, the rest of your work unit is looking over your shoulder, waiting to see what you're going to do.)

SOMETHING TO THINK ABOUT

There are two reasons for firing an employee who doesn't follow work directions:

- She's demonstrated that she doesn't intend to follow workplace rules. In other words, she's past reasonable rehabilitation.

- She may or may not be salvageable, but the rest of your unit is near enough to anarchy that you have to take the action to maintain order in the work unit as a whole. Open insubordination on the part of an employee may be sufficient reason for termination.

Always consider *both* reasons when you're faced with a serious offense.

No. 68 Your Authority Is Challenged

She ignores your directions to cooperate with another staff member

THE SCENE

"What's wrong with that Sartini woman on your staff?" Joe asks indignantly. "All I asked for was expedited handling of *one little data request*, and you'd think I'd asked for the moon and the stars. I thought you told me you were stressing customer service to that group of yours upstairs!"

Well, actually you can empathize a little with Elaine Sartini; Joe's not the easiest manager to get along with. *On the other hand*, you explicitly told her to cooperate with him since you're trying to get *his* cooperation on something else. Wasn't she listening?

POSSIBLE CAUSES

Elaine may have misunderstood your directions.

She may not have meant to be uncooperative, but simply didn't know what you were asking her to do.

Elaine may not realize why it's important to cooperate with the other manager.

Even if she knows why it's essential to keep customers satisfied, she may not have grasped the concept of "internal customer" or the importance of peer relationships.

Elaine may be deliberately ignoring your instructions.

She may not agree with you; she may not respect your decision-making capabilities; she may have let her dislike of Joe interfere with her good judgment; or she may be out to get you. But regardless of her underlying motive, in this case she's clearly made a conscious decision *not* to follow your direction.

> ***Hint:*** At all levels of the company, good peer relationships are critical to a successful career. But that fact is often not obvious to your employees who are most concerned about protecting their own parochial interests. Regardless of any individual employee's attempts to undermine your efforts to establish and maintain those relationships, it's important that your staff in general understand why they're important and what they can do to foster good relationships between units.

YOUR RESPONSE

If Elaine didn't understand what you were asking her to do:

Review with her the limits of her authority—to bend the rules or to make other accommodations in response to "special requests." Make sure she understands which rules or procedures *may not* be violated and why, as well as those over which she exercises some discretion.

Then discuss with her the particular case with Joe. Explain what she could have done better and how. Rehearse with her how she should handle similar situations in the future and why it's worth her while to make a special efforts to be cooperative with Joe—and other staff members she's not particularly fond of.

Suggest that she consult with you the next time this kind of situation arises. And when she does, instead of *giving* her an answer, ask first how she thinks it should be handled. That way you'll foster her own independent resolution of cases, while ensuring that there are no more foul-ups while she's developing her judgment-making skills.

SOMETHING TO THINK ABOUT

You can't assume that every incident in which an employee fails to follow a direction is a conscious attempt to undermine your authority. Frequently, there's a real possibility that the employee was trying to help out—that she thought you were mistaken and could save you by doing things differently.

In dealing with failures to follow instructions, it's important to explain to employees as well as you can *why* you've made the decisions you have. Of course, they also need to know that it's not acceptable for them to substitute their judgment for yours when you've required a specific course of action. But you're much more likely to get their wholehearted cooperation in the future if your decisions appear to them to be the well-reasoned judgments they are, rather than capricious whims.

If Elaine doesn't understand why it's important to cooperate with the other manager:

Describe to her the relationship between Joe's unit and yours. Explain what benefits you get from him, either as a regular part of the work or because of special efforts he may make for you. You may have to go into considerable detail here, especially if Joe and his unit don't affect Elaine directly. In that case, you'll need to make sure that Elaine also learns something about the different functions of your unit and in particular the areas where Joe can help, or hurt.

If the message doesn't seem to be getting across, you might ask Elaine to list the people that she personally relies on to get her work accomplished. From there you should be able to make a general point regarding the interdependence among units, including yours and Joe's.

In the end, although it's better for you *and* Elaine if she understands why it's important to cooperate, your basic concern must be that she *does* it. If you can't convince her of the necessity of fostering good relationships with other units, then you'll simply have to *direct her* to follow you instructions. You can't afford to let one employee's lack of understanding alienate an important ally.

If Elaine is deliberately ignoring your instructions:

Failing to follow an order is tantamount to *refusing* to follow it. See the first challenge in this chapter for how to deal with a blatant case of refusal to follow work directions.

No. 69 Going Over Your Head

He goes over your head when you give him work he doesn't like

THE SCENE

You pick up your phone and give your routine greeting, "Hello. This is Eleanor Wilkins."

But what you get in return is not routine. Your boss is on the other end, and he's got that "I'm not the least bit amused by this" tone.

"Eleanor, are you and Eddie Daniels having some sort of fight?"

"I don't think so, Jeff," you answer, with growing anxiety. "Why do you ask?"

"He came up here to see me—as a matter of fact, he just left. He was complaining about some work you assigned him, said you were loading him up and letting the others off."

"I really don't know what that's all about, but I'll take care of it," you say, as bravely as you can.

"I expect you to."

"Damn!" you mutter to yourself as you hang up. You knew Eddie didn't like the assignment, but you hadn't expected him to run right to your boss.

POSSIBLE CAUSES

In Eddie's eyes, you're mistreating him so badly that he believes going over your head is the only way he can get things straightened out.

What he did was an act of desperation.

Eddie believes that what you told him to do is so bad that your boss ought to know about it.

He isn't getting what he wants, so he tried to "end-run" you.

When Eddie doesn't get what he wants, this is his habitual way of dealing with the situation.

The difference between the last two is that, in the latter, this is Eddie's *pattern* of dealing with these situations.

> ***Hint:*** This is irritating, of course, but there's something more than the immediate nuisance to fret about. You need to deal with this one quickly and effectively so that your authority doesn't start to erode. If other employees see that Eddie can get around you, well . . .

YOUR RESPONSE

No matter what the cause is:

This is another situation where your first response is likely to be anger. But wait until you have your anger well under control, then review the situation as objectively as you can. If you've contributed to the situation, you need to realize it up front.

Once you've objectively analyzed the situation, have a discussion with Eddie. You want to listen carefully to him, so you can get a good feel for what's going on.

If Eddie believes you're mistreating him and this is the only way he can deal with it:

Be careful with this one. You need to listen carefully and be honest with yourself: Are you mistreating him? Is this something he did only out of desperation?

If Eddie apparently believes this in all honesty, deal with that problem, whether you think he's right or not. Why does he believe it? What have you done? What can you—and he—do to correct it? Do your best to get to the bottom of the situation and deal with his concerns and lay them to rest.

Has Eddie voiced his concerns to you before? If so, why didn't you listen? If not, why didn't he? Unless he had a good, realistic reason for not talking to you, counsel him strongly that you expect him to do so next time. If necessary, tell him that if he goes over your head without talking to you, you'll write him up or take even more serious action.

You may have noticed the following pattern in other problems: First make sure that you really listen when an employee comes to you with a problem or complaint. Then make sure that he comes to you before he talks to anyone else or takes any action. If you do the first, you have every right to require the latter.

If he believes what you told him to do is so bad your boss should know about it:

We don't need to tell you this is serious. Why would he believe that? Again, look at the situation calmly. Did you tell him to do something because you were angry or trying to prove a point? Might Eddie have misunderstood your request and thought you were directing him to do something unsafe or illegal? If so, you need to apologize, get straight with yourself about why or how you did it, and then determine to avoid the problem in the future.

If the assignment you gave Eddie was an acceptable one, why did he react so strongly to it? There could be a number of reasons for this; the burden of proof is on him to persuade you that his was a legitimate one. (If it wasn't, see the next response for suggestions.)

Your relationship with Eddie obviously needs some work. If he believed that you told him to do something you shouldn't have, that's a strong indication that the relationship isn't very good. How can you correct that?

You also need to talk to Eddie about his responsibility to talk with you first. Use the suggestions in the preceding response.

If he tried to "end-run" you because he didn't get his way:

(The difference between this situation and the next one is that in this one Eddie is pulling an end-run as an isolated occurrence, whereas in the next situation, it's the way that he habitually deals with not getting what he wants.)

When you've established that this is the case, the mildest thing you can do is counsel Eddie in no uncertain terms not to repeat it. Then promise him that if it happens again you'll take much stronger action. You want to stop this before he starts to make a habit of it.

Your side of this action is to make sure that you haven't contributed to the problem. For instance, some employees—some very good ones—have a highly developed sense of what's reasonable. What looks to you like Eddie trying to get his way may seem to him like an attempt to get around your "unreasonable" assignment. (This is similar to the circumstances in the preceding response, but not really the same thing.)

You also need to speak to Eddie about the importance of coming to you first. See the suggestions in the first response to this challenge.

If this is the way Eddie habitually deals with not getting his way:

This is where you make crystal clear that you won't tolerate his behavior. You may not be able to take any formal corrective action this time, but you can certainly admonish him and then take stronger corrective action against him if he tries it again.

Why so strong an approach? If this is the way Eddie usually reacts when things don't go his way, he'll keep on doing it. He won't change unless the cost of doing it becomes too high.

Keep this in mind: Eddie may be used to going around supervisors because he's had one or more who wouldn't listen to his problems and complaints. What you see is the habit; the frustration that may have driven him to it is not so clear. It's worth probing for. If his approach is based on frustration, you can try to show him that you *will* listen to him and try to deal with his problems.

SOMETHING TO THINK ABOUT

We've left out an entire element in the situation: your boss. Once you get Eddie dealt with, you need to deal with your boss. If the two of you have a good relationship, be honest about the situation. If not, put the best face on it that you can. The key is to assure your boss that this was an isolated incident, that you've dealt with it firmly and fairly, and that it won't happen again.

Then make sure it *doesn't* happen again.

No. 70 OPEN SCORN FOR YOUR AUTHORITY

An employee publicly criticizes you

THE SCENE

"Just who does she think she is?" grumbles Peggy to Mike in the hall outside the restroom. A group of workers begin to gather as Peggy expounds her litany of grievances: "She couldn't find her office without a map and here she is telling *me* how to manage a project I've had for years. On top of that, she's *insisting* that I coordinate with Paul Preston next door. We'll never get anything done now, and all because the old bat has to have things *her* way!" As you head in the direction of the impromptu gathering, Peggy and a few others see you, and the group begins to disperses. But you've caught enough of the scene to know what's going on.

POSSIBLE CAUSES

Frankly, it doesn't matter *why* Peggy is criticizing you in front of the rest of the staff. This is an action designed specifically to undermine your authority. You cannot tolerate it—regardless of what provocation Peggy may have had or of how limited her influence is over her coworkers.

YOUR RESPONSE

This is one situation where immediate action is important. You've seen and heard Peggy in action, and your workers know it. If you ignore the situation or put off dealing with it, they'll interpret your inaction as a sign of weakness, and you'll add another nail to the coffin Peggy is working so hard to build for you.

At the same time, you cannot stoop to the tactics Peggy has employed. Public criticism is always out of line, barring a direct threat to human life or safety. It doesn't matter whether it's Peggy criticizing you or you criticizing Peggy. You cannot allow yourself to engage in the behavior for which you're about to chastise Peggy. But you *can* make it clear to the group at large that this is a serious matter with which you will deal swiftly and firmly.

Calmly but firmly call out to Peggy in front of the group, "Peggy, I'll see you in my office right now!" This should convey the message—to Peggy and the others.

Explain to Peggy exactly what she did that you consider inappropriate. She probably already knows, but it's important that you define the specific things she did that are unacceptable. Explain also why they're unacceptable. Nothing long or complicated is required here, just a short statement about the need for respect and courtesy for managers, as well as customers and coworkers.

If this is the first time Peggy has publicly criticized you, warn her that you will not treat such incidents lightly and that repetitions will likely result in a severe response—perhaps even termination. Also explain why it's important to have someone in authority, and that authority and authoritarianism aren't synonymous. Make sure she understands the consequences of a "leaderless" organization and the confusion and lack of focus that result.

If Peggy has criticized you or other supervisors in public before *or* if this criticism is likely to result in real damage to your credibility or effectiveness, a warning is not sufficient. You should try to obtain a public retraction from Peggy, but, even after retraction, you may decide that Peggy has done enough irreparable damage that you can't afford to keep her on the staff.

Public retraction does not necessarily mean public apology. While it's certainly desirable to get Peggy to admit to her audience that her behavior was inappropriate, this is not an opportunity for you to exact revenge by humiliating Peggy. Public retraction should be done as sensitively and tactfully as you can arrange it.

SOMETHING TO THINK ABOUT

While public criticism is clearly inappropriate behavior, public disagreement is not. In fact, as a good manager, you should invite open and honest discussion, including disagreement, on issues that arise.

The difference between unacceptable criticism and acceptable disagreement lies in the setting and the manner of presentation. Public disagreement should be in a setting where both sides of the question are represented so that there can be real debate on the merits of each position. It should not be done behind your back or the backs of other employees who hold the opposite position. And acceptable public disagreement *always* focuses on the issues, never on personalities and *never* descending to insults or name-calling.

No. 71 A Cozy Alliance with Your Boss

A staff member brags that you can't do anything to him because of his friendship with your boss

THE SCENE

"Look, it doesn't really matter *what* you think I ought to do. I'm not going to do it, and there's nothing you can do about it! Ernie Eckert and I are old friends, and he'll do anything I ask—and if you push me one more time I'm going to ask him to get you off my back. Understand?"

With that, Andy turns and stomps out, leaving you even more frustrated than before. How are you going to maintain discipline when an employee openly flaunts his friendship with your boss?

POSSIBLE CAUSES

Andy is bluffing.

His friendship with Ernie Eckert is an exaggeration, or even a pure invention.

They are friends, but Eckert is too professional to participate in Andy's childish workplace politics.

They are friends, and what Andy said is exactly right.

Eckert cares more about the friendship than Andy's productivity or keeping order in your work unit.

> *Hint:* It doesn't sound good, but don't panic yet.

YOUR RESPONSE

No matter what the cause is:

We often begin with the recommendation that you talk with the employee. Not this time. This time you talk with your boss, Ernie Eckert.

Your goal is to find out just what the relationship is between him and Andy. You might start the conversation something like this: "I understand you know Andy pretty well, and I was wondering if you could help me. I've been having some problems with his productivity and . . ."

Listen carefully to Ernie's response. If he's honest with you, you'll know just what to do. But he may not be completely honest. If he speaks in generalities such as "I want you to treat him just like anyone else," you can't be sure of his true intentions. Be tactful, but try to probe for his real feelings.

If Andy is bluffing:

He just tried to play hardball and failed. Now it's your turn to play hardball. Call him in, make it perfectly clear you don't buy his "friendship" routine, and tell him what you expect. Then make sure he delivers.

Needless to say, you don't take this course of action unless you're *sure* that Ernie has no interest in what happens with Andy.

If they are friends, but Eckert won't give Andy unfair special treatment:

Call Andy in. Explain that you just talked with Ernie Eckert and found that he expects the same thing you do—an honest day's work from Andy. Be tactful and reasonable and be clear. When Andy leaves, he should have no doubts about what you expect from him.

Keep in mind that Andy will probably relay his version of the conversation to Eckert. You'll help accomplish your objectives if you take these two steps:

- When you talk with Eckert in the first place, explain to him the problem you're having and what you intend to tell Andy. If any of it troubles him, change it and get his okay before you leave.

- As soon as you finish talking with Andy, give Eckert a call. Tell him you and Andy have had your conversation, and that he can probably expect a call or a visit from Andy. Depending on Eckert's response, you might want to summarize the conversation for him.

If they are friends, and Eckert will support Andy:

Don't conclude this until you've probed very carefully in your talk with Eckert. He probably won't ever tell you he'll side with Andy, but he may say something like "Oh, yes, he's a good man. I expect you to treat him well." A few statements like this, and you've got the picture.

If Andy can get Eckert to block you, your choices are very limited. Challenge 112 discusses a similar situation in some depth.

SOMETHING TO THINK ABOUT

A good rule of thumb is to treat all of your employees as though they intend to do a good job. That prevents a lot of misunderstanding and helps you get the best from each of them.

There are exceptions, employees who really do intend to get away with everything they can, any way they can. When you've got one of those, take your kid gloves off. Don't do anything immoral or illegal; don't break the rules. Just be very smart and very tough.

By the way, this is where it pays off to have good working relationships with your employees. If the group as a whole thinks well of you, they'll help you create a culture that doesn't tolerate employees who don't want to do their fair share.

No.72 Politics Behind Your Back

A member of your team tries to sabotage you with other employees

THE SCENE

"Boss, I think you should know what's going on behind your back," offers Carolyn after staff meeting this morning. "Frank is running around the office trying to get people stirred up against you and your decision to take us off flexible hours for the next two months. Most of us know why you had to do it, and, while we're not thrilled, we're willing to go along with you. But Frank is talking about a slowdown—kind of a 'you can't make me if I don't wanna' trick. He thinks if he can make you look bad enough, he can drive you out of this unit!"

POSSIBLE CAUSES

Frank may believe that you're damaging the organization.

He may feel so strongly that what you're doing is wrong and so powerless to change it by working through proper channels that he's willing to descend to guerilla tactics.

Frank may be out to get your job.

He may see discrediting you as a way to get you out of the organization and open up chances for his own advancement.

Frank may not like you.

It may not be that he thinks you're doing a terrible job from which he has to save the organization or that he wants your position, he just wants you to be gone. Maybe your personalities clash; maybe he doesn't like the way you dress, or wear your hair, or talk. But for one reason or another, he doesn't want you around anymore.

> ***Hint:*** This situation, like most of the others in this chapter, involves overtly hostile acts toward you by your subordinates. Regardless of the motives, which may (as in the first cause listed above) be essentially good, the methods are unacceptable. Organizations can't run without leaders;

someone has to set directions and make decisions about policy and values. Undermining authority never solves a problem; it only creates additional ones.

YOUR RESPONSE

If Frank believes you're hurting the organization:

His motives are basically sound, even though his methods are not. Before you talk to Frank, you need to get your own emotions under control. It's not pleasant to realize that someone's out to get you, no matter what the reason is. So think before you act. Try to find out from trusted coworkers what Frank is concerned about. Then in confronting him, deal with the issues, not your own pain.

Let Frank know that you're aware of what he's been doing and that you disapprove strongly, not just because of the personal harm it's causing you, but also because of the damage *he*'s doing to the organization. Sabotage only works when it's undiscovered; once it's out in the open, it's a useless tactic.

Give Frank a chance to explain why he believes you're harming the organization. Listen carefully. If he believes it that strongly, there may be something important in what he says. Tell him specifically what you intend to do to allay his concerns, and what acceptable redress is available to him if he's still not satisfied.

Explain to Frank how his efforts damage the organization at least as much as anything you may have done. Talk to him about why mutual respect and trust are so critical and how his actions have undermined both your respect for and trust in him.

If Frank wants your job:

As before, the best way to get Frank to stop his campaign against you is to let him (and others, as appropriate) know that you're aware of what's going on. Because Frank's motives are not nearly so pure in this case, it's not so important to direct your efforts toward reestablishing the relationship. Frank has made it clear that his ambition is paramount, and your reasonable, understanding approach is going to have no effect on him.

Confront Frank. Let him know that what he's done has destroyed the trust and confidence you had in him, and that you see no way for him to regain them.

He may apologize and offer to make amends. If so, you'll have to make a judgment call as to whether he's destroyed the relationship so thoroughly that it's unsalvageable or whether you're willing to give it another try. If you do decide to work with Frank, watch him carefully. He's betrayed you once, and he may again—especially if he *really* wants your job.

He may not offer to make amends, or he may offer and then step back into his old maneuvering. At this point, you have no choice but to show him the door. As long as he's around to sabotage your efforts, your effectiveness will suffer.

SOMETHING TO THINK ABOUT

If you find that several of the challenges in this chapter sound familiar to you, then you're probably working in an organization that is essentially sick. Disagreement and dissension among workers is not that uncommon—particularly in organizations undergoing unusual stress or change, but deliberate attempts to undermine authority, overtly or covertly, *are* very uncommon.

If individual workers resort to these kinds of tactics because they are dissatisfied and don't know more constructive ways to accomplish what they want, then you must address the problems specific to those individuals. But if you begin to see patterns of this kind of behavior, either within your own unit or across organizational lines, then you need to look hard at the company itself. *Something* is operating to make employees believe that this is a good way for them to get what they want. For your good and the good of the company, it's essential that you get to the root of the problem and remedy that to convince them otherwise.

If Frank doesn't like you:

Once again, begin by bringing the covert behavior out into the open, but as unemotionally as you possibly can. At this point, you don't know whether the underlying cause is something you can work out with Frank or not.

Make sure Frank understands why his actions are unacceptable, and their impact on the trust and confidence you have in him. At the same time, explain that you know people don't always get along and offer to discuss with him things that the two of you can do to mend the relationship.

If Frank trusts you, he'll probably be willing to tell you what it is that bothers him. Then you can decide whether it's something that you can and are willing to change. If so, work out with Frank what you're willing to do and what you expect from him. Remind him that one of the things you expect is that he won't engage in this kind of conduct again and warn him of the consequences if he should.

If Frank won't talk to you about the underlying causes of his dislike of you, then you won't be able to salvage the relationship. He's already undermined your trust in him and now, in effect, has refused to do anything to fix things. If he's a worker you would otherwise want to keep, offer him a position in another part of the company if one is available. If not, let him go.

No. 73 An Employee Refuses Overtime

An employee refuses to work emergency overtime

THE SCENE

"Chris, we can stand here and argue until quitting time and it won't change anything. I won't work until 9:00 tonight. May I go now?"

You nod. You really need Bonnie to work late, and the example she's setting by refusing to do so may encourage other employees to refuse, too. Now what do you do?

POSSIBLE CAUSES

Bonnie has personal commitments that keep her from being flexible.

She may have to get her children at a fixed time or go home to take care of elderly parents.

She may have special plans for this evening.

She's organized her life so she doesn't have any flexibility.

Bonnie has a second job.

She starts work soon after she leaves this job.

She's not a team player.

Hint: Sorting out just what the situation is may be a challenge.

YOUR RESPONSE

If she has personal commitments that keep her from being flexible:

In Challenge 65 we looked at an employee who was late because of personal commitments. You might want to look at that discussion for additional thoughts.

More and more workers have demanding personal responsibilities. If Bonnie has to pick up an elderly parent from an elder-care facility, she may have to do it no matter what. There's no point in getting upset about it; she simply doesn't have flexibility.

Does this mean you let her refuse to work overtime? Perhaps. But there are other alternatives (though probably not for today). Maybe she can make other arrangements if she gets advance notice of the overtime, or come in early in the morning instead of staying late. The important point is for both of you to know what, if any, flexibility she has and then make your plans based on it.

There's a moral to this story: You should know what flexibility each of your workers has *before* a situation like this comes up. That way, both your expectations and theirs will be realistic. You'll avoid these last-minute confrontations.

If she has special plans for this evening:

What you do depends more than anything else on the practices of your work unit. Is this the first time last-minute overtime has come up in months? Then it's reasonable for her to have had plans for that evening. On the other hand, have you made employees aware that they'll be needed to work overtime, sometimes on same-day notice, with the expectation that employees will be available to work it? That's a different situation.

In other words, there's a lot to take into account in this circumstance. If Bonnie knew from past practice that she was taking a gamble, she should be counseled about refusing the overtime. Otherwise, it's not reasonable to expect it from her.

Is the situation apt to arise again, with Bonnie or someone else? Then you (and your employees, if possible) should establish a reasonable policy that gets the work done with the least disruption to their personal lives.

If she's organized her life so she doesn't have flexibility:

Sometimes it's hard to tell the difference between this and the first cause. She may be locked in to responsibilities after work, but she may have had options regarding whether or not to do it that way. Does she have to pick up a child from day care? She may have been able to get a neighbor to do it for her. It's important to find out how much flexibility she really has.

If she has made most of the decisions that have taken away her flexibility and you need her to work last-minute overtime periodically, then make it clear that you expect her to reorganize her life to accommodate the overtime. This may take several discussions, and you may have to help her think it through. If she can reasonably do it, though, you have the right to expect her to.

If she has a second job:

Is this her primary job? If the answer is yes, then this is the job she owes her primary allegiance to. You have the right to expect her to accommodate reasonable requests for overtime.

It's probably not wise to deal with the situation any more today. But call her in tomorrow and discuss the situation with her. Make it clear that you expect this job to come first. If you need her to work overtime, you expect her to be available to do it. If she's not able to work the hours this job demands, then you may not be able to retain her in this position.

Having said that, here's a strong *but*: But many people, especially unskilled workers and/or heads of single-parent families, have to work two or more jobs to make ends meet. Even though this is Bonnie's primary job, she may need the other one to survive. This means that while you should expect Bonnie's cooperation regarding overtime, you should also recognize that Bonnie may have no real choice in the matter, in which case, the two of you can just look at the situation closely and try to work out an arrangement that accommodates your needs and hers.

If she's not a flexible person:

If she's a good, well-motivated worker who doesn't have the emotional flexibility to make last-minute changes, your options are almost as limited as in the first response to this challenge.

If you can arrange the job so that she doesn't get last-minute overtime, fine. Perhaps she can work the overtime if given a day or two advance notice. Can you accommodate that? Can someone else learn her job and take the necessary overtime? Can you take the duties that require the overtime out of her job and give them to someone else who can work the overtime?

If it's not possible to prevent last-minute overtime for her job, you may want to look into reassigning her to another job. If all else fails, you may have to deal with it as a performance problem.

SOMETHING TO THINK ABOUT

There are two "deep" and somewhat contradictory issues here. On the one hand, most families are now two-worker families. This means that each spouse has more before- and after-work responsibilities and less flexibility about working extra hours. On the other hand, the organization has to get its job done; this often means last-minute changes in schedule. There's no easy solution for this.

What will help? If frequent unscheduled overtime is a fact of life in your line of work, be clear with employees what your expectations are—before they're hired or transfer into your unit. And to the extent you can, plan ahead so that last-minute overtime is absolutely minimized.

No. 74 COASTING TO RETIREMENT

An older worker has stopped performing to your standards

THE SCENE

Charley Moore was never a stellar worker, but he's always been okay—in all the years he's been with the company he's been dependable, reasonably conscientious, a good solid worker who's carried his share of the load. Lately, though, you've noticed more errors and a lot less work coming from his desk. There doesn't seem to be any cause you can really point to—no new assignments or changes in procedures, no personal or health problems that you know of.

Charley hasn't said anything to you, but you suspect that he intends to retire in a few months. Could these mistakes and work slowdown be a bit of an "early retirement"? And if he's really leaving, is it really worth doing anything about Charley's lax performance?

POSSIBLE CAUSES

Charlie may really be getting ready to retire and is losing interest in the job.

As he makes plans for his retirement, the work he's been doing may be less and less meaningful to him.

Charlie may be losing interest in the job—but without any plans to retire.

Some workers believe that after they've spent a lot of years on the job the company "owes" them time off—on the job.

Charlie may have personal or health problems not obvious to you that are affecting his performance.

Many employees have very strong needs for privacy, and so may keep personal difficulties hidden from you or the other workers in your unit.

YOUR RESPONSE

If Charlie is getting ready to retire and losing interest in work:

Take into account the severity of Charley's performance deterioration, its effect on the work of the unit and the other workers, and the length of time until Charley's projected retirement. Then decide whether you need to take any action to correct the situation. If Charley's plans seem firm and he's retiring in the next couple of months, any attempts to correct his performance will probably be futile and result in bad feelings in his last few months on the job. If you decide that the problems are severe enough that you must deal with them, be as sensitive to Charley's situation as you can. He's entering into a whole new phase of his life. The transition from work to retirement can be very traumatic for some workers—particularly if the employee has been working for a long time, is wrapped up in his career or derives a lot of his identity from his career, or needs the structure of the work environment as the backbone for the rest of his life.

If Charley is losing interest in work, but isn't retiring soon:

Deal with this as you would any other instance of deteriorating performance. Chapter 6 describes a variety of situations in which supervisors are challenged to improve their employees' performance.

If Charley has personal or health problems:

Discuss with Charley the performance problems you've observed, being as specific and detailed as you can. Tell Charley exactly what he has to do to improve his performance and, if necessary, identify what acceptable performance is for the tasks he's been assigned.

If at this point Charley tells you that he has a personal or health problem that's affecting his performance, then accommodate his concerns to the extent that you can, referring him to medical or counseling help if he needs or wants it. Challenge 26 discusses in more detail methods for dealing with an employee who has health problems that affect his or her work.

SOMETHING TO THINK ABOUT

Almost never is "nothing" the appropriate response to deteriorating performance. Even if you think Charley has stopped performing because he's getting ready to retire, you can't turn a blind eye to the situation. Whether you ultimately decide to take corrective action or let Charley continue at his reduced performance level, you need to pursue the issue at least far enough to analyze the real cause of the change in performance. What seems like innocent slacking off may be a symptom of something much more serious—to Charley's health or to the health of the company.

CHAPTER NINE

Maintaining Morale During Uncertain Times

No. 75 ANXIETY OVER LAYOFFS

Rumors are rampant that the company is going to go through another round of layoffs

THE SCENE

It is mid-afternoon on a hot August day. You've just offered what should have been an exciting training opportunity to four of your best employees. But no one's excited. Is this the "Dog Days" blahs? Mid-afternoon nap time?

"I don't know why you think we should get all excited about learning something we'll never even be able to use," complains Jackie. "We all know the company's newest merger means we're going to have even more positions cut. What good is it to go to training and then come back the next day to find a pink slip in your in-basket?"

"She's right, you know," Lena adds. "We thought we were safe because we kept our jobs through the first round of layoffs. Now we don't know where we stand, and we don't know how many more times we're going to have to go through this again. That kind of anxiety doesn't make us feel like putting out any more for the company. We just want to lay low and try to keep the jobs we have."

POSSIBLE CAUSES

The rumors may reflect employees' continued anxiety about losing their jobs even though the worst is already over.

Even after layoff actions have been completed, the "survivors" have emotional adjustments to work through, too.

The rumors of a new round of layoffs may be true.

You may already be aware of the company's plans, or word may not have filtered down through official channels.

> ***Hint:*** Although a little suspense may be invigorating, anxiety, especially about keeping a job, can really sap employees' motivation and energy. Even if your employees are likely to be affected, they will be able to deal much better with what they know than with what they don't know. To alleviate their anxiety, provide your staff members with whatever information and support you reasonably can, both to make them feel better and to keep up the performance of your unit.

YOUR RESPONSE

If the rumors are groundless but reflect employees' continuing anxiety:

There are several steps you can take to improve morale. First, put your employees' immediate fears to rest by reassuring them that the rumors are false. But check out the facts before you speak. Employees often expect their managers to reassure them—and then issue pink slips the next week. If you're to have any credibility with your employees, you need to be absolutely sure that they won't be affected before you attempt to allay their fears.

If there will be layoffs that affect some other section of the company, explain what conditions in your unit are insulating it from the damage.

Then make sure that the employees who survived the previous downsizing actions get some professional help and counseling to help them deal with the situation. Their reactions will range from relief that they haven't been hurt to feeling guilt that they were spared although others were hit, from being too hard on themselves in an effort to protect themselves from any future cuts to being paralyzed by their fear of future harm so that they can't produce anything. These are serious emotional reactions that often can't be handled by even a sensitive and well-intentioned manager. Get your people the help they need to overcome this "survivor syndrome" and return to high-performance work.

If the rumors of a new round of layoffs are true:

Make sure your employees get all the information they need to make plans for their futures. There is a fine line here between telling them too much and too little. At any stage in the planning process, some decisions will have been finalized, while other issues will still be under consideration. And some things that sound like firm decisions may still be subject to change. Tell your employees what you can, subject, of course, to the company's policies about release of information. And don't speculate. The worst thing you can do is feed your employees' already present anxieties; they'll pick up enough false rumors without your help.

Find out as much as you can about the severance packages your employees will be offered. Help them understand the technical legal terms in which such offers are often couched and how the offers translate to benefits for the individual employees. If your company has a human resources department, its staff will be able to help you with this.

Let your employees know what training is available for staff members who will be affected by the layoffs. Encourage them to take advantage of whatever the company offers, either in the way of formal training or skills-enhancing job assignments. The better employees' skills are and the better they have performed during their tenure with you, the more likely they are to beat the competition in the job market.

Identify available outplacement services (and if the company doesn't already have outplacement contacts, push them to develop some) and direct your employees to them. Many companies offer affected employees help in preparing resumes, in improving interviewing skills, and in identifying new employment opportunities.

Most important, keep talking to your employees. Be as reassuring and helpful as you can, but most of all be informative. One of the worst parts of any bad situation is not knowing the real story. Replacing fiction from the employee rumor mill with truth, even unwelcome truth, is probably the single most valuable service you can offer your employees.

SOMETHING TO THINK ABOUT

Much of the success of your efforts to dispel rumors and to help employees work through the effects of the many mergers and acquisitions in which corporations are engaged depends on how much they trust you. If there have been times in the past when you've not been true to your word or when the information you've given employees has turned out not to be reliable, then your employees won't have a lot of trust in you now. And unless your work-group trusts you, you won't be able to do anything to relieve their anxieties, for their sake or yours.

So for now and for the future, resolve that your word will be your bond. Trust is not something you're entitled to as a manager, it's something you earn.

No. 76 Overworked Employees

You hear that your workgroup will file grievances if it gets more work to do

THE SCENE

"Now, look, Nan—we don't have anything against you. You're a decent person and you're fair to us. But we just can't do any more work than we're doing now. We keep hearing rumors that the company is going to dump new work on us because of this latest round of layoffs. If we get anything more to do for at least a month or two, I promise you you'll have a dozen grievances on your desk Tuesday morning, and that's just a start. If you've got any pull with management, you'd better use it now. We're not kidding!"

When she finishes, Sandy walks out of your office without even waiting for you to answer. It's clear she means it. Now what do you do about it?

POSSIBLE CAUSES

Your workgroup is unhappy with the company because of the continuing layoffs, and this is their way of showing it.

They may or may not be able to take on more work, but they don't intend to.

Your workgroup's productivity is much lower than it ought to be.

The group could increase its productivity, but chooses not to.

The unit's productivity is high, but management has been increasing workload without regard for productivity.

So the workgroup is being penalized for its high productivity.

The unit's productivity is acceptable, but it could absorb another increase without being overloaded.

> **Hint:** This is a classic example of the situation that a first-line supervisor gets caught in. On the one hand, you owe loyalty to management to support the production increase. On the other, your people think it's unfair and are up in arms against it. You're right in the middle.

Remember that all you have so far is a rumor. The layoffs and/or work-load increase may or may not happen. You want to look at the discussion here for ideas, but you also need to find out whether there really are going to be more layoffs and whether they will affect your workgroup.

YOUR RESPONSE

If they're unhappy with the company because of the continuing layoffs, and this is their way of showing it:

This isn't so unusual a situation, but it's a difficult one. If the real cause of their anger isn't the specific increase in workload itself, nothing you do about the increase is apt to help.

You know at least something about why they're unhappy with the company, but is there more to it than just the layoffs and acquiring new businesses? Has the company made the restructuring harder on employees (at least in their eyes) than it needed to be? Has management cut employees and cut employee benefits but feathered their own nests? Be sure you find out all the factors behind your employees' unhappiness.

Once you know the factors for sure, what can you do? If the unit's productivity is relatively low (see the next response), not much. But if it produces at a continually high level—and if you can show this—you may get any workload increase headed off. (See the second response after this one.) You need to walk a narrow path, supporting your workgroup without appearing to be fighting higher management.

If your unit's productivity is much less than it ought to be:

No matter how strongly they may feel about the workload increase, you can't defend their reaction to higher management. Your job is to get them to accept the increased production. If you don't, both you and they will suffer.

Your most important job is to persuade your employees that they need to increase their productivity, because you're not going to be able to defend their not getting more work done. You know this is going to be difficult, but it has to be done. If you have productivity statistics from other groups similar to your own, use them to show your workers why they need to improve. If not, do whatever you can to get the point across to the workgroup.

If the group's productivity is low, attempting to avoid more work when other groups are already producing more will be a disaster. You must avoid this at all costs, and with any luck, you can convince the workgroup to do so.

If the unit's productivity is high, but management has been increasing workload without regard for productivity:

Here we have the reverse problem: Your people are productive, but they've gotten stuck with the same increase as the rest of the organization, which is less productive. If you don't do something, they're going to be punished for doing so well. You can figure what that will do to their productivity and motivation in the future.

How you deal with this one depends on how your company deals with productivity. If there are established goals that your people have been exceeding, you can at least show higher management that an increase isn't fair. It should also be easy to show them if your employees have a higher rate of production than other similar units.

What if there aren't records that will show how productive your unit is? Here's where your boss's confidence in you comes in. If your boss believes that you've been getting production from your unit, he or she may go to bat for you.

Your other alternatives aren't very good ones. Do what you can to talk management out of the increase and to talk your employees into being patient. Then find a way to demonstrate how high their productivity already is.

If the workgroup's current productivity is acceptable, but it could absorb another increase without being overloaded:

This is another challenging situation. You wouldn't be embarrassed if you sided with your employees and tried to persuade higher management to drop the increase. On the other hand, you wouldn't be out of line to try to get your people to accept the increase.

From your employees' perspective, the basic question is this: Why should they increase their output if it's already acceptable? That's the question you'll have to answer for them if you want them to change. Will taking on the new work make their jobs more secure? Is it really just their fair share, so that other units don't see them as slackers?

What if you can't find a reason for them to increase production? As you might suspect, you'll be in a difficult situation. Higher management will be expecting the increase, but your employees won't be willing to produce it. This is a true impasse, and one that's not easy to resolve. You'll have to dig more deeply for reasons for the workgroup to change. Here's where credibility with your boss and your employees will stand you in good stead. If you have credibility with both sides, both of them may be willing to give you some time to find a solution. If you don't have credibility? Wish we could help, but. . .

SOMETHING TO THINK ABOUT

When a company must increase productivity to make up for layoffs, it can easily run into trouble. Employees can fight back by filing grievances, "working to rule," refusing to cooperate with other units, and in a dozen other ways. They can also work faster and turn out more products with a higher rework and rejection rate.

How do you prevent this backlash?

- One alternative is to get greater productivity by training employees more effectively. They may not know the best ways to perform their tasks even if they've been doing them for some time. High-quality training in the best procedures might enable them to produce more with no more effort or strain.

- Another way: Involve workers in improving the processes and procedures they use. They know their work better than anyone else, and if they choose to do so they can improve how they do it better than anyone else. If your organization has a continuous process improvement program, find out about it and find out how your workgroup might be able to use it.

No. 77
NONPERFORMANCE IN THE FACE OF LAYOFFS
Expecting a layoff, one employee stops producing

THE SCENE

"Juan, I asked you to have those budget figures for me two weeks ago, and you still haven't completed them. What's the problem here?" you ask in obvious frustration. "Don't you know that with these layoffs going on all around us, this is the worst possible time for us to slack off?"

"Well, Darryl," replies Juan, "it looks to me like it doesn't make any difference one way or the other how much work we do or how well we do it. Look at Lillian over in public relations—one of the best representatives the company ever had—and she's out the door. And Bill in marketing, and a whole slew of people on the floor. I figure my number's up any way you look at it. So why should I put out for the company if they won't put out for me? I'm just making the transition from working to not working a little early."

POSSIBLE CAUSES

Juan may believe that his performance will have no impact on his chances of being laid off.

He may not recognize that, even with notice in hand, his prospects for being retained in this job or getting a good reference for another job depend on his performance in the time he has left here.

He may be using lack of production on the job as a way of venting his anger over being laid off.

And, within bounds, this may be one of the less painful possible ways (for him and for you) to work through that anger.

He may be using lack of production as a "self-fulfilling prophecy."

That way, if he does get hit by the layoffs he can tell himself it was because he stopped producing, not because the company doesn't value him anymore.

> *Hint:* If you didn't know before, you need to understand now that being laid off is much more than an economic blow. Government unemployment compensation and "golden parachute" deals help to soften some of the financial loss, but there isn't much of an emotional safety net for workers who lose their jobs. The loss of self-esteem and the depression and anxiety can be devastating. So workers will cope in whatever way they know how, which may not be the most productive coping mechanism for either the company or the workers themselves. There's a major difference in how you'll need to respond to the fairly rational reaction described in the first situation and the emotionally driven reactions in the second and third situations.

YOUR RESPONSE

If Juan thinks his performance will have no impact on his chances of not being laid off:

In this situation, a heart-to-heart chat with Juan may be all it takes to get his work back on track.

- If there's a chance that some of the termination notices may be withdrawn before the layoffs become effective (usually because other workers get placed somewhere else or because of retirements or resignations), then let Juan know that the better his performance is, the better his chances of being kept on. Call-backs from temporary layoffs may also be affected by workers' performance, especially in a system that's not driven exclusively by seniority.

- Even if it's a virtual certainty that Juan will lose his job, you can talk to him about the effect a good reference can have on his ability to get another job—especially another job in the same industry where many of the managers know one another and rely on referrals from each other.

If this is the reason Juan's been slacking off, your explanations and encouragement may be all that's needed to get him back to his normal productivity.

If Juan is working out his anger at losing his job:

Your task here is harder. You're dealing not with a rational response to a situation, but with a purely emotional response. Juan may not be able to work past his anger without some professional help. Your coaching and explanations may fall on deaf ears.

You should also be on the lookout for more than this passive response, such as Juan's sabotaging the work or acting out his anger in abusive language or even violence.

Anger is a normal and healthy reaction to misfortune. If it lasts only a few days, or even a week or two, you can be fairly sure that Juan will work through the rest on his own. Your encouragement and support will help, along with occasional reminders of the benefits to him of continuing to produce even when things get rough.

But if the angry reaction seems to go on for a long time and Juan doesn't seem to be working through it by himself, then you need to make sure he gets some outside help, through your employee assistance program or referral to an outside counseling service.

If Juan is working against himself by performing poorly:

You'll need to deal with the problem on both a rational front and an emotional front at the same time.

If there's still not a final decision about who will stay and who will go (and if performance *does* count in determining who stays), you need to talk to Juan to make sure he understands how the system works and that his lack of production may be hurting him. Even on an entirely rational basis, Juan may not realize that he is his own worst enemy when he doesn't produce.

You also need to help Juan get some outside assistance to work through his anxiety and depression so that he can deal with whatever comes constructively, rather than self-destructively.

SOMETHING TO THINK ABOUT

You need to consider what kinds of messages you're sending your workgroup by your own attitude toward impending layoffs. If your job is also on the line and your anger or anxiety or depression is affecting how you approach the work, those emotions will be obvious to everyone you work with, just as Juan's emotional responses were obvious to you. And, as in Juan's case, you yourself may not be aware of how you're being affected. Mergers, acquisitions, layoffs, restructuring, and the changes that accompany them are traumatic for *everyone*, workers and managers alike. One of the best ways you can take care of your employees is by taking care of yourself too.

No. 78
A TALENTED EMPLOYEE LOOKS ELSEWHERE

An ambitious employee you can't promote starts job hunting

THE SCENE

"Donna, I know there's nothing you can do about this," begins Tony, "but I think I owe it to you to let you know that I'm looking around. I think I've taken this job about as far as I can go. There don't seem to be any new challenges to meet, and it's all getting pretty routine. But it doesn't look as if there's anywhere for me to go as long as I stay with Smart Systems. I know it's not your fault—there just aren't any openings higher up right now, and it doesn't look as if there are going to be any soon either. I think it's time for me to move on."

You're not surprised. You hate to admit it, but Tony's right. But you'd really hate to lose him. Isn't there something you can think of to get him to stay?

POSSIBLE CAUSES

Tony may not feel appreciated in this job.

He knows he's done well for the company, but he believes the company hasn't done well by him. He believes that the contributions he's made ought to buy him some recognition, preferably a better job with more money.

Tony may not feel challenged in this job.

He's mentioned that he thinks he's taken this job as far as he can go. If there are no new worlds to conquer, doing the same old work day after day can get pretty boring. Tony's looking for something where he can regain the excitement and challenge.

> ***Hint:*** The best way to find out the cause of Tony's dissatisfaction is to ask him. He's been honest with you about wanting to leave. He'll probably also be willing to tell you specifically why.

YOUR RESPONSE

If Tony doesn't feel appreciated in this job:

Even if you can't promote Tony, chances are there are other ways you can recognize his outstanding performance—a bonus, a gift certificate, mention in the company newsletter or local newspaper, recognition as "Employee of the Month" or "Employee of the Quarter." Identify those things you can do, and choose one that you think Tony will like and that's appropriate for his contributions.

You may be able to change Tony's title or stature in the office without giving him a real promotion. Maybe he could be a lead worker or a "special assistant." This "no-cost" promotion, accomplished with a significant amount of fanfare and accompanied by a more tangible bonus or reward, may let Tony know that the company and his employer do appreciate him.

Finally, make sure Tony understands the way promotions work in your company and what you are able (and willing) to do to help him get promoted, either within your section or elsewhere in the company.

If Tony doesn't feel challenged:

Identify special projects or assignments you could give Tony that aren't a regular part of his job but that would give him a chance to expand his skills. Be careful in what you assign Tony. Don't give him anything *too* much higher than what he's doing now, otherwise he may feel that you're taking advantage of his special skills and talents without compensating him appropriately.

Talk to Tony about his long-term career goals. Would he like to continue to expand his technical expertise, completing progressively more demanding assignments? Or would he prefer to complement his technical skills with managerial assignments? Try to structure additional responsibilities around the things he's most interested in.

At the same time that you're enhancing Tony's assignments to give him greater challenges, look into taking away from his job some of the more routine work (or work he's mastered so that it's become routine). Assign those duties to someone else in the organization who you believe will be able to perform them creditably, so that new work isn't being piled on Tony without relief from existing responsibilities. While a good employee consistently looks for greater challenges, he also resents being overburdened because "you can always count on Tony."

What if there is no more challenging work in the organization you can offer Tony? In that case, you need to have a straightforward discussion with him and explain that he's already doing the most interesting work the unit has to offer. Then do what you can to help Tony find the kind of work that will satisfy him, preferably retaining his skills within the company, but going elsewhere if that's what he needs.

SOMETHING TO THINK ABOUT

As we've discussed in the responses, there are some things you can do to encourage Tony to stay, at least for a while. But you also need to ask yourself at some point if the effort's worth it. If you can't give Tony what he thinks he wants (a promotion) the things you *can* give him may not satisfy him for long. Or he may be becoming so resentful of the company's failure to recognize him that he won't do as good a job for you as he has in the past.

In either case, the best you can do is to let Tony leave: Express your understanding of the difficult situation Tony is in, acknowledge your inability to satisfy him, and offer your help in finding him something better elsewhere. You can't be all things to all people.

No. 79
YOUR TEAM MUST TAKE ON MORE WORK
Your workgroup gets a new function dropped in its lap

THE SCENE

"Hey, I need a minute of your time," Margaret says as she sits down across from you.

"Sure. What's up?"

"I've been looking at the files we just got with this new assignment, and I gotta tell you that I'm confused. How in the world did we end up with this stuff, anyway?"

"I wish I knew," you reply. "Supposedly it has something to do with the special projects we did last year, but it doesn't make any more sense to me than it does to you.

"So what are we going to do?"

POSSIBLE CAUSES

The organization probably gave you the new function either because it was cutting back staff or because it has acquired a new business—and so it's spreading the work around. Was your workgroup picked for this work because its current work is similar, because it's viewed as talented and capable, or because it currently doesn't have enough to do? What matters is whether or not you can successfully integrate the new function.

YOUR RESPONSE

Assign an individual or small group to learn and perform the new function:

If you can spare an individual or, if necessary, a small group, have them learn the new function. Get training for them if it's available. Have them talk to individuals who previously performed the work if you can. Just make it their mission to get up to speed on the task as quickly as possible.

Once they've learned how to perform the function, do you have the individual or group of workers continue to perform it themselves or teach the rest of the workgroup to perform it? If the function is different from the rest of the work of your unit, it's probably better for the trained group to continue to perform it. (You should train a backup individual or group in the function if you can, of course.) But if it is related to the group's primary work, perhaps you want to gradually train everyone to do it.

Here's another way to look at the new function: Is the regular work of the group getting somewhat boring for employees? Would the new function be more interesting and challenging? Would it let them learn and use new skills? Then use the new function as a way of expanding workgroup jobs and making them more interesting. If you can do this, you can turn the new function into a plus for the workgroup.

Try to trade off the function for another one the workgroup understands better:

Don't try this unless the first is too impractical. If you really don't believe the workgroup can integrate the new function with what they're already doing, see if you can find another function—one easier to learn—that the group could pick up in place of it. Be sure that this function fits better, though; it won't help much to find another function and then discover that it's just as hard to learn as the first one.

Try to persuade the company that your workload is too heavy to accept the new function:

Don't even *think* of taking this approach unless you can show, on the basis of production reports or other solid measures, that your workgroup has more work than others and that it's handled everything else that's come its way. Every workgroup is probably having to take on new work, and every workgroup is probably as overworked as your own.

Suppose you can show that your workgroup has a heavier workload than others. Do you automatically try to get rid of the new function? No. First you ask yourself if you can squeeze it in. If you can, look again at some of the potential benefits from the new function that we described earlier. Are these benefits worth the extra work and stress of the new function? They may be, and if they are you should do what you can to take on the function. Remember, if higher management believes your workgroup is more productive than others, you and all your employees benefit, particularly if job cutbacks are a possibility.

If none of this seems relevant, bite the bullet and show the organization how the new function imposes a greater workload on your group than others have. But be sure you can *show* them, with objective measurements. If you can't, you'll get the reputation for not wanting to shoulder your fair share of the load, and that's a reputation you want to avoid.

SOMETHING TO THINK ABOUT

You need to protect your workgroup from a workload so heavy it can't produce a quality product. You don't need to protect it from improving to the point that it can handle a heavy workload effectively.

Workgroups often let themselves get caught in the trap of comparing themselves to other workgroups. They think that if they're producing about the same as other workgroups, they're producing enough. The problem is that this way of thinking prevents the workgroup from distinguishing itself from other workgroups. It will just be "one of the pack."

Especially in a highly competitive environment, the workgroup may be cut or abolished for no better reason other than there's no reason not to. To prevent that, help the workgroup keep improving so it can take an increasing workload in stride. Then make sure that higher management knows how heavy the group's workload is and, therefore, how valuable the workgroup is to the organization.

No. 80
YOU INHERIT AN UNQUALIFIED WORKER

You need someone who's fully trained but instead must accept a "newbie"

THE SCENE

"Well, Jill," your boss begins, "I see you're looking for a new buyer." Then he drops the bombshell: "You know, we've got a lot of people here who are going to lose their jobs if we don't do something to help them. So I've arranged for Claude in sales promotions to come over to work for you. He's taken some business courses in college, and I'm sure he'll work out fine."

"But, Karen," you stammer, "I've got a backlog I won't be able to work through for several months even if I can find somebody who knows what he's doing. I can't afford to take someone who doesn't have any experience at all. A lot of money passes through this department. If we buy the wrong stock or at too high a price, we can lose a lot of money too. We *need* to have somebody experienced!"

"I hear what you're saying," Karen replies. "But you'll just have to do the best you can. I'm sure if you were the one being cut from the staff you'd be grateful for a second chance. And Claude might work harder for you than someone who hasn't been so close to unemployment."

POSSIBLE CAUSES

This is one of those situations where the cause is clear: Your boss has made a decision and you need to live with it. Maybe it's company policy to find jobs for displaced workers before new employees are hired. Maybe Karen has a personal interest in seeing that as few people as possible lose their jobs. Her motivation doesn't matter. Placement of unqualified or marginally qualified people in new jobs is a common side effect of corporate restructuring. The only question you have to answer is how you're going to cope with the situation with the least possible loss of productivity.

> *Hint:* Don't pick just one of the following responses. Use as many of them you can.

YOUR RESPONSE

Provide intensive training to your new worker:

Many offices don't have established training programs. New employees either learn from watching and working with experienced workers, or the firm normally hires nothing but trained workers. If your company doesn't have an established training program, find out quickly if there are some training sources you can tap. Look into a local college or junior college, courses in the area given by a professional association or an organization that specializes in training, even a video course you can rent or buy. Finally, don't forget to find books on the subject. There are often dozens, even hundreds, of books on a given occupation. Can you find one or two that deal with your kind of work and see that Claude reads them? Perhaps you and he could meet once or twice a week to discuss them.

Match your new employee with a "mentor":

Whether or not you can get formal training, you need to see that Claude has a chance to learn the specific skills he'll need on *your* job. One good way to do that is to identify a worker in your area who does a job that's very similar to the one Claude is going into, someone who's very good at doing that job and who can explain things well to somebody who doesn't know the area, and who's *very* patient. In other words, someone who can serve as a mentor for Claude.

Before Claude arrives on the job, sit down with the mentor and explain what his or her role will be. Typically, the mentor will be expected to help orient your new employee to the work, show him how each task is performed, review work and provide advice and assistance, and answer questions.

It's helpful if you have time to work with the mentor to break down the job into steps or processes, then decide how well Claude should perform on one task before he goes on to learn the next. You can sequence the tasks or processes in whatever way seems most logical to you (for example, you can teach the most important tasks first, or the simplest ones first, or use some other order).

The mentor will work with Claude on tasks one or two at a time, teaching and coaching until he becomes proficient in those one or two before moving on to the next ones.

Provide the mentor with some relief from his or her own workload and emphasize the importance of training the new employee. Then follow up with both the mentor and the trainee often enough to be sure that the training is progressing on schedule and to reinforce to the mentor how important this training assignment is. If you just dump the assignment on the mentor and never follow up, you'll give the impression that you don't give the task much importance.

Separate out the simpler work and give it to the new employee:

When everyone in an organization is well qualified and well trained, the most difficult work is often distributed among all the workers. That means that each employee also does some of the simpler work. If this is the case in your unit, a little job redesign will let your new employee become productive quickly.

Get together with your best workers—or perhaps even all your workers—and identify enough of the routine work to make a separate job, and assign Claude to that job. You can count on your employees' cooperation, because most of them will be happy to get rid of this work.

While Claude handles the simple tasks he's been assigned, you can train him in the other areas of the position he was originally intended to fill. After a few weeks or a few months, you'll have to decide whether to let Claude continue doing just the simpler work, or bring him along to become a full performer? That depends on many factors, one of which is his progress in the job. Keep that decision in mind as you evaluate his performance from the beginning.

SOMETHING TO THINK ABOUT

Every manager likes to have the best qualified employees possible. It generally makes life much easier. However, there's a down side to that. What happens if your people are highly qualified and motivated, but much of the work is boring? They may lose their motivation and look for more challenging jobs elsewhere.

How do you combat this problem? Concentrate the simpler work in one or a few jobs. Then you can hire less qualified, lower paid employees to fill these jobs. If they have the ability and the motivation, they can move up into the more skilled jobs. If they don't, they can still make a contribution doing the less demanding work. You win two ways: You get your work done while keeping your best workers challenged, *and* you have an opportunity to "test" the work of newer employees before you put them into jobs with greater responsibilities.

No. 81
A VIOLATED NONCOMPETE AGREEMENT
A valued employee is going over to the competition— with your customer list

THE SCENE

"Roy, I think there's something going on with Iris Chang that you should know about," confides Mary one evening at the close of the day. "I've overheard some of her conversations in the past couple of days and answered the phone on some 'hang-up' calls, and, well, frankly, I think she's trying to move over to Clark, Dawes, and Somerset and take some of our best customers with her."

"What?!" you reply in disbelief. "If she takes our customer list and starts courting all our clients, we'll go under like a torpedoed submarine. There's got to be something I can do to stop her."

POSSIBLE CAUSES

Iris may believe her job is in jeopardy and wants to protect herself.

Corporate restructuring creates a climate of anxiety. Iris may believe that she's more likely to get a job if she takes her client list with her, or she may think it will be easier to get started with a new employer if she has her own customers.

Iris may be angry with you or the company, and this is her way of getting even.

She may not have been recognized when she thought she should be, or maybe she didn't get a raise or a promotion she thought she deserved, or she may resent what she feels are needless layoffs.

> *Hint:* This is a very serious charge you're making against Iris. Investigate as thoroughly as you can (as quickly as you can so no real damage is done) before taking action.

YOUR RESPONSE

Regardless of the cause:

Confront Iris as soon as you have a reasonable basis for believing that Mary's report is accurate. If Iris is not negotiating to take the customer lists to your competitors, you can back off. But if she is negotiating, you may be able to shock her into reconsidering. Customer lists are crucial to many organizations, and armed competitors will know exactly whom to target to increase their business and damage yours. You must take immediate action.

Regardless of the cause, as soon as you are convinced that Iris is negotiating, you should also consult your legal counsel to find out what protections the company already has in place. Many companies whose customer base is limited and exclusive require their employees to sign "noncompetition" agreements before they start work. These are often enforceable as regular contracts, and Iris could be liable for damages the company can prove it suffered because she used the client lists to compete.

Even if new employees aren't required to sign noncompetition agreements, are there other mechanisms in place to protect customer lists? Are they considered "confidential" or "proprietary" company lists? Is taking your company's customer lists treated like other thefts (such as thefts of equipment or trade secrets)? Has the company had similar problems in the past, and, if so, how did it protect itself?

Your legal counsel should have the answers to these questions and may even need to handle the situation. But assuming the ball is still in your court . . .

If Iris believes her job is in jeopardy and wants to protect herself

In this case, she's more likely to deal rationally with the situation than if she's out for revenge.

First, tell her to stop negotiating to take the customer lists with her when she leaves. Make sure she knows that you know what she's planning, that you will deal with her actions severely if she doesn't stop her negotiations voluntarily, and that action against her will continue even after she leaves your employment—through your company's lawyers.

If Iris promises to stop, and if you believe her, then you can back off, and let her continue her assignment and her job hunt. But, of course, keep a watchful eye on her activities.

If you can't get a firm commitment from Iris that your customer list is safe, or if you don't believe her commitment is real, you'll need to take stronger action. Move her out of the job—that's right, completely out of the job. You can move her out of the department or into a less sensitive job in the same unit, but get her into a job where she doesn't have access to your customer lists any more. Even if she promised to stop using the lists as a negotiating tool, if you can't take her at her word, then that's a sign that her actions have destroyed the trust that's essential in the employee-employer relationship. That's all the reason you need to have her taken out of the job.

If Iris is angry with you or the organization and is trying to get even:

Your first step here is clear. If Iris wants to hurt you or the company, then you have to separate her before she can do any more damage. As in the preceding cause, she has broken your trust and confidence in her. In addition, she's acted purposefully to sabotage the company.

As you work through the termination process, you should consult with your lawyer, security division, or employee assistance program coordinator to see whether there is any potential for Iris to react violently to her separation. Her acts of sabotage were obviously hostile, and that hostility can take many forms. Although for many people in Iris' situation such industrial sabotage substitutes for violence, it could also be a first step toward more violent behavior.

You also need to consider what else Iris might do (or has already done) to hurt the company. Then take precautionary measures. If you believe she's dangerous enough, don't give her time to do more damage after she's been notified of her termination. Give her the notice papers, then escort her to her office to pack up her personal belongings under your scrutiny, take away her keys, company identification card, and parking pass and walk her out the door. Even if your company insists on a formal notice period before the termination is effective, you can carry Iris on paid leave and still keep her out of the office.

If you believe Iris has done other damage (like fouling up computer records or "fixing" accounts or reports), investigate the areas where she could have done some harm. If you find evidence of misconduct, talk to your company attorney about whether there is some action you can take, even after Iris is terminated, to recover the company's losses.

SOMETHING TO THINK ABOUT

While you don't necessarily want to publicize the *extent* of the damage Iris has done, you *should* make sure your employees know that you identified a serious threat to the company and dealt with it swiftly and decisively. This sends two important messages to your unit. First, it lets others know that negotiations with competitors to take them the company's customer lists will not be tolerated and that you will follow up. Second, it lets the unit know that you'll do what's necessary to protect the company, and thereby the employees, from such threats. They need that reassurance.

And if you don't already have a policy in place and your customer lists *are* closely held information, you should suggest instituting protections like non-competition agreements for your workforce.

No. 82
MISUSE OF PROPRIETARY INFORMATION
An employee is using company data to help his own private clients

THE SCENE

What several other employees have told you is true. You pause outside George Maripolis's cubicle and listen to his phone conversation. He is clearly talking to someone who isn't a customer of the company, and he just as clearly is giving the caller confidential company information. It's bad enough that he's dealing with his private customers on company time. It's even worse that he's giving them company information. You know you can't ignore the situation any longer.

POSSIBLE CAUSES

George has been doing his own business on company time with company clients for a long time.

This is just the first time he's been caught.

Recent talk of more layoffs has caused George anxiety about his job, and he's trying to set up a business to support himself if he's one of the people laid off.

He wants to protect himself from the threat of the organization's continued restructuring.

George has specific reasons to believe he'll be laid off and is trying to provide a continuing source of income.

> *Hint:* None of these reasons justifies what George is doing. Remember, though, that continuing restructuring and layoffs are tremendously hard on the workers who remain. If your company doesn't have a program to work with remaining employees and help them cope with the situation, at least you should talk with them and help them through the rough times. And they are rough times.

YOUR RESPONSE

No matter what the cause is:

Your first task is to get data. Talk with George. Tell him what you heard. Give him every chance to respond. But be sure you ask the hard questions: How long has he been doing it? What makes him think it's okay to use the company client list? It may be uncomfortable for both of you for you to ask the hard questions. But your job is to ask them.

Then ask other members of the workgroup who have observed him. Again, you and they will be uncomfortable, but this is your job.

If George has been doing his own business on company time with company clients for a long time:

You don't know George's motivation for what he's doing or how long it's been going on. What you do know is that George has dealt with his clients on company time using company information. The natural assumption that goes with this is that he has done so in the past. So begin with that assumption. And go with it unless he and other members of the workgroup present clear evidence—not assertions, evidence—to the contrary.

What if he has been not only transacting his business on company time but using the company's client list to do so? He has seriously violated his employment contract with the company. The question is: Should he remain with the company any longer?

If you're in a large company, you can talk with someone in the company's human resources management office to see what usually happens in situations like this one. If your company is smaller, then you or your boss will need to decide what happens to George. At the minimum, George needs to agree to stop using company time and the company customer list at once and permanently. And he needs to be disciplined, with no less than a suspension without pay. Whatever happens, the message needs to be clear to him and other members of the workgroup that the organization won't tolerate this kind of behavior. Period.

If recent talk of more layoffs has caused George anxiety about his job, and he's trying to set up a business to support himself if the worst happens:

George may genuinely be reacting to the company's serious reductions, though it's up to him to persuade you of that and to do so with something other than promises and contrite words. What he's done is serious, regardless of his reasons for doing it.

Suppose he does make a case that he was doing this because he was afraid of more layoffs? Is he competing with the company, offering generally the same services? That's extremely serious, no matter what his reason was. Or has he been careful to offer very different services, ones that might even lead customers to want more services from your company? How much he's looked out for the company's interest as well as his own carries a lot of weight in judging his actions.

He has to stop, unless the company is specifically willing to authorize him to do it. Unless you're the company's owner, *you* can't authorize him to do it; that will only get you into the same trouble once the company finds out about the situation. (It will also suggest to other members of the workgroup that they can get away with the same thing.) George has to stop and guarantee you that he has done so.

You also need to take some corrective action, though if he's protected the company's interest as well as his own, the discipline can be much less severe than in the preceding situation. But George still needs to get the message loud and clear that he shouldn't have done it and can't do it again.

If George has a specific reason to believe he'll be laid off and is trying to provide a continuing source of income:

George has still acted wrongly, but perhaps you and the organization can afford to be somewhat more understanding in this situation, especially if he has protected the company's interests (as in the preceding response).

Does the organization permit individuals who will be laid off to look for jobs on company time? If so, George has jumped the gun. Perhaps a stern lecture is enough to address his behavior. And if he's genuinely taking the company's welfare into consideration, you and the organization might be willing to let him continue pursuing a new business opportunity.

Note that we've put in a lot of "if's." Here as everywhere else, the burden remains on George to demonstrate that his actions weren't as serious as they seemed.

SOMETHING TO THINK ABOUT

Every manager must walk the sometimes-narrow line between looking out for the interests of the organization and responding to the needs of workers. But when workers break the rules and endanger the company's well being in the process, disciplinary action is sometimes necessary. There are extenuating circumstances at times, and effective managers develop the ability to tell these circumstances from more ordinary ones. They also develop a feel for how these circumstances need to be handled so that they don't set precedents that someone will apply to more normal circumstances.

Always begin with the assumption that the circumstances are ordinary and breaking the rules can't be excused. When this approach doesn't seem fair in a particular situation, begin considering that you may truly have extenuating circumstances on your hands and act accordingly.

No. 83 Job-Hunting on Company Time

Lately she spends most of her time looking for another job

THE SCENE

Marla quickly changes her computer screen as she sees you walking by. "Well, she's at it again," you reflect silently. "Marla was always a pretty good worker, but I can't get a bit of work out of her anymore. All day long, she's either typing up a new resume or calling for job openings or taking a 'long lunch' to go on another interview. I can't afford to keep paying her for doing nothing, and I can't stand to hear another complaint about her not carrying her share of the load. I guess I need to get tough and hope I don't get a grievance in return!"

POSSIBLE CAUSES

Marla may believe she's being hit in the next round of layoffs.

She may have heard rumors or she may have reliable sources who've given her a "heads up" that she's next on the list. In either case, she's trying to protect herself.

Marla may have lost interest in your job or decided that it's time to move on to greener pastures.

Very few people stay in the same job for more than a few years any more, and Marla may have decided she's learned all she can where she is.

> *Hint:* There are really two areas of concern here. First, because Marla's spending so much time job hunting rather than producing you need to address her lack of productivity. If Marla is a good worker whom you'd like you keep, you also need to address the "why" of her job search. What made her decide it was time to leave? If her reasons are in areas within your control, you'll need to decide how much you want to change her situation to encourage her to stay. (Of course, if Marla was never a great worker to begin with, your major concern is to keep her producing for as long as she's still on the payroll.)

YOUR RESPONSE

If Marla believes she's being hit in the next round of layoffs:

Talk to your boss to find out what you can about whether the information Marla is working from is accurate. However, keep in mind that as a matter of company policy sometimes your boss or the personnel office can't disclose upcoming layoff plans until all the notifications are ready to be delivered, to keep some employees from having an unfair advantage over others. If your company has such a policy, or if you suspect that the information you're given isn't reliable, you will need to dig deeper to find out whether Marla's concerns are well founded.

Talk to Marla about her own sources of information. Use whatever informal information network you've already developed to find out what you can about Marla's situation (and the situation of everyone in your unit). If you find out that Marla or others you supervise are likely to be hurt in the next round of layoffs, then even if you can't divulge specific information to them, you can be especially sensitive to their personal needs over the next few months.

The key here is balance. If Marla really is about to lose her job, the company has some moral obligation to Marla to facilitate her job search; therefore, you must balance your continuing need for production in your unit with Marla's need to find a new job. On a very practical level, you're likely to be limited in what you can do at this point to enforce Marla's performance.

Once you find out that Marla's job really is in jeopardy (and you can talk to her openly about it), discuss with her accommodations that will allow her to look for a new job while she continues to produce for you.

Find out what the company's policy is concerning employees' use of computers, copiers, and other equipment to prepare job applications. Even if the company generally doesn't allow employees' personal use of its equipment, there may be special policies for workers caught in layoffs. Once Marla receives official notice of termination, refer her to outplacement and job training facilities for help.

If your investigations reveal that Marla is not likely to lose her job, and if you're confident that your sources are reliable, talk to Marla to reassure her that her employment is secure. Make sure she knows that you'll let her know if you get any information to indicate that her situation has changed and that you'll keep checking. At the same time, be sure Marla understands that since her job's not in danger, you expect her to return to her previous high level of production. Then enforce that expectation.

If Marla has decided it's time to move on to greener pastures:

In this case, it's appropriate for you to take a stronger stand. Marla is job hunting entirely for her own benefit, and the company bears no responsibility for putting her out on the street if she doesn't find a job.

Remind Marla that her duty is to her current employer as long as she's on the payroll, and that you expect full production during the time she's at work. If there are occasional calls to or from prospective employers, that's okay. If her job search is approaching a full-time occupation, that's not.

For many companies, interviews must be taken on vacation days or personal days, not on long breaks when the employee "slips away" for an hour or two. Check to see what your company's policy is and make sure Marla understands. For most employees, a simple explanation (or reminder) of what your expectations are will serve to correct the situation.

If Marla's a good employee and you genuinely don't want to lose her, discuss what you could do within the bounds of her current position to meet her needs.

SOMETHING TO THINK ABOUT

When you're trying to find out why Marla is looking for another job so that you can entice her to stay, keep in mind that it may take some time for *her* to figure out why she wants to leave. Many employees begin a job search whenever boredom or a vague, ill-defined dissatisfaction sets in, without knowing exactly what the problem is. Finding out the source of Marla's dissatisfaction may take some sensitive, but not intrusive, questioning, and patience.

Keep in mind, too, that the reasons why Marla wants to leave may have nothing to do with the job or the company or the work environment at all. She may have personal reasons (like a commitment in another town) or she may be making a career switch to an area that's completely different from anything your company's involved in.

But whenever an employee notifies you that she's leaving, or planning to leave, your unit, you should discuss with her why she wants to make the change. You may find a pattern developing—in response to unchallenging work, lack of opportunities to advance, or some other obstacle to a fulfilling work experience. That final interview probably won't keep Marla from leaving, but it may give you clues for reducing turnover in the future.

Find out first what her needs are (obviously, they're not the same for every employee). Does she want more challenge and a chance to grow in her assignment? Does she want more recognition for the things she's accomplished? Does she want to branch out and learn about other areas, get some experience in a related field? Is she leaving because of the pay, or benefits, or working conditions?

Once you know what's given Marla the urge to move on, you can see what it's possible for you to do within your own company to entice her to stay. However, be careful not to give Marla "perks" that aren't available to every other employee in her situation unless you can back up her special treatment with solid reasons: higher performance levels, greater expertise, or similar job-related reasons. The fact that Marla's ready to leave, by itself, is *not* a reasonable excuse for giving her special treatment.

And if Marla is someone you'd just as soon see leave the company, you need to make a decision about how hard you want to come down on her job hunting activities. On one hand, a strict approach toward your performance expectations may nudge her into intensifying her search. On the other, she may comply with your demands—and so not find another job.

In general, it would be best to treat Marla's job search as you would any other performance problem. Other sections in this book can give you ideas.

No. 84 Indifferent New Boss

Your new boss refuses to learn anything about the work

THE SCENE

"Hey, see you have a new boss," Jeff remarks as you're having coffee together. "What do you think of her?"

"Well, it's much too early to tell," you reply, "but I think there's going to be one serious problem. She called me in the first day and explained that she doesn't know much about what my workgroup does, and since she doesn't expect to manage us for that long she doesn't intend to learn. She made it clear that we're on our own."

"That may not be all bad."

"I don't know. Carol sure gave us a lot of help when she was our manager. I'm not sure what will happen without that kind of help."

POSSIBLE CAUSES

The reasons for your new boss's unwillingness to learn are evident. What we're concerned about here is how to manage effectively with a boss who (1) is new and (2) has made it clear she doesn't intend to learn your work. You need to deal with these two key aspects of the situation.

Hint: Don't forget that there are a number of things you *don't* have to worry about: You already know the work, not only your general technical area, but the specifics of how to do business in this company and how to get things accomplished. You've also already established relationships with your peers and superiors throughout the organization. So you have time to adapt to the new situation, and even without your new boss's support you can keep the work of the group on track.

YOUR RESPONSE

First, deal with the fact that you have a new boss:

First impressions *do* count—a lot! While you can destroy a good first impression later on by screwing up something important, it's very hard to do the reverse and overcome a poor first impression. In your first few meetings with your new boss, you need to convince her that:

- You're a loyal subordinate;
- You're not a threat to her;
- You and your workgroup know your business, and she can count on you for consistently good and timely products

How do you do that? Well, *not* by making a sales pitch for yourself. What you need to do is *demonstrate* those things by what you say and do in the course of normal business.

These are some specific things you can do to make the transition as easy as possible for both you and your new boss:

- Find out as much as you can about your new boss before she starts on her job. Talk to other people in the organization and any contacts you have in the organizations where she's worked before. If you have a good relationship with *her* boss, you might also ask him or her what to expect. Consider all of this as background information. Don't rely exclusively on other people's opinions in forming your own, but use what you learn to try to make the best first impression you can.

- Schedule a meeting where the two of you won't be rushed and you can ask specific questions about how your boss likes things done. Does she prefer information in written form; does she like to converse about the work; or does she like a combination of the two? Does she intend to hold regular staff meetings where you'll report on status, or would she prefer to meet with you individually? Does she want you to report on a scheduled basis, or just whenever you think something's going on she should know about?

These questions about style preferences are legitimate questions to ask, and your boss herself is the best source of information. Better to ask now than to spend months giving her things she doesn't want (or not giving her what she does).

- This first meeting is *not* the best time to ask questions about how to handle specific work problems. If there are pressing issues, try to keep them on "hold" for a week or two. If you can't, let your boss know what the issues are and what you plan to do about them. Then let her know at what stages in the future, if any, she'll have the opportunity to reverse anything she's uncomfortable with. If she gives you specific direction, that's fine. If not, don't press her; she'll probably be uncomfortable because of her lack of knowledge, and you'll have made a tactical error right at the start.

- Use the information you've gathered beforehand to identify any areas where your management style is likely to conflict with your boss'. Try to work in some opportunities during your discussion to probe those areas to see how she reacts. If there's a possible conflict (for example, she likes to control things closely, but you give your people a lot of autonomy as long as they produce), don't press the issue. Wait until you can come up with a strategy for negotiating specific areas where you will be likely to get what you want without causing conflict.

Then deal with her desire not to be involved in your unit's work:

Your first task, of course, is to find what she means when she says that she doesn't intend to learn your unit's work. Is she going to keep completely hands-off and basically act as though she weren't supervising you and the group? Does she want to do the administrative management, so that she expects you to clear all personnel decisions with her? Just what does she intend the relationship to be? The sooner you find this out, the better both of you can deal with the situation.

Does she want to be briefed about your unit and what you do in the company, so she'll have a basic knowledge? Set up a summary briefing with her, preferably with your workgroup present and taking an active part. As part of the meeting, find out what kinds of reports, if any, she wants on the workgroup's work. Arrange to provide her any that she wants promptly.

Does she want to be involved in the administrative decisions? See that she meets every member of the workgroup as soon as possible and give her information on different employees whenever you get the chance. You don't want her overseeing your personnel and other administrative decisions without some understanding of the different workers as individuals.

Does she simply want to be a supervisor on paper, with no involvement at all with your unit? Although this places extra responsibility on you, it also gives you extra opportunity. For example, this might be an opportunity to make changes you've wanted but your previous supervisor wouldn't let you make. Whatever the disadvantages of the situation, having more responsibilities can give you a chance to hone your own managerial know-how, and that's a definite advantage.

SOMETHING TO THINK ABOUT

We cannot stress enough how important having your own boss's confidence is to your effectiveness as a manager. When you have a new boss, you have a golden opportunity to establish that confidence from the ground up. Sure, things will never be the same as when "Good Old What's Her Name" used to run things here. But if you deal with your new boss as you should, they may be even better.

So spend the time and attention necessary to get off to a good start with your new boss. At the same time, make sure that she knows how good you and your workgroup are. She may not want to spend time learning the group's work, but if she thinks well of you and the group she'll support what you do.

Remember, your first job as a manager is to make your workers successful and your second job is to make your boss successful. All else is optional.

CHAPTER TEN

Surviving and Thriving During Corporate Restructuring

No. 85 COMPETITION IN YOUR WORKGROUP

High pressure makes employees compete with each other, not cooperate

THE SCENE

You take a few minutes before the end of the day to glance through the papers accumulating in your in-basket and find to your dismay that the proposal you asked for on new product designs has come in duplicate—one version from Rita and another from Chris.

"What's going on here?" you wonder, as you leaf through each submission. "These look like the same ideas, just in different words and different format. Why can't they get together on some of this stuff? They know I'm going to have to meet with them to work out whatever picayune differences there are; they know I'm going to be ticked off that I have to spend my time arbitrating between them; but they seem to think that one of them is going to come out a winner. Don't they know that when they can't work together they both come out losers?"

POSSIBLE CAUSES

Your unit has become accustomed to letting you work out their problems rather than working them out themselves.

If they know that they don't have to cooperate with one another because you're a willing arbitrator, then they won't cooperate.

There's no payoff for teamwork, but big payoffs for individual performance.

Whatever else may be wrong, you can be sure that this is a major part of the problem. And the problem won't go away until you solve this.

Your staff members have weak cooperative skills.

We talk about people having "interpersonal skills." Actually, there are a wide variety of interpersonal skills. Some people are very good at giving and taking directions. Others are good at the give-and-take of cooperative relationships. Your people may be short on cooperative skills.

> **Hint:** When workers are under a lot of pressure, they tend to follow the most comfortable, least demanding paths to get the work done. Restructuring and reorganizing create a lot of pressure on workers who remain, because they often have to take up the slack caused by the loss of jobs elsewhere in the company. If you haven't structured the work of your unit in such a way that cooperation is more comfortable (and rewarding) than individual efforts, it will be much harder to get your staff to change at a time when demands on them are highest.

YOUR RESPONSE

If your staff has become accustomed to letting you work out their problems for them:

If this is a long-established practice, you can't just suddenly back out on them. First you need to establish a reason for them to want to change. The following response addresses this. Then you need to develop in them the skills they will need to work together constructively. The last response to this challenge discusses this process. But first, you must address the most immediate concern: changing your own behavior.

Once your workgroup is ready to assume responsibility for their own success in teaming, you need to give them the opportunity to practice their skills. Assign group members a project that is too much for one person to accomplish in the time allotted. Then stand back.

Arrange for regularly scheduled progress reports from the team to see that they stay on track. But when conflicts or questions arise and team members come to you for resolution, throw the ball back in their court. Tell them that you expect every problem presented to you to come with a single recommended solution, agreed upon by the group. If you continue to get multiple recommendations or reports from the individual members of a group rather than a group report, send those individual responses back to the group. Stand firm that your expectations are for cooperation, not competition.

If the rewards are for individual performance rather than for group performance:

Take a cold, honest look at what the rewards really are for your people. Are the individual "stars" the ones who get the promotions? Do pay increases depend solely on individual performance rather than overall group success?

In some cases answering "yes" to both questions is appropriate. Do you really *need* cooperation? That's not a silly question. In some lines of work or work environments, it's best to put up with the friction and let people handle projects independently. If that's the way it should be in your workgroup, though, don't expect your employees to be team players. Don't make joint assignments unless you're forced to.

On the other hand, if you need cooperation, reward cooperation. Revise your reward structure so it pays for cooperation. Make cooperation with group members one of the factors that pay increases depend upon. Give bonuses or rewards to people who help others get their jobs done. You can borrow an idea from some sports teams and let your employees give stars to other employees who have been particularly helpful to them. Each month or quarter, reward the employee(s) with the largest number of stars a day off or a gift certificate to a local restaurant.

Expect flak, listen to it, and keep on track. If individual performance is what has been paying off, your people have been "trained" to compete. It will take time to change, so be patient, but firm.

If your employees have weak cooperative skills:

Get your employees together and tell them how the way they work is going to change. Make it clear that cooperation will be important, that it will be rewarded, and how it will be rewarded. Make sure your employees know *why* you've decided that cooperation is now more important than individual performance—what in the work situation has changed, what has happened to change your own perceptions. Link the change in work method to some objective happening within the organization or its industry so your employees won't think you're just being fickle and try to outwait you rather than change.

Arrange to provide training support for the change. To make the change effectively, you'll probably need several courses or workshops spread over several months. Training will be most productive if your employees can attend the sessions together so they'll have a chance to practice in class with their own workgroup members. You may also need to identify someone who can provide on-site support—offering observations or consultation as the group puts its new skills into practice.

Identify some assignments that require your people to work in twos or threes, so they can start practicing cooperation. Tie this in as closely as you can to the training they get. Give them a chance to practice what they're learning as soon as possible after they learn it.

Expect your employees to be anxious. They're not only changing the way they work, but they're having to learn and practice a whole new set of skills. Encourage them, and give them guidance, but make sure that they keep moving in the direction you want.

SOMETHING TO THINK ABOUT

People do what they have the opportunity to do and what they know how to do, *if* it pays off for them. As a manager, it's up to you to provide the opportunity, the training (if necessary), and the rewards. Whenever you want to change your employees' mode of operating or introduce a new process into the work environment, you need to develop a plan that will address all three of these areas. Without opportunity, training, and rewards, almost no change will be possible.

No. 86 An Employee on the Edge

He seems to be coming unglued from work stresses

THE SCENE

You walk back to your office, shaking your head. Martin Kaminsky has always been a little weird, but lately he's been acting truly crazy. You just heard him accuse Sandra Wilson, a new clerk, of hiding the notes from his latest audit. When Sandra left the room in tears, Martin turned to the others and yelled, *"You* think I can't keep up with you, but I can. I'll show all of you!"

POSSIBLE CAUSES

Martin may be reacting to a temporary stressful situation outside work.

Perhaps his home life is bothering him. Perhaps it's as simple as his attempting to quit smoking or drinking.

He may have periodic episodes.

All of us go through "phases" in our emotions, more "laid-back" at times, more "up-tight" at others. Martin's swings may be more pronounced than normal.

Stress resulting from changes in the corporate environment and the resulting additional work may be getting to him.

His strange behavior may be a sign that on-the-job pressures are making him irrational and unstable, to the point where he needs professional help.

> *Hint*: The worst reaction you can make is to give vent to your frustration with Martin. Whatever is happening, your emotional response will only make it worse.

YOUR RESPONSE

No matter what the cause is:

First, as we already said, remember to keep your cool. Observe carefully. Then, if necessary, find someone who's familiar with emotional disturbance and learn all you can from him or her.

Talk to other employees. Learn everything they've observed about Martin. How has he changed? Has this ever happened before? What happened then? How was it handled then? How quickly did he recover?

Talk with Martin. Yes, this is going to be stressful, and, no, you're not going to play psychiatrist. But you are going to try to get a "feel" for his situation. You want to talk with him about the problem, if possible. If he can talk about it, that increases the chance that it can be resolved with a minimum of stress. If he can't, well, that's important information, too.

How do you talk to him? You talk about his performance and his actions on the job: "Martin, you really laid into Sandra out there. From my perspective, you were more strident than the situation called for. What's going on?"

There's another side to the picture. If the situation is deteriorating, you may have to act without knowing all you need to know. It may be a tense time, for Martin, your other employees, and you. But if you act on the best information you have, trying to do the best you can by everyone, you'll bring about the best solution possible under the situation.

If he's reacting to a temporary stressful situation outside work:

How will you know this? You won't, for sure. But if the problem is a specific situation that doesn't involve work, Martin should at least be able to assure you that the problem has nothing to do with work. He may not want to talk about the specific problem, particularly if it's something very personal, such as a divorce or a terminally ill individual close to him, but he will probably be willing to work with you to the extent of assuring you that it's personal.

Is Martin getting help to see him through the situation? If not, you should suggest, as tactfully as possible, that he get help. While you want to support him, and his fellow employees probably will want to also, he has to take reasonable steps to keep his job performance from deteriorating.

Be as supportive as you can. Simply be available to listen to him, and encourage your other employees to do the same.

Should you suggest he take time off from work? You can offer him the option and make him aware of his rights under the Family and Medical Leave Act, but be careful not to imply that you're insisting that he take time off to resolve his personal situation. He may depend on work to take his mind off his off-the-job crisis. If he does want to continue working, though, you have the opening you need to suggest that he needs to have control of himself at work, and perhaps to suggest again that he get professional help.

If this is a periodic episode:

Your best guidance is what Martin has done before when he's had similar episodes. How long have they lasted? How severe were they? However, bear in mind that knowing how the situation played out in the past is no guarantee of what you can expect this time.

It's important to find out whether Martin understands what's happening. If he does, it may be even easier to resolve than the preceding situation. Many people are able to realize when they're having an episode such as this and respond realistically to it.

You'll probably want to suggest that he get professional help in this case also. You may also want to encourage him to take some time off. That depends, of course, on the severity of his condition. You'll have to walk a careful line between supporting him and insisting that he take whatever actions are necessary to help himself.

If stress resulting from corporate changes and additional work may be getting to him:

If you ask Martin about the reasons for his actions, he may understand what's happening and describe it to you. Or he may show it by denying the situation, responding inappropriately, or becoming very defensive—signs that he feels caught in something he can't control.

If he does understand what's happening, determine whether he is taking steps to counteract it. Is he getting professional help? Or is he sinking more and more deeply into inappropriate behavior? If he's taking appropriate steps, your most effective response is to give him room and to see that other members of the workgroup do so also and watch for improvements.

If he doesn't improve, or if he's not doing anything to prevent his on-the-job behavior from deteriorating, you need to take swift, effective action. If he's being disruptive, you may have to insist that he take sick time off, use vacation time, whatever is necessary to get him out of the work situation. If company policy permits, you may need to send him for a psychiatric evaluation. Remember, you're not doing this to punish him, but to relieve a condition that's painful both for him and for your other employees. Make sure your words and actions in handling the situation make this clear to Martin.

If Martin in any way threatens or implies violence to others or himself, respond to that *immediately*. Don't ever assume that it's "just talk." Get counsel from your company physician or any other professional you can reach. Call the company security office or local law enforcement officials if violence seems imminent.

SOMETHING TO THINK ABOUT

Corporate restructuring produces additional stress for most organizations, their managers, and workers. Unless individuals are accustomed to handling this level of stress, it may affect them severely, even to the point of serious emotional disturbance. One of your basic jobs is to help your employees deal with this stress.

One concrete, early step you should take if your company is undergoing this turmoil is to find out if your company offers stress reduction training available. If it does, get it for your workgroup. If it doesn't, find a course through a commercial firm or a local community college and use it. But get help, and get it quickly. For individuals like Martin, a course is too little, too late. But it may help others in the workgroup avoid the extreme reaction that Martin had.

No. 87 YOUR BOSS PUSHES TOO HARD
You face unreasonable demands for quality or quantity of work

THE SCENE

Just who does your boss think he is? It doesn't seem to matter how much the staff works themselves to death, he's never pleased. He was bad enough a year ago, but now with the company's recent acquisition of TechTemp and staff reductions he's becoming impossible. Whatever your group does, it's never fast enough, there's never enough of it, and it's never good enough. You've *never* worked for such an unreasonable boss. Doesn't he have any idea what you're up against? After all, your workgroup has taken its share of reductions.

POSSIBLE CAUSES

Your unit may not be producing a reasonable quantity or quality of work.

Maybe this isn't your boss's problem at all. Maybe it's yours.

Your boss may be reacting to the pressure for greater productivity from those above him.

Not every demand is a reflection of your own boss's needs or desires. Just as you may have to push your people to make the boss happy, sometimes he has to push you to make *his* boss happy. And with the staff reductions as a result of the restructuring, he has to do more of it now.

Your boss may not understand what is reasonable to expect of you and your unit.

This is particularly likely if he's been transferred recently from a unit that does different work or is operating in a different environment.

> *Hints*: Remember, when an organization has to make staff reductions and cut costs to survive competitive pressures, everyone gets affected. The old standards of what constituted a good day's work aren't valid any more. This doesn't automatically mean that everyone has to work harder, though that may be the case. It does mean that everyone has to work as smart as possible. There's no room to just do things the way they used to be done, or to use an inefficient process just because you know it. Everyone must be constantly engaged in process and performance improvement.

Although the third possible cause may be the most tempting from your point of view, it's also the least likely. (That's why it's last on the list.) Most second-line managers have worked their way up through first-level supervisory jobs. They have a pretty good idea when they become second-tier managers what's reasonable to expect and what isn't. If there's a disagreement about how much your unit ought to be producing, or what quality of work it's reasonable to expect, chances are it's your problem, not your boss's. In the interests of retaining the position you've worked so hard to achieve, it's in your best interests to assume that you're the one who's got to change.

YOUR RESPONSE

If your unit isn't producing a reasonable quantity or quality of work:

This is a major problem. You should approach your boss *immediately* and talk candidly with him about where the workgroup is falling short. Don't be defensive or argue with him; get the clearest picture you can of where he thinks your unit can do better. What are his production goals? What does he consider adequate quality? What does he consider "complete staff work" in the assignments he gives you to perform? Maybe you've misunderstood his expectations of you.

If it's still not clear after talking to him what quantity or quality of work he expects, you might consider talking to a colleague who also works for him (or who's worked for him in the past). You might get some ideas about how much or what kind of work it takes to satisfy him.

Once you know what he's looking for, it's up to your workgroup to produce it. Maybe you're not organized as efficiently as you could be. Maybe you've let some of your own people slide and haven't expected as much of *them* as you should. Now's the time to tighten up. You can't produce any more than the people in your unit produce for you; your leverage is through them. So make sure the people who work for you know what you expect and the consequences of their failure to meet your expectations.

If your boss is reacting to the pressure for greater productivity from those above him:

You have a narrow line to walk. You can't refuse the work, but you also have to be realistic. As in the first response, sit down with your boss and find out exactly where he believes you're falling short. Again, listen—don't argue. You want all the information you can get on how he sees you and your workgroup.

Then get together with either a few key workers or your entire work-group and fill them in on your boss's expectations. Go over each item specifically and ask for suggestions on how they can give him the productivity and/or quality he wants. If they don't believe they can do it all—and if they persuade you they genuinely can't—find out in detail what tasks they don't think they can get done and why. Don't let the group off easily, but don't let them overestimate what they can do. The best strategy: Be confident in your workgroup's ability that you'll set challenging goals, but be reasonable in your expectations.

Now it's time to talk with your boss again. If you see how you can provide him what he wants, tell him so and show him how you intend to do it. If you can't meet all of his expectations, now is the time to put all of your negotiating skills to work. What does the workgroup need to concentrate on? What must be done well and on time? What might slide a little or be done without quite as much care without causing problems? Is there anything your workgroup is doing now that could be streamlined—or not done at all? (Almost every unit does some work that's a carryover from some prior period, but no longer relevant.) You want to help him look good to his boss; concentrate on what you need to do to do that.

The two of you will probably be able to agree on a workable course of action. But don't dare stop there. Your workgroup will almost certainly pick up more work, so you need to start thinking about ways to do what you're doing now better and faster. Remember, every time you say to your boss, "It'll be tough, but we can do it," both your job security and his go up a notch.

If your boss doesn't understand what is reasonable to expect of you and your unit:

Your goal is still to satisfy your boss, but you may be able to negotiate down his requirements. What kind of relationship do you have with him? Does he seem to respect you and your abilities? Or do you think he may be looking for an excuse to dump you? Will he listen to your ideas?

If you have the kind of relationship that allows you to discuss with him the problems you're having in meeting his demands, then talk with him. Find out as specifically as possible where he thinks you're falling short. If you have previous production charts or performance-review results that show other observers' satisfaction with the quantity and quality of work your unit has produced, show him. Try to find out if anything has changed in the company's priorities that changes your own unit's work priorities. And remember that he may be under pressure from those above to increase productivity. Then work out the most realistic work agreement possible with him. After that, your job is to sell your workgroup on the agreement and carry through.

What if your boss really is being unreasonable, but you can't get him to change his mind? You've shown him your production records and commendations from previous supervisors or audit teams, but he just won't be persuaded. He's convinced that you can do more and better than you are, and he expects you to improve. If you really can't find any way to meet his demands, then your best bet may be to try to get out of the job. This is a no-win situation, where it looks as if there's no way to satisfy him. Rely on your previous good record, go to other managers, and sell your services elsewhere. In the meantime, do the best you can to satisfy him, so he won't sabotage your efforts to find a better situation.

SOMETHING TO THINK ABOUT

It's important to keep in mind that in a lean organization, particularly one that's still adjusting to more work and fewer people, everyone needs to look for ways to increase productivity. Don't wait for the next round of additional work to hit, or for your boss to get upset with your current productivity. Encourage your workgroup continually to keep finding ways to improve their quality and quantity—and help them do it.

No. 88 Hiring Freeze
You're told not to expect more hiring, even though workload is increasing

THE SCENE

"They're at it again, Trudy. We have to cut our staff by another 10 percent, and because you have two vacancies, I'll have to start there. I'm afraid you can't fill them until at least the first of next year.

"But, Carrie, I need those people to meet all the new assignments our unit absorbed when you abolished Pete McNamara's unit six months ago. I can't do more work with fewer people."

"That's exactly what you'll have to do, Trudy. If I don't stop hiring now, I'll have to start thinking about whom to lay off later. I'm sorry about the bind this puts you in, but I'll let you know if anything changes."

Just when you thought you were going to catch up, this happens. Now what?

POSSIBLE CAUSES

Your boss is setting the stage to get rid of you or your unit.

Other units have already been abolished. That's how you got all this extra work to begin with. If you and your group can't perform under the extra pressure, you'll probably go too. Your boss may think the easiest way to find out how much you can handle is to create a situation that taxes your resources; you'll either be a star *or* you'll self-destruct.

Your boss is making the right decision from her point of view.

Otherwise, she really would have to start letting permanent employees go.

> *Hint:* This is one of those cases where the cause is generally less important than what you need to do to handle the situation. Regardless of why your boss is taking positions out of your unit, the consequences to you and the group are the same.

YOUR RESPONSE

In either case, the only course you can take is to make the best of a tough situation. Here are some ideas:

- If your employees understand that the alternative was to let current employees go (including perhaps some of them), they may be willing to work longer and harder, at least in the short term. After a few months, though, this may start to sound a little hollow to them.
- Whether your employees can produce more or not, you need to see that the highest-priority work gets done. Be sure you and your employees know what the priorities are. Talk to your boss to see that the two of you understand them the same way. Then pass this on to your employees and spend as little time as possible on the low-priority items and as much time as possible on those at the top of the priority list.
- Challenge your group to come up with better and quicker ways to get their jobs done. In this circumstance, they certainly won't have to worry about working themselves out of a job if they become more efficient. In fact, the

more efficient the group becomes, the more indispensable they will be to the company. When group members come up with good ideas, see that they get recognized and, if possible, paid handsomely for them.

- Spend even more time than usual making sure your people have the equipment and supplies they need. If they've been needing some new equipment, this may be the time to try to get approval for it, as long as it doesn't cost so much that the budget cuts rule it out. If fluctuations in the work you receive from other units make it harder for your people to do their job, work with those other units to smooth out the work flow. You might try a sharing arrangement where your group helps others who have peaks in workload in return for those units helping you when your group gets overloaded.

- If you start to get seriously behind in the work, explore more formal borrowing arrangements. (After all, the cut you took may have saved jobs in someone else's group.) If your output is the input to another unit, they may be particularly willing to help you.

- If your unit really has to stretch to make up for the vacancies you couldn't fill, and especially if the group comes up with ways to really work smarter, make sure your boss knows. Nothing could be worse than her believing that you handled the cuts efficiently because you were overstaffed to start with.

SOMETHING TO THINK ABOUT

Like several other challenges we discuss in this book, your boss's actions here put you in a real bind. But fighting the situation won't help much. Whenever your group is hit with a significant challenge, your role expands to include "cheerleader." Practice your motivational skills and use them to concentrate your energy as well as that of your staff on the new situation. If you and your unit can successfully deal with this challenge, you may enhance your reputation significantly and ensure your long-term survival in spite of staff cuts.

No. 89
STUCK WITH A LOW-PERFORMING WORKER
Your boss refuses to let you fire a nonperformer, despite a mandate to run lean business units

THE SCENE

"Sheila, Bev simply isn't working out. She gets sloppier and sloppier every day, she accuses me of picking on her, and she's disrupting the other employees. I've got to get rid of her."

"I understand how you feel, but I'm not at all sure you've given her a fair chance. Work with her some more. I think you can bring her around."

"But I'm already short two workers. I need everyone left in my workgroup to be fully productive.

"No more. I've made my decision. Now you go back and shape her up."

POSSIBLE CAUSES

Sheila believes you really haven't given Bev a fair chance.

She thinks she has to intervene to see that you don't compound the problem you've caused.

She may be unwilling to fire employees.

She's concluded it isn't worth it, for one reason or another. And she may not understand how important it is in a lean organization for everyone to carry his or her part of the load.

Sheila may have organizational reasons for not firing Bev that have nothing to do with your situation.

The organization may not yet have faced the requirement for everyone to be fully productive.

She may be friends with Bev and unwilling to let you take any action against her.

Her friendship is more important to her than any damage that Bev's poor performance can cause.

Hint: The situation has the potential to create two very undesirable results. First, it can undermine your authority in your work unit. Bev may see that no matter how strongly you talk, you can't really deliver. Second, others may ask themselves why they're working so hard if Bev can get away with poor productivity. Neither of these situations is tolerable in an environment in which you're already threatened by cutbacks (or even elimination of your unit). You want to prevent or minimize both these problems, no matter what their causes are.

YOUR RESPONSE

If Sheila believes you really haven't given Bev a fair chance:

This is serious. It means you don't have Sheila's confidence in an area that's key to your success in your job. In the other three causes, the problem is Bev and—at least in your eyes—your boss. In this situation, the problem is your relationship with Sheila, and perhaps with Bev.

First, you need to review the situation in your own mind. What's happened that might make Sheila think Bev hasn't gotten a fair chance? Then find out why she thinks you haven't been treating Bev fairly. If possible, ask Sheila. Don't argue or defend yourself; concentrate on finding out exactly how she sees the situation. Has Bev gone around you and complained to her? Does Sheila suspect that you may be prejudiced against Bev because she's female or a minority? Look for any other reasons why she thinks you haven't given Bev a reasonable opportunity to succeed.

Is there a chance Sheila is right? Is it possible that you have been treating Bev differently from other employees? Do you perhaps not like or trust her, or is she difficult for you to get along with? Once you have an answer that seems right, you can start to correct the situation. Talk with Bev and try to get her to open up with you about how she sees the situation. Then try to make a mutual agreement that both of you are willing to follow. As part of the agreement, arrange regular meetings with her where each of you can review how she seems to be doing.

And then make sure that Sheila knows that the two of you are working together to ensure that Bev's being treated fairly. Remember, it's just as important that Sheila knows you're working on the problem as it is to work on it.

Suppose you honestly believe you've treated Bev fairly? Now you need to figure out why Sheila doesn't see it that way. The next step, of course, is to plan what you need to do to help Sheila change her mind. Perhaps you haven't mentioned to her when Bev has failed at an assignment or been late on one. See that Sheila knows that now.

One word of caution: Don't give the impression that your goal is to prove Sheila wrong. Your goal is to treat Bev fairly and help Sheila see that you are. Then when she sees that you are managing as you should, she will (probably) let you take whatever action you need to take.

If she's unwilling to fire employees:

You'll know if this is the reason either from your prior experiences with Sheila or from what other managers have told you. In the long run, it makes a difference whether she won't fire employees in general or is just responding to immediate organizational pressures. In this situation, it makes no difference. She has developed an approach as a manager that isn't workable in the current high-pressure, high-productivity situation. You need to deal with that.

So what do you do? You analyze your unit's work and then show Sheila as specifically as possible how Bev's failure to produce is handicapping overall productivity. If possible, explain how it almost kept the group from meeting an important deadline or almost caused them to submit an unacceptable product. You should know what Sheila's priorities are. Show her how Bev's performance is interfering with achieving those. In short, do the best possible job of showing that Bev's poor performance directly affects Sheila's success in her job. If you can get that across, you may get the authority you need to take action to get rid of Bev.

And if you can't change Sheila's mind? Ask her to take Bev off your hands and find her another job—or let you arrange for her to move to another unit. If Bev is a poor enough performer, offer to get along without a replacement. That may persuade Sheila either to let you do something or finally to do something herself.

If none of these work, give Sheila regular updates on how Bev's poor performance continues to interfere with your workgroup's ability to do its job and with Sheila's ability to succeed in hers.

If Sheila has organizational reasons for not firing Bev that have nothing to do with your situation:

She may be responding to pressures that have nothing to do with you or Bev. The organization, for whatever reason, still doesn't believe in firing people. And Sheila may not feel that she needs to tell you the reason, or that she can tell you.

Use some of the suggestions from the preceding response. Ask Sheila to let you find Bev another job. Give her regular reports, which she might want to share with her own boss, of how Bev's poor performance is interfering with the group's productivity. Keep the issue alive.

There is one consolation in this situation: Bev probably doesn't know that you can't fire her, at least not yet. You still have some leverage with her. Use it. Keep insisting that she perform satisfactorily. If she won't, take corrective action to the maximum extent that your boss permits. Who knows—if you do the most that you can do it may be enough to get her to start performing more effectively.

If she's friends with Bev and unwilling to let you take action against her:

Make sure Sheila knows exactly what problems you're having with Bev and how they affect your unit's ability to do the work. She may know Bev primarily from a social perspective. And if no one's complained to her before (with hard facts to back up the complaints), she may really not know what the problems are. Her attempts to protect Bev may spring from her lack of knowledge rather than a conscious decision to protect her no matter what. She may decide to let you deal with Bev's performance without regard for their friendship.

But probably not, in which case you should ask Sheila to let you find a position for Bev in another workgroup or identify one for her. You don't want to be caught in the middle. She may agree to try to move Bev, but if she doesn't, follow the suggestions in the preceding response and make sure she stays constantly aware of Bev's impact on the workgroup and on her own success.

SOMETHING TO THINK ABOUT

Very few aspects of your job as a manager are more important than making sure that your boss has confidence in you. This overall confidence is more important than almost any specific situation that can arise. If you have it, you will be able to deal with any problem, even one where you may need to fire an employee. If you don't have it, you may have trouble getting your boss' support for even minor actions.

Maintaining your boss' confidence doesn't mean becoming a "yes person," or letting your boss run your workgroup. It does mean understanding what's important to your boss and supporting this in every way you can. In other words, one of your basic responsibilities is making your boss look good. Do that, and you'll have her confidence.

No.90 Losing Talented Employees

Your best workers are leaving for other jobs

THE SCENE

"Well, Paul, we're sorry to see you go, but I understand how you feel. If I had kids getting ready to go to college, I'd be looking for more security too."

Although you're being gracious, inside you're feeling panic set in. Three of your best workers gone in as many months. Not that you can blame them; the rumors of layoffs are flying fast and furious. But how are you ever going to get all this work done? And if you can't, that makes you and the rest of your staff even more vulnerable.

POSSIBLE CAUSES

It's fairly clear why your best workers are leaving the company. They believe that they'll be out of a job sooner or later, and they've decided to get out while the getting's good. But how reliable are the rumors that are floating around?

If the rumors are accurate and there will be more restructuring and lay-offs, including your unit, there's not much you can do to entice your workers to stay. In that case, your main concern is to keep up production (and morale) in the rest of your unit.

But if the rumors are false, or if the planned restructuring isn't likely to hurt your group, then you have considerably more leverage to stop the drain of talent.

> *Hint:* Talent drain during corporate reorganizations and restructuring can be a real killer because you often can't do anything to replace the people you're losing. Be careful not to take out your frustration on the staff, either the ones leaving or the ones staying. The ones who leave are reacting to their situation in the best way they know how and so are the ones who stay. Your continuing support is important to both groups.

YOUR RESPONSE

If the rumors of more layoffs are true:

Recognize that there probably isn't a lot you can do to keep your workers from looking for other jobs if the ones they have now are likely to disappear. But that doesn't mean that your situation is hopeless. You have several avenues you can try to keep up production and morale in your unit in spite of the frequent departures.

- Talk to your manager or your personnel department to try to find out who's likely to be hurt in the layoffs and who's likely to be more secure. Within the limits imposed by your company on disclosure of information, reassure the people whose jobs are most secure. Emphasize the need for everyone to continue to produce and to pull together to keep that security.

- Find out also what authority you have to offer retention bonuses to workers who have other jobs lined up but who may be able to delay their reporting dates for a few weeks or months. Your company might have options available to give those workers an incentive to stay for a little longer to give you time to adjust the workload in your unit.

- Talk to other managers in your organization to see if you can arrange to borrow some workers, even part time, to get over the hump until the layoffs and reorganization are complete. Depending on the kind of work your unit does and how easily other people can learn to perform, you may even be able to offer overtime hours to workers in other units who'd be willing to do some work for you after they've completed their full-time jobs each day.

- If it looks as if your options for additional help are running out, meet with your staff to review all the functions they perform. Decide which ones are critical and which ones aren't (or are less critical). Review each employee's work assignments. Prioritize the work within each job·and move assignments around as necessary to ensure that all the high-priority work gets done and that all your workers are actively involved in the high-priority assignments. Develop some contingency plans to cover any of the less critical areas that may suddenly become "hot," but let everyone know that you don't expect the remaining group to perform everything that the full group did.

- Is being short-staffed likely to be a long-term situation? If so, consider doing a process reengineering study of some of your key functions. In a reengineering analysis you can analyze all the work involved in each function and the process you use to perform it, then evaluate whether there are better or more efficient ways to get the same work done. There may be ways to rework your unit's processes themselves to get more work accomplished with fewer people and without burning out the ones you have.

If the rumors of layoffs are false:

Pass on to your staff all the information you can about the company's plans and how secure they are. Reassure them that you'll let them know if anything changes to put their jobs in jeopardy and make sure they know that they're valued members of your staff. If you're able to get to staff members who have accepted other jobs or are negotiating with other companies for positions, see if you can offer retention bonuses to entice them to stay.

Most of all, make sure that the information you give your staff is accurate and timely. If the jobs aren't secure, don't give false hope. Not only is that unfair to staff members who've been loyal to you and the company, it's also very likely to backfire once your workers find out the truth.

SOMETHING TO THINK ABOUT

Workers change jobs for lots of reasons, sometimes because they are seeking better opportunities and sometimes because they're not happy where they are. If your company is contemplating layoffs and job security is in question, the reason for the mass exodus is obvious. But what if your unit's jobs are secure and your workforce is still leaving? Take a look at your work environment from your employees' point of view. Is it too structured? Not structured enough? Is the work challenging? Or are employees burnt out because there's too much work? Identify the disincentives and correct the ones over which you have some control.

Sometimes several workers will decide to change jobs at about the same time just by coincidence. But sometimes it's because there's a problem where they are. Your first concern should be to make sure *you're* not the problem!

No. 91 Scene-Stealing Boss
Your manager takes credit for what you do

THE SCENE

"Look here at the company newsletter," Craig offers at lunch.
Fred Newton's been interviewed about that new order-processing system you put in a couple of months ago. And see what he says:

"I thought we needed. . ." and "It seemed to me. . ." and "I decided this. . ." and "I created that. . ." Reading this, no one would ever know you had anything to do with the project at all—and it was your idea to begin with!"

"Don't you know?" Alice adds, "Newton's been doing that to all of us lately. He seems to think he can secure his job by grabbing all the glory for our work."

POSSIBLE CAUSES

Newton may really be trying to enhance his own image by claiming credit for what his subordinates accomplish.

This could be a strategy to make himself more competitive in an uncertain corporate climate or it could be because he really believes he deserves the credit for anything his staff does. In either case, the behavior is guaranteed to make him plenty of enemies and may backfire when his staff starts to fight back.

Newton may believe that when he speaks of himself, his listeners understand that he's referring to his staff also.

He may not realize how important it is to the people who did the work to get specific credit for it and that his superiors will give him credit for assembling a good staff, perhaps even more than for coming up with ideas himself.

> ***Hint:*** This is a tricky situation. Part of the job of any subordinate is to make his or her boss look good, but preferably not at the expense of other employees. Your goal here is to make sure your boss gets lots of credit for what you and your unit do, but for his excellent leadership of the effort, not for the idea or the work itself.

YOUR RESPONSE

If your boss is trying to enhance his own image by claiming credit for others' work:

During a period of corporate uncertainty, it's important that the decision makers know who in the organization is making a significant contribution. Obviously, the problem here is that your boss is taking credit for contributions that others are responsible for. So it's critical that you protect yourself somehow. You need to make sure your company's decision makers know how valuable you are, and your record will look dismally bare if all your accomplishments appear to be your boss's.

Try to work out an informal arrangement with your boss that you won't complain when he takes the credit for things you do, as long as he does what he can to boost *your* career. This doesn't even have to be a spoken agreement, as long as you both know what the rules are and live up to them. Drop a few hints here and there that you're on to his game, and see what reaction you get.

If subtlety doesn't work, and if you can't come to a more open agreement about what he'll do for you, then you need to be more assertive. Document your ideas and accomplishments. When you have something new to suggest, do it in writing rather than in informal conversation. Make formal proposals rather than oral requests—and early enough in the process that it's obvious later whose idea this really was. Prepare regular progress reports that identify, specifically and in detail, what's been done and who did the work. Keep records, and whenever possible, make sure your documentation becomes part of the unit's official files.

As much as you can without appearing to brag, let others know what you've accomplished. You can always tell friends and co-workers what you're contemplating and what you've completed. If your boss' other subordinate supervisors are suffering the same treatment you are, they'll be glad to share their accomplishments with you and help you establish your own contributions. As opportunities arise in conversations with casual workplace acquaintances, mention work you've done that's especially noteworthy. In doing this, you must maintain a delicate balance. You don't want to look like a braggart or a "know-it-all," and it's best not to upstage your boss or contradict him too openly. But it's important to engage in a little defense publicity from time to time.

Keep your sense of humor. If you're a talented and dedicated manager, especially if you have a proven track record in the company, people will already know who's *really* doing the work. They'll soon recognize your boss for the scene-stealer he is and begin to discount his tales of great feats.

If your boss believes his listeners understand that his staff shares in the credit for the work:

Make sure that when you report progress or accomplishments to your boss you include the names of the major contributors. Give him the information he needs to pass credit along when he has occasion to talk about the project to other people.

Make gentle encouraging statements to him about the positive effects of recognizing employees' contributions. Let him know how your employees react (such as with greater enthusiasm or productivity) when they know that someone above them is aware of their efforts. Your occasional hints may be all it takes to raise your boss' consciousness.

If gentle reminders don't work, and if your relationship with your boss is generally good, you might try a more direct approach. Tell him how discouraging it is for you and your staff when it appears that he's taking credit for others' hard work. If he's a sensitive manager, he'll get the message.

Of course, you *won't* want to be this direct if you suspect that he really does want to claim credit for other people's efforts. It's likely to make him even more aggressive in grabbing the glory from you and your group.

SOMETHING TO THINK ABOUT

While you're concerned about the credit your boss is taking for your accomplishments, are your employees concerned about your taking credit for *their* work? You can't expect workers to do their best if all their efforts go to your greater glory. Just as you want your boss to be generous with his praise and credit, your workers want the same from you.

Whenever your employees accomplish something of note, make sure they're recognized for their contributions—both with a "thank you" from you and with some public recognition. That recognition doesn't have to be monetary; it can be a mention in a staff meeting, a congratulatory note on the bulletin board, or an acknowledgment in casual conversations with other employees. But, regardless of the method you decide to use, praise your employees often and sincerely.

CHAPTER ELEVEN

Making the Most of Technology

No. 92 WASTING TIME ON THE WEB

Your employees spend their work time surfing the Net

THE SCENE

"Krystal, what's going on here?" you ask. "Every time I glance at your computer screen, you seem to be tuned into some Web page. Your work hardly calls for spending time online. How come you're spending so much time on the Internet?"

POSSIBLE CAUSES

Krystal may be looking for ways to make her job more efficient by using Internet resources you've never though of.

She may have found some resources she could use and is now looking for even more job helps.

She may be testing her limits.

She's not sure how much personal time she can spend without some word from you, and now she's found out.

She may not have enough work to keep her busy and this is how she uses her free time.

This may be a problem, or it may not, depending on the nature of the job.

> *Hint:* The Internet is a great work tool—and a great temptation as well. Your challenge is to keep people interested enough to use it for the company's work, but not so fascinated that the rest of the job suffers.

YOUR RESPONSE

If Krystal is looking for ways to make her job more efficient:

First, confirm that this is the case. Is Krystal a conscientious employee who would want to make use of the tools available to her to do a better job? If so, accept her explanation, congratulate her on her initiative, and ask her whether she's learned anything worth passing on to other members of the unit.

Encourage her to put together a list of resources others can use—with Web site addresses and brief descriptions of information to be found at each site. Enlist her help in coaching other employees who may not be quite so adventurous on the Internet so that they also can use the tools available there.

If Krystal is testing her limits:

Why would she feel the need to test? Haven't you made it clear to employees what your policies, or the company's policies, are on computer usage? If not, establish those policies now. Here are some areas you might want to address:

- *Personal use of company computers:* You could limit your employees' use of computer systems to business use. Alternatively, you could permit your employees to use the company's computers for personal reasons as long as they don't abuse the privilege, or you could permit personal use of computers as long as it's not on company time. These restrictions can apply to any computer equipment or services paid for by the company, whether they're physically located at the workplace or in an employee's home.

- *Software and data files:* You could limit employees' ability to add software or data (personal or business) to the system without express permission—so that your system doesn't get overloaded.

- *Virus protection:* You could require employees to run all files they receive from outside the company through virus-scanning software before they're loaded on the company's system, regardless of whether the files are attached to e-mail or on disks.

- *Confidential files:* You can limit employees' access to certain data files, such as payroll or personnel records or confidential client information, by using passwords or other mechanisms. And your policy could notify employees of any penalties for unauthorized entry into the company's confidential files.

- *Internet use:* You could ban employees' use of the Internet altogether or limit it strictly to business purposes. You could also prohibit employees from accessing material on the Internet that you, or the company, consider inappropriate for the workplace, such as obscene or pornographic material.

Regardless of what policy you adopt, first make sure that everyone knows what the policy is. Post it on the bulletin board, broadcast it on the company's internal e-mail system, give paper copies to each of your employees, or use some combination of these approaches. Remember, you can't hold people responsible for policies they don't know about, and you can't enforce limits you haven't set. If you see Krystal whiling away her workday surfing the Net *after* you've disseminated the company's policy on technology usage to your employees, you can make it more forcefully clear that's not what she's being paid to do.

If Krystal doesn't have enough work to keep her busy:

This is a different problem. In this case, Internet usage is just incidental to the real issue, which is that you have an employee who doesn't have enough to do.

Perhaps Krystal is in a job where there are substantial fluctuations in workload and not much you can assign her during the slow periods to even it out. In that case, you're probably resigned to a certain amount of "down time" and your main concern should be that she doesn't offend customers or other employees by flaunting her lack of work. Suggest that instead of surfing the Net or playing games on the computer, she should bring reading material that she can more discreetly peruse at her desk. Or even better, assign her some of the jobs that often get put off until that "someday" that never comes, such as sorting through old files or organizing reference materials.

If Krystal has too much time on her hands simply because there's just not enough work to keep her busy, then it's time to do some job restructuring in your unit. Chances are there's someone who *is* overloaded and could really use the assistance. If no one else in your unit needs help, then this may be a position you could offer up to another unit, switch to part-time to cover the amount of work that is assigned, or abolish altogether.

SOMETHING TO THINK ABOUT

Although Internet access is becoming increasingly common for employees across all levels of an organization, the Internet is a business tool just like any other that belongs to the company. Further, time employees spend surfing the Net for their personal usage is time they are not spending contributing to your unit's—and the company's—productivity. You have every right to establish policies for Internet use and to enforce those policies. If you don't have policies in place, set them now. If you do have policies, enforce them evenhandedly. If you don't, it's hard to complain when employees abuse the system.

No. 93
UNREASONABLE EXPECTATION OF PRIVACY

A worker complains that others are using his computer when he's away

THE SCENE

"Hey, look here," you overhear Ivan accusing your secretary, "I was out of the office for a couple of days and when I got back, I could tell you'd been snooping through my e-mail. You may think you can get away with that, but it's no different from opening my personal mail. Now, just stay away from my computer when I'm gone, or you'll be sorry."

"Hold it," Kiki replies. "My computer was out of commission for three days running last week—starting even before you left. So it shouldn't have been any surprise that I'd be looking for another machine to work on."

POSSIBLE CAUSES

Ivan is touchy about other employees using any of his work tools.

He has everything in his work area arranged "just so," and it disturbs his sense of order when other people use his office or equipment.

Ivan may have had a bad experience previously with Kiki's use of his work tools.

She may have lost files or left his office in disarray or divulged confidential information.

Ivan may have personal files on his computer that he doesn't want anyone else to see.

He might keep his tax records on his computer, notes from his girlfriend, or risque jokes his buddies send him.

YOUR RESPONSE

If Ivan is touchy about other employees using his work tools:

Talk to Ivan about his concerns. Explain how important it is that employees be able to share resources—especially when one worker's equipment is malfunctioning. Explore whether there's a way Ivan can "protect" the files or equipment he's most concerned about while allowing other employees access to what they need.

If Ivan is a team player, he'll understand the necessity of what you're requesting, even though it's at odds with his personal work style. And because Ivan is a good worker, you'll want to try to devise solutions that will give you the flexibility you need while respecting that work style. Perhaps you could agree that employees will use his office or equipment only after clearing it with you. You could agree to give Ivan as much advance notice as possible if someone else will be using his computer or other equipment so he can organize his desk and his files for the least disruption possible.

If Ivan isn't a team player and is adamant that no one else should be able to use "his" things, remind him that they're not "his" things, they're the company's. And look at the last response to this challenge for more information on privacy policies.

If Ivan's had a bad experience with Kiki's use of his work equipment in the past:

In this case, Ivan has a legitimate complaint, and your issues are more with Kiki than with Ivan. Reassure Ivan that you'll see that his work equipment is protected, but remind him of the necessity for employees to be able to share equipment from time to time. Then address the problem with Kiki.

Admonish Kiki that when she uses other employees' equipment or offices she should leave them in the same condition she found them. Make sure she understands that although she may have been in a bind with her continuing computer problems, you may have to deny her access to other employees' work areas if her use of their equipment damages their productivity.

Require her to check with you before using any other employee's equipment, and as a part of your permission, you should check the condition of the equipment both before and after Kiki uses it. That way, if you receive any complaints, you'll be able to determine whether or not they are legitimate.

This might also be a good time to see whether Kiki may have contributed to the problems she's having with her own computer. Talk to her about the malfunctions and what she thinks may have caused them. Look into a computer training course for Kiki that will help her to use her computer more effectively and teach her what computer matters she should leave to the experts.

If Ivan has personal files on his computer that he doesn't want any one else to see:

Communicate clearly to Ivan and the rest of your workgroup that employees have no expectation of privacy in their computer files. If you don't have a policy on computer privacy, adopt one. The policy should inform your employees that data on the company's computer systems is not protected and may be reviewed by the company's managers at any time and without warning. In the policy, you can reserve the right to monitor all e-mail, Internet use, and data transmission. You can also require that any passwords, user IDs, or other data protection information be kept on file with the company—either with your computer systems personnel or with you—so that the company can access any of the information on the computers.

Give Ivan and your other employees some reasonable period of time, maybe a week or two, to remove any personal or confidential files they wouldn't want anyone in the company to see. Then implement the new policy.

SOMETHING TO THINK ABOUT

Unless you tell your employees otherwise, they're likely to expect privacy in their offices, computers, and communications. In order to have adequate access to your employees' computer systems and data, you need to have policies in place that define just what privacy, if any, employees can expect and what the company considers its property. If you don't have those policies in place now, develop them. Your personnel department or legal counsel can help.

No. 94 Lewd E-mails

She complains about offensive e-mail from a coworker

THE SCENE

"Becky, I'm getting some really raw stuff in the office e-mail from Larry," Cheryl complains. "I wouldn't ask you to look at it because it's so disgusting, but I want it to stop. Does he think I'll be interested in him if he keeps sending me that trash?"

"Larry?!" you ask in surprise. Of all the members of your workgroup, Larry is the last person you could image sending lewd e-mails. But you know that appearances can be deceiving, and that your job is to prevent harassment no matter what form it takes.

"I'll take care of this immediately," you assure Cheryl.

POSSIBLE CAUSES

It really doesn't matter why Larry is sending material to Cheryl that she finds offensive. You need to stop it. Treat this as you would any other complaint of sexual harassment. The fact that it occurred on the computer doesn't make it any different from harassment that occurs in print, in person, or in any other medium.

YOUR RESPONSE

Whenever you have an allegation of sexual harassment:

The basic approach is the same, regardless of how the harassment occurred:

- First, investigate the allegation. Look at the material Larry has sent Cheryl. Is it really sexually offensive, or do you think Cheryl is overreacting? (You also need to verify that Larry has sent anything at all to Cheryl. At least initially, you can't discount the possibility that Cheryl is making unfounded allegations against Larry for some reason.) Make copies of the materials Larry sent to Cheryl. Find out from Cheryl whether she's shown the materials to anyone else or if she's confronted Larry about sending them.

- Let Cheryl know that you've taken her complaint seriously and that you intend to deal with the situation promptly.

- Make sure Larry stops. Whether you find the materials offensive or not, Cheryl does. In terms of your directions to Larry, it doesn't really matter whether other people would find the materials offensive. The fact that Cheryl does is reason enough to have Larry stop sending them. What if Larry refuses? Then you have two issues to address with Larry—insubordination and allegations of sexual harassment. Your safest move may be to let Larry go.

• Notify your boss, your personnel department, and your legal counsel of Cheryl's complaint. Follow whatever steps they direct.

• If you don't already have a sexual harassment policy in place, develop one. If you do have a policy, make sure it addresses computer and Internet issues. Again, your boss, your personnel department, and your legal counsel can help.

SOMETHING TO THINK ABOUT

The Internet and your company's internal networks offer a broad range of options for broadcasting messages to coworkers and outsiders. It didn't take long for pyramid schemes to pop up on the Internet; pornographic sites are legion; and the ease with which materials, both innocuous and offensive, can be sent to myriad recipients is staggering. If you've been lax in developing and disseminating policies for your company against discrimination and against sexual harassment, recognize that the potential for problems multiplies as each new communication tool is introduced.

Develop policies now, and be sure the policies address inappropriate usage of electronic communication tools. See that they're communicated to your entire workgroup. And enforce them conscientiously.

No. 95 Too Attached to Company Property

A terminating employee won't return the company's notebook computer

THE SCENE

"I've tried three times again today to get in touch with Adam," Natasha reports. "Either he's hardly ever at home or he's ducking my calls. And the certified letter I sent out last week has come back as unclaimed. I know perfectly well that *he* knows we're trying to get that computer back. Does he think we're just going to give up and go away . . . or that we've forgotten he was allowed to take it home with him?"

"Well, I haven't forgotten we loaned it to him," you reply. "And being allowed to keep the computer was not part of his resignation package!"

POSSIBLE CAUSES

Adam may not have any idea that you're trying to get your computer back.

He's been busy and didn't even think about the fact that it's sitting in his closet, or he may think it was his to keep.

Adam has no intention of returning the computer.

He knows it's not his, but he intends to keep it anyway. Maybe he thinks nobody will notice, or he may be angry about his treatment by the company. But for whatever reason, he's not planning to give it back.

> *Hint:* How you approach Adam in this instance, at least initially, depends a lot on the circumstances under which he left employment with your company. Did you part amicably or was he disgruntled when he left? It's also important to know what the company's past practice has been. Have other employees, especially any other employees Adam would know about, been permitted to keep the computers the company issued them? Even if the employees purchased the computers from the company at a discounted price, Adam may know only that the employees ended up keeping the computers, not that they paid for them.

YOUR RESPONSE

If you think Adam doesn't realize that you expect the computer to be returned:

Keep trying to get in touch with him. Leave messages on his home answering machine and send a letter or two by regular mail that can be held or forwarded if he's away from home.

Keep your tone cordial but clear. Let him know that the computer is company property and needs to be returned. Set a day by which you expect to have the computer back.

If past practice has been to allow employees to purchase the computers they've used, you can make the same offer to Adam. However, unless you have a standing agreement with your employees that they can purchase the computers, you don't have to make the offer to Adam. If you do allow the purchase, set a price and a deadline for response. Make it clear that you expect to see either the money or the computer by the date you've established.

If you conclude that Adam has no intention of returning the computer:

You may decide, based on the circumstances of Adam's resignation or his history with the company, that he knows quite well that he should return the computer. Or perhaps you've reached this conclusion after your repeated requests for its return have gone unanswered by Adam. In either case, your next step is to make a more firm demand for the return of the equipment.

Prepare a written demand letter. Don't accuse Adam of stealing the computer; don't impute motives to him; and don't threaten. Outline the conditions under which he was loaned the computer for his work, state clearly that the computer remains the property of the company, and require its return by a specified date.

If you don't receive a response to your demand, you may want to consider taking stronger action, perhaps even filing suit to recover the computer. You'll want to discuss your options with your boss and with your legal counsel.

And what about the computers, personal hand-held devices, cell phones, pagers, or other equipment of significant value that you've issued to the rest of your employees? How can you make sure that what's happened with Adam won't be repeated when you try to recover those items?

We can't guarantee that no other employee will ever try to keep equipment he's not supposed to have, but the following safeguards should minimize your risk:

- Whenever you issue an item of equipment, have the employee sign a receipt. The receipt should identify the equipment with a detailed description, including model and serial numbers. The receipt should also clearly state that the equipment remains the property of the company and must be returned upon demand.

- Give a copy of the signed receipt to the employee and keep a copy in your files. Now everyone knows what the rules are.

- As an added precaution, have employees sign receipts for equipment that's already in their possession. Ask everyone to bring in equipment they've been issued, and prepare receipts with the same detailed descriptions that you're using for newly issued items.

- Consider issuing a policy statement on company-issued equipment. Alert employees that anything the company gives them for their use remains company property. Include your policy on personal use of company equipment and, if you have a program for employee purchases, explain that as well. Give a copy to each of your employees, whether or not they currently have company equipment in their possession.

SOMETHING TO THINK ABOUT

A recurring recommendation we've made in this chapter is that you should develop policies regarding how the company intends to handle certain issues and inform employees of those policies *before* problems arise. Now you should consider pulling all of those policies together, along with descriptions of the company's goals, organization and structure, rules, benefit plans, and resources into a single employee handbook. There are many information sources you can use for guidance on developing handbooks for your staff. Look at several to decide whether an employee handbook would be helpful in your company.

No. 96 Tug of War Over Personal Use

An employee uses company property at home for his personal use

THE SCENE

"Nice poster," you observe as you walk past the bulletin board. "I see Steve's neighborhood association is having a rummage sale next weekend."

But wait! That type style and those graphics bear an uncanny resemblance to those promotional fliers we prepared for the launch of our new appraisal service. Steve took the laptop home to finish that design proposal a couple of nights ago; it looks as if he finished something else while he was at it. That's not supposed to happen. One thing they're firm about here is company property for company use—only.

POSSIBLE CAUSES

Steve may not be aware of company policy.

Especially if he's new to the company or if he just began taking the equipment home to work, he may not know what the rules are.

Steve may not agree with the rule.

He may have made a conscious decision to violate this company policy.

Steve may have a disregard for rules and restrictions in general.

This may not be an isolated incident, but Steve's usual mode of operation.

> *Hint:* As with any suspected violation of company rules, it's critical that you get the facts before you act. Is the software that Steve used commercially available? Might he have bought software identical to what you're using at work for his own use? Can you prove that Steve used company property? Especially if he made an honest mistake or if he made a conscious decision to break the rule, he may tell you. But you can't do anything until you know what the real situation is.

YOUR RESPONSE

If Steve isn't aware of company policy:

A word of instruction is probably the only action you need to take in this situation. Tell Steve what the company's rules are and, as clearly as you can, explain why the rules exist. If you have any authority to make exceptions to the rules, explain what the limits of your authority are and how Steve should request an exception.

You should also take this opportunity to make sure *everyone* in your unit knows what the company's policies are—on this and maybe one or two other things that people seem to have trouble remembering. The rules may not seem all that important to the employees who have to follow them, so a friendly reminder now and again doesn't hurt.

But don't make the mistake of issuing only the general reminder to the entire staff without talking to Steve individually. Steve clearly violated the policy, even though it was a policy he wasn't aware of. You can't be sure he'll get the message unless you deliver it personally.

If Steve doesn't agree with the rule:

Find out Steve's reasons for not following the company's policy. Explain the purpose of the rule and what it is intended to accomplish; listen to any ideas Steve has about how the same purpose could be accomplished differently. Let him know that you'll try to push for changes in those areas where his ideas show promise. (If your company has a formal suggestion program, encourage Steve to submit his ideas through that channel so he can get credit for them.)

At the same time you're listening to Steve's criticisms and recommendations for improving the current system, remind him of his obligations as an employee. Regardless of his opinions about company rules and policies, as an employee of the organization he's expected to follow directions first and then question them. Make sure he understands that refusal to obey a company rule or policy is insubordination and could have significant consequences for him.

If this is the first time Steve's failed to follow the rule, your warning and explanation are probably sufficient. However, if this is a behavior pattern for Steve, you'll need to take stronger corrective action. (See the next response.)

If Steve has a general disregard for rules and restrictions:

This is a serious problem. An organization without rules and limits suffers from disorganization and confuses and disturbs people—it doesn't "free" them from anything except a sense of purpose and order. If Steve does have a general disregard for rules and restrictions, chances are this isn't the first time he's exhibited it. You may even have warned or corrected him in the past for similar incidents. Your specific actions in this case depend considerably on his history with the company.

If this is the first time you've personally had to deal with Steve in this kind of incident, and if this offense is relatively minor, a warning is appropriate, preferably one documented in his employee records, either in your office or in the personnel department.

If this is not the first problem of its kind you've had with Steve, stronger measures are necessary, such as a formal write-up in his personnel file, or perhaps an even stronger approach if this has happened several times before and lesser remedies haven't corrected the misconduct.

SOMETHING TO THINK ABOUT

In any case where you have to warn or correct an employee (whether for failing to follow rules or for something else), it's crucial that you explain why you're taking the action. The purpose of discipline is almost always to correct behavior rather than to "punish" employees. Therefore, at the same time you impose a penalty, make sure the employee understands not only what he did wrong, but what you expect in the future.

CHAPTER TWELVE

Working Through
Your Own Issues

No. 97 NEGLECTING YOUR BOSS'S BUSINESS

**Your boss gets caught up in a problem you should
have warned him about**

THE SCENE

"You knew that Sam Wollenski was going to complain to the old man about
my trip to Rochester?!" your boss asks you angrily.

"Well," you stammer, "he did say something about taking it higher in the
organization. . ."

"And you didn't say anything to me?!"

"Uh. . . no."

"Why in the world didn't you. . . Oh, forget it. I don't want to hear anything more about it. Get back to work, and I'll talk to you later."

POSSIBLE CAUSES

You didn't think you needed to say anything to your boss.

After all, Sam didn't say for sure that he was going to talk to "the old man."

You meant to say something, but it slipped your mind.

Your boss can look out for himself.

You have problems of your own. You can't look out for him all the time.

Hint: Regardless of the cause, you are in hot water at least up to your eyebrows.

YOUR RESPONSE

If you didn't think you needed to say anything to your boss:

Did you think that Sam was just "blowing smoke," that he would cool down? Or did you not think it was that serious?

It doesn't matter. In case you haven't learned it, here is one of the fundamental commandments of organizational life:

No matter what else you do, always see that your boss knows about any matter that may affect him. Period. No exceptions. And doubly true if the "matter" is negative. Letting your boss be "blind-sided" by a problem you knew about is a major employee mortal sin.

There's a simple way to handle this. When your boss calms down, go see him. Tell him you goofed, that you should have picked up on Sam's comment and warned him. Don't make excuses; just apologize. Then promise him that it will never, ever happen again.

What if he's upset and yells at you? Let him. Again, don't make excuses. Do your best to direct his attention to the future—the future in which you won't ever let it happen again. With luck, he'll give you one more chance.

If you meant to say something, but it slipped your mind:

This is a first-class oops! There's no excuse for it, and you should offer none.

Follow the suggestions in the preceding response. Are you skilled at being abject? Good, because you'll need to show plenty of that.

But you have an additional problem. How do you make sure that you don't forget to warn your boss the next time you've got a clue and he doesn't? There are dozens of ways. You can stick a note on your desk or computer monitor; add an item to your "To Do" list, if you keep one; or use your electronic scheduler and memo pad—complete with alarms if you can. The important thing is to make sure that you find a way that works and just *do* it. Set up a system so that you never forget to warn your boss again. In this game, it's two strikes and you're out.

If you think your boss can look out for himself:

Bad misunderstanding! Apparently no one has taught you this first law of effective "subordinateship":

You have no responsibility greater than that of helping your boss be successful. None. Nada. Zip. Period.

Does this sound harsh and manipulative and scheming and otherwise unsavory? Stop and think a moment about what you expect from your employees. Don't you want them to help make you successful? Is there something wrong with that?

It really doesn't matter if you think there's something wrong with it—your boss probably doesn't. He just provided you with a useful learning experience. Take advantage of it.

When you talk with your boss, admit that you just didn't think. Tell him how much you've learned. Assure him that this failure was the "old" you, which he won't ever see again. Then make sure that you become and remain the "new" you.

SOMETHING TO THINK ABOUT

In many challenges we describe in this book, finding and using the right response is difficult. Not in this case. It's as simple as realizing you fouled up, admitting it, and then making absolutely, lead-pipe-cinch sure it never happens again. There, that was easy, wasn't it? (And, with luck, your boss will still speak to you.)

No. 98 Charges of Sexual Harassment

An employee accuses you of sexual harassment

THE SCENE

You answer what seems to be a routine telephone call from an employee. But instead you hear: "Mrs. Pierce, this is Bert Essmann from the EEO Office. I'd like to come over and talk to you tomorrow afternoon, if possible. Don Segali has filed a sexual harassment complaint against you."

Shocked and stunned, you replace the handset. What happens now?

POSSIBLE CAUSES

The specific cause of the sexual harassment charge isn't important here. There are only two possible conditions: Either you harassed Don Segali or you didn't.

A charge of sexual harassment is justified if you made unwanted overtures, either physical or verbal, to the employee making the complaint. It does not matter whether the actions or words were *intended* to have sexual overtones. What matters is that a reasonable person, objectively viewing the facts, would construe the actions or remarks as sexual in nature.

Likewise, confirmed sexual harassment does not require a superior-subordinate relationship. Although the situation is worse if you supervise Don, particularly if he alleges that you threatened to take or withhold actions based on his cooperation with you, the absence of such threats or of a supervisor subordinate relationship doesn't mean that sexual harassment hasn't occurred. Sexual harassment occurs whenever an employee is the object of unwanted overtures, regardless of the employment relationship between the employee and the person alleged to have harassed him or her.

So the first thing you need to do is find out the specific content of Don's complaint against you. As the person alleged to have harassed Don, you are entitled to know, specifically and in detail, what Don is alleging. You have a right to know not only what charge Don has made against you, but also what evidence he's offered in support of his charge. If he's cited specific incidents of harassing behavior, you have the right to find out the details of those incidents as he recounted them—names, dates, places, what happened.

Before you respond to any of Don's allegations, think carefully about what he's said. Did the incidents occur as he's described them? If not, in what respects do your recollections differ from his? If your recollections are essentially the same, do you see how Don could have interpreted the incidents as sexual harassment? What did you intend?

Only after you know what you're being accused of and have had some time to think over the situation can you respond appropriately to these *very* serious allegations.

> *Hint:* Specific procedures for dealing with sexual harassment complaints differ somewhat from organization to organization. Because sexual harassment charges, justified or unjustified, are so serious and potentially so damaging, one of the first things you'll want to find out is what specific rights to representation you may have before you answer any questions the investigator may pose.

If you have the right to be represented by an attorney or other representative, explain to the investigator or EEO counselor that you're very concerned about clearing up these allegations without damage to you or Don. Then defer answering any questions until your representative can be present. You need to protect yourself as much as you can. Even if you're completely innocent, you'll benefit from the assistance of an experienced representative.

YOUR RESPONSE

Because the circumstances under which sexual harassment charges arise differ so much, we can only provide you with general guidelines to dealing with them. Most important is that you talk to your representative about the specifics of your case and follow her advice. If you're not comfortable with the advice your representative gives you, get a second opinion, but don't strike out on your own. Sexual harassment charges, justified or not, have much greater potential for ruining you personally than any other category of discrimination charge. Our best advice is "Watch your step!"

Your representative will probably want you to address specifically and in detail each charge and incident the complainant has raised. Any documents you have that were prepared at the time the alleged harassment occurred that would support your recollection of events will be particularly helpful.

Wherever you can, identify other people who may have witnessed the specific incidents that Don alleges were sexual harassment. Even if no one was with you at the times Don claims you harassed him, you may be able to identify other employees who could make written statements about the general nature of your relationship with Don and with other men in the company that would help refute the charges.

You should *not* interview or discuss the situation with any of these witnesses personally. One of them could later claim that he or she was coerced into a particular position. It's much better if you provide the names to your representative or to an EEO investigator or counselor, describe the kind of information you expect the witnesses to provide, and then let someone else do the interviewing.

In addition, do not approach Don yourself to try to resolve the complaint. If Don has filed a sexual harassment charge against you, it's clear that the relationship with you is badly strained. You cannot trust that anything you say to him informally about his complaint won't end up as a reprisal charge later on.

Once you've helped your representative assemble your defense against the charges, there's not much you can do except to sit back and wait as calmly as you can. Sexual harassment charges are difficult to prove if there are no witnesses and no previous history of discriminatory or unethical behavior. In those cases, the final decision depends greatly on the credibility of the people involved. If you've been an open, honest, trustworthy person all along, you have a good chance of refuting the charges even if you don't have witnesses who can contradict Don's statements.

In the meantime, treat your employees as you always have—fairly, impartially, and objectively. You don't need to avoid Don, but you should exercise some prudence in how you talk to him (and where you talk to him). And what if, upon reflection, you decide that you did something that Don could reasonably interpret as sexual harassment? Let your representative know *right away*. Then follow the advice your representative gives you regarding how to make Don "whole" without ruining your own career.

SOMETHING TO THINK ABOUT

If you decide that you really did sexually harass Don, there are two decisions you should make *soon*.

The first is a private decision that you will never engage in that behavior again and that you'll be on your guard against behavior that, however well intentioned, could be interpreted as sexual harassment.

The second is a career decision: If you've been found to have sexually harassed Don, intentionally or unintentionally, it's going to be difficult for you to function effectively in the future as a manager in your current position. You need to begin to look around for a new position where you can put your past mistakes behind you and start fresh. No one who's worked with you in this situation is likely ever to trust you again. The stigma of sexual harassment is *that* powerful.

No. 99 Missing the Deadline

You dropped the ball on a major project

THE SCENE

"Millie, would you please see that Art Nomura gets this project summary?"

"The one for the general ledger update? Just a little late, aren't you?"

"Actually, it's less than six weeks behind. I think we'll have it up and running for real in another week or so. You know, that's not so bad for a project like this."

"Nomura isn't so nonchalant about it. When you told him you'd have it by two weeks ago without fail, he promised it to the comptroller by then. He's already been chewed out once—I'd try not to run into him for a year or so if I were you."

POSSIBLE CAUSES

One of your key programmers left you right in the middle of the project.

It took you more than six weeks to replace him.

There turned out to be more coding than you expected.

The old system was in worse shape than you thought.

Several key managers in the comptroller's office were late reviewing the preliminary outputs and getting them back to you.

They deserve part of the blame for the system being late.

You did your best, but too many small things went wrong.

No one could have anticipated the sheer number of glitches you had to deal with.

> ***Hints:*** None of the above matters. You promised to deliver a system by a certain date. Your boss relied on you and made a commitment to his peers. Now the date has come and gone and there's no system. You've embarrassed your boss, not to mention fouling up the comptroller's plans. The excuses don't matter.

Now, let's get to what does matter:

- *Your planning was unrealistic.* You counted on everything (or most things) going right, and they didn't.
- *You didn't control the project effectively.* Even if your planning was okay, your execution was faulty.
- *You didn't warn your boss in advance that the project was in trouble.* This might at least have saved your boss the worst of his embarrassment, and let the comptroller revise her plans.

YOUR RESPONSE

If your planning was unrealistic:

You'd better do a detailed "post mortem" quickly. What happened that you didn't anticipate? Where should you have known better? Where should you have built in some slack just on general principles? Did you get good input from the team of people who were assigned the work or did they (or you) just invent deadlines?

If you don't have clear answers to these questions, you'd better find some first-class training in effective project planning.

If you didn't control the project effectively:

If your planning was realistic (and perhaps even if it wasn't), you let something get away from you. When did the slippage begin? Did anyone realize what was happening? If so, did you listen when you were told there was a problem? And why wasn't it corrected? If not, how long did it slide before someone finally understood there was a problem? You'd better get the answers to these and similar questions in detail.

Again, it sounds as if you need some training in actual project management. It might be a good idea to find it and sign up for it as quickly as possible, preferably before you talk with Art.

If you didn't warn your boss in advance that the project was in trouble:

There's a lot we might say about this. Most of it is said in Challenge 97 in this chapter. Take a look at that challenge and the suggested responses.

No matter what the cause is:

The most serious problem is the impact of this on your relationship with Art. You've let him down *badly.*

If you don't realize how badly, let us help you understand. One of your most valuable assets as an employee—regardless of your level in the company hierarchy—is the absolute confidence of your boss. If your boss *knows* that he can count on you to produce what you promised, when you promised it, you're halfway home. If he doesn't know this—sorry, but you're not even on the team yet.

What approach should you assume when you approach Art? "Abject remorse" is one phrase that comes to mind. *Don't* even think of making excuses or offering explanations. You blew it, period.

What you need to do more than anything else is to direct Art's attention away from the past and toward the future—a much improved future. That's why it's important to analyze *why* and *how* the project failed, quickly and in detail. Then plan what you need to do to prevent that kind of failure ever again. (Your steps to prevent it should involve a significant amount of your personal time, not just on-the-clock time.) Get started on these steps right away. If you're lucky, you'll be on your way by the time you talk with Art. Then you can show him concretely what you've learned and how you're going to see that nothing like this ever happens again. Will it be enough? Who knows? We do know that nothing less is apt to help.

SOMETHING TO THINK ABOUT

Stop and think. Aren't your really valuable employees the ones to whom you can give a job and then never worry about it again? You assign the project and—unless they warn you in advance—they deliver what they promised. They're the people who make a manager's life bearable (and occasionally even satisfying).

Do you have something more important to do than to be this kind of person where your boss is concerned?

No. 100
YOU'VE BOUGHT THE HYPE, NOW WHAT?
You've taken over a supposedly well run unit that's actually on the verge of disintegration

THE SCENE

This is the third time this week you've found someone *almost* doing something incredibly stupid, but managed to stop it in time. First, John Bolling told the division chief's assistant there was "no way" he could get her the materials she needed for the CEO's conference on Wednesday. (Luckily the assistant complained to you first, rather than to her boss, so you could fix things up.)

Then, Gary Robinson deleted (but did not destroy!) most of his supply orders. So you had to have data processing down to "undelete" them.

Finally, yesterday afternoon Paula Stellman "lost" a shipment of hazardous chemicals on their way to disposal (which, fortunately, someone found in a hallway, just before the trash pickup came).

Those are just too many near misses, especially for what was supposed to be a "good" group.

POSSIBLE CAUSES

There may have been a lot of recent turnover in the unit.

The workers on whom the unit's good reputation was based may no longer work there, leaving you with a group of new people who don't know their jobs very well yet.

The group may have relied on the previous supervisor to keep things going.

Especially if the previous supervisor had a strong directive style and was technically very competent, she may have been the glue holding the whole operation together. The workers themselves may not be accustomed to being held responsible for their own work.

The unit's performance may have been deteriorating for quite a while.

The last supervisor got out just in time, leaving you to deal with the mess.

> **Hint:** Early on, you need to decide just how bad things are in your group. Are there just a few key players who are doing poorly, but whose performance affects the entire unit's production? Or is almost everyone doing worse than you'd like? Is there likely to be "mission failure" if you don't step in immediately? Is there likely to be some noticeable "mission failure" even if you start working the problem right now?
>
> If things are bad enough that you expect people outside the unit to begin noticing problems, then you need to let your boss know soon what you've found. This is delicate because you don't want to sound as if you're slamming your predecessor, or setting yourself up to look like a hero. But if there are likely to be complaints, your boss should hear about them from you first.

YOUR RESPONSE

If there has been a lot of recent turnover in the unit:

To some extent, time will cure many of the problems you're facing now. But there are some actions you can take to speed the process along.

Review your files and ask other employees in the unit to see if there are standard operating procedures for the jobs that have been filled recently. Read over the procedures yourself and ask experienced employees to look at them also to be sure that they're still current and that they reflect a reasonable way to do business. If the operating procedures are usable, they're a good starting point for your training efforts. You can go over them with the new workers. Make sure they understand what they're supposed to do and then have them use the operating procedures as job aids when they encounter situations they're not sure about. With any luck, the operating procedures you have in place will cover much of the day-to-day work of the unit.

Ask some of your more experienced workers to work with the new people for a while until they're more comfortable in their positions. The more experienced staff shouldn't plan to do the work for the new people, but should be prepared to "look over their shoulders" for a while—to review work and answer questions when unfamiliar situations arise.

If the turnover has been especially heavy, leaving you with few people who know the operation, you may be able to arrange to borrow a few workers from other units. You'll be looking for people who have previously worked in your unit and know the work well enough to be able to get your new group off on the right foot. If there aren't enough current employees who can help out, maybe a recent retiree would be willing to lend a hand. Ask to keep the additional workers for a few weeks, just long enough to get your new people started right, but not so long that they become dependent on the extra help.

If the group relied on the previous supervisor to keep things going:

You have a real challenge here, but one that can reap rewards if handled well. The key is to teach your staff how to accept delegation. This may not be pleasant at first. You'll be asking them to take responsibility for things they've never been personally accountable for in the past. But once they've tried it, most of them won't ever want to go back to the old way.

Sit down with your staff and talk to them about how your style differs from that of your predecessor. Without criticizing her style, explain what you see as the advantages to them and the unit of delegated responsibility. Stress the freedom they will have to run their portion of the process pretty much as they see fit once they've demonstrated to you their competence and willingness to accept responsibility.

The next step is just to jump in and do it. Begin by assigning specific tasks to individual workers. Agree on what you'll expect to see at the end of the assignment and when it will be due. Make a note on your calendar, and then *go away*. Don't initiate a contact with an employee again about the assignment until the day *after* it's due.

When employees come to you with questions about how they ought to do something, unless it clearly requires a policy or precedent-making decision, *do not answer them*. Respond with something like, "I'd have to think about that. How do *you* want to handle it?" You don't have to prove your technical competence. Your people know you know the work. They need to show you *they* know it. So resist the temptation to find answers for them. Their job is to come up with answers. Your job is to say "yes" or "no."

If you've explained your requirements clearly and stayed out of your employees' way as they've carried them out, they should begin very soon to deliver what you want. If not, a few repetitions of this assignment pattern, punctuated with reminders of your basic philosophy of delegation, should get the message across. What if repeated efforts don't result in a turnaround in your employees' willingness to accept responsibility for their own work and improvement in their products? You may need to talk to some of them about a career move—out of your unit.

If the unit's performance has been deteriorating for quite a while:

As we discussed in the problems dealing with individual poor performance, the longer performance problems go unattended, the harder it is to correct them. If performance has been deteriorating over a period of time and is just now reaching the critical point, you cannot afford to delay another day.

Although the situation is not quite as dire—yet—the responses presented in Challenge 18 outline the basic steps you need to follow in dealing with ongoing organizational performance problems.

SOMETHING TO THINK ABOUT

Sometimes greater responsibility is seen as a reward for employees' good performance. In this challenge, though, you'll note that we've suggested delegation of responsibility as a way to achieve better performance. Whenever you have a group that has the skills and experience to perform well but something is clearly getting in the way, consider that the problem may be you. Delegate progressively greater levels of responsibility to each employee, and you'll likely see your employees shine like stars.

No. 101 Telling Tall Tales

You lied to your boss about finishing a project and now she's found out about it

THE SCENE

"Sit down," Anne Menza, your boss, says. You sit. She is obviously mad, so you sit quietly, listening as she continues. "You told me that you had finished the material for Jack Lukas. He called me ten minutes ago and asked me where it was. First, tell me where it is, and don't lie to me again."

"I really have almost finished it. It'll be in his hands by noon, I promise."

"Why did you lie to me about having it done?"

"I really thought I'd have it done soon enough that I could give it to him. But something came up and. . . "

"Something came up, nothing! You lied to me! And I don't like having people around who lie to me. Now make damn sure Mr. Lukas gets what you promised." Your boss looks back at her papers, obviously done with you—for now. You hesitate a moment and leave.

POSSIBLE CAUSES

You're performing poorly.

The fact that you're performing poorly doesn't justify your lying to your boss (or to anyone). But you may have felt that you needed to cover for the poor performance.

You felt pressured and lied your way out of the situation.

Individuals tend to make promises they can't keep and even to lie about what they have done when they feel pressured to deliver something they don't believe they can deliver. You may have felt this way because your boss was pressuring you very hard to get Jack Lukas what he needed. So, to get her off your back, you promised what you knew you couldn't deliver and then tried to lie your way out when you didn't deliver.

You don't take your commitments seriously.

Apparently you're not reliable.

Hints: The three causes don't exclude each other. In fact, all three could be true.

If you were working for either of us, you'd be one step away from unemployment. Your boss probably sees the situation the same way. Act accordingly.

YOUR RESPONSE

No matter what the cause:

You lied to your boss. You have a few hours to persuade her that this will never, ever happen again. If you fail to do that. . . well, you can figure out for yourself what will happen.

The three causes are listed to help you understand your own behavior. If you understand it and can explain to your boss why you lied *and how you will correct things so that you won't lie again,* you may keep your job. Just remember: The causes aren't excuses. They're conditions that you can change—that you will commit yourself to change—so you won't be tempted to lie again. Use them as such.

Don't even think of making excuses or trying to justify what you did. That's guaranteed not to work. Simply admit that you lied and that it was completely wrong. Your boss will almost certainly ask you if you've lied to her before. If you have, come completely clean about that too. Your only real chance is to own up to everything and then convince your boss that you can and will change.

If you're performing poorly:

When you and your boss consider your situation, you need to deal first with the fact that you lied and resolve that. Poor performance is no reason for lying, nor will promising to cure one cure the other. First you need to deal with the lying, then with the performance.

When you get to the performance, what do you do? You ask your boss to go over your performance and point out any deficiencies she's noted. Then you need to go over your performance, being even harder on yourself, until you're sure you understand just what you're doing (or not doing) and why.

Then make a clear improvement plan. Depending on your boss's preferences and your relationship with her, you may want to ask her to help. Remember, though, that the responsibility is totally yours (you can be sure she'll remember). Work out the plan, put some realistic milestones on it, and give it to her. Then do exactly what you say you'll do. (For more on this, see the last response to this challenge.)

If you felt pressured and tried to lie your way out of the situation:

Of course, this doesn't justify the lying either, but it may be something that needs to be dealt with when the truthfulness issue has been resolved. Do you believe that your boss puts too much pressure on you? Discuss it with her. Be specific about some of the consequences of the pressure.

Your boss may pressure you because she believes that otherwise she won't get an appropriate amount of work out of you. How do you reassure her on that? She may believe you're unreliable; if so, look at the next section. Perhaps the problem's mostly with your response to the situation rather than the situation itself—in which case you might want to go to some stress-management training and learn how to handle the pressure.

What you do need to learn, no matter what, is to not make commitments unless you're sure you can keep them. And that takes us to the next response.

If you don't take your commitments seriously:

This may be the key to the whole situation. If you want people to trust you and believe that you are dependable, you need to do two things. First, you make every commitment with the full intention that you will keep it exactly as you made it. Second, you either keep the commitment or renegotiate it *well in advance of the due date*. That's all you have to do, and it's something everyone is capable of doing.

Clearly, however, you haven't been doing it. Just as clearly, you need to start doing it immediately. Here's how:

- Whenever someone asks you for a commitment, or you volunteer one, think carefully before you make it. Can you realistically keep it? If so, by all means make it and then keep it. But what if you can't keep it? Then don't make it. If your boss or someone else is pressuring you to make it, resist the pressure and ask for the person's help. Explain that you don't want to make a commitment you can't keep.

- As hard as it may seem, and no matter how great the pressure, don't make a commitment you don't believe you can keep—ever. If you have to, say something like "Okay, I'll agree that we'll do this by August 15th. But I don't believe we can. What are you going to say when I come to you on August 15th and tell you we need another ten days?"

- If someone wants a commitment you don't believe you can make, be as specific as possible about why you can't meet it. Go into detail if you have to. Use past records. Do whatever will help negotiate a reasonable deadline.
- Once you negotiate the commitment, keep it. If you can't? Well, that should happen only if something occurred that you couldn't reasonably anticipate. Renegotiate the commitment immediately. Don't ever wait until just before it's due and then announce you can't produce. Negotiate the change as soon as you can and make as small a change as possible from the original schedule.

This may sound terribly difficult for you now. Nevertheless, you certainly have ample reason to practice it. As you begin to make and keep your commitments, you'll find that it gets easier and easier. In part, this happens because people now see you're serious about keeping commitments so they're willing to trust you more. It's a virtuous circle.

SOMETHING TO THINK ABOUT

Nothing justifies dishonesty between individuals who need to work together and trust each other. This is simply one of those things that needs not to happen, and to be dealt with quickly and firmly if it does.

Your own employees will never understand that lying is absolutely forbidden unless you set the example. You need to do so in order for your boss to trust you and give you some independence. You need to do so in order for your workgroup to be clear that you expect the same from them. And you need to do so in all your other job relationships.

Keeping commitments, making your word your bond, is only slightly less important. (Promising to deliver something and then not delivering it is essentially a form of lying itself.) If you insist on both in yourself and in your workgroup, and try to get the same from your boss, you will have taken a giant step toward building a successful workgroup with a great reputation.

No. 102 Who's In Charge Around Here?

You often can't answer your boss's questions about work status

THE SCENE

"What's this I hear about your group having been asked to do some follow-on work on the Petersen project?" your boss asks after the staff meeting.

"I'm not sure," you reply. "I'll have to find out more about it."

"You mean you don't know what's going on in your own section? From what I hear, and it's all over the building, you've got a couple of real stars on that project. How could you not know what they're doing?"

POSSIBLE CAUSES

Your boss may want to know more details than you would normally be expected to keep up with.

Especially if she came from the area that you now supervise, and if she had a number of years of experience there, she may be interested in more of the guts of the operation. And especially if your technical strengths are *not* in that area, this puts you in a real bind.

Your people may not keep you informed about what's going on in their assignments.

They may be accustomed to working independently and seldom think to tell you about things unless there's a problem brewing.

You may be a "hands off" manager who doesn't want to know details.

> **Hint:** How much do you *really* need to know about what's going on in your workgroup?
>
> In general, you need to know enough to make reasonable work assignments (both kinds of work and amount of work each of your employees are currently assigned), to review work for overall quality and adequacy, to solve problems that arise, and to appropriately correct and reward your employees for their performance.

But, above and beyond that, how much you really need to know about the details is however much your boss is likely to want to know. Much of what your boss thinks of your performance as a manager is going to be based on two criteria: the feedback she gets from other sources (whether those are statistical reports or input from customers and other managers) and the reliability of what you tell her about what's going on in your group. If she ever gets the impression that you don't know as much as she thinks you should about your group's work, you have a real image problem with your boss.

YOUR RESPONSE

If your boss wants to know more details than you would normally expect:

Now you know. After a couple of episodes like the one we just described, you should have a pretty clear idea of the kinds of things your boss is going to want to know about your workgroup. Maybe she has a favorite area she always asks about (such as if she used to handle workers' compensation cases and asks periodically what the latest court decisions have said). Or maybe she wants you to know the exact status of each project in your section, rather than just that they're "on target."

But whatever her level of interest is, you should have a good idea fairly quickly what it is she's looking for.

Then learn enough about the details of those areas that you can answer most of the questions she's likely to pose. If your boss is particularly interested in an area where you don't have much technical expertise, sit down with the senior worker in that area and get some tutoring. Don't get in the habit of sending your boss herself to that worker for information, though. You'll just reinforce her impression that you don't know enough about what's going on. But what if you're still stumped occasionally? It's probably not a problem if you don't know the answers only once in a while. Most managers realize that the reason you have a staff is so you can delegate the nitty-gritty work to them. And if your boss has a keen interest in one or two projects, so that she wants to know everything that's going on in them, you can sometimes take your senior worker along with you to give her periodic status updates.

What does all this probing do to your staff's morale? Especially if you've empowered them to run the project themselves? This can be a bit more tricky. So far, your boss hasn't asked you to *do* anything different; she just wants to *know* more details than you've been able to provide. Explain her interest to your staff and let them know that you'll try, by providing her all the information she could possibly want, to keep your boss' actual involvement in the accomplishment of the project to a minimum. If she gets enough information to reassure her that the project is running smoothly, she's less likely to want to intervene, and after a while she may even stop asking so many questions.

If your staff isn't keeping you informed:

As we discussed in Challenge 4, both traditionally managed and empowered work groups are still responsible for keeping their managers informed about what's going on in their projects. Look at Challenges 1 and 4 for ideas about how to manage your delegation of authority to ensure that you get the information you need from your group.

If you have a "hands off" management style:

In Challenge 103, we refer to the "if you don't hear anything, everything's okay" performance standard. Is that how you manage your workgroup? If so, then you really don't have enough information to manage well. Not only will your boss be disappointed that you can't answer her questions, unless you have an exceptionally talented and motivated group of people, you're also likely to have performance problems in your group.

We've already outlined what you need to know to manage effectively: You need to be able to assign work, considering the skills and current assignments of your people. You need to be able to evaluate the adequacy of the work that your section produces. You need to be able to solve problems. And you need to be able to shape your workers' performance by rewarding and correcting them appropriately.

Do you know everything that everyone in your section is working on? Do you know whether everyone is fully occupied and whether anyone is truly overloaded? Do you know how they're doing with their milestones or whether production is at the level it needs to be? Do you know what the error rate is for production work, and whether there are certain kinds of errors that seem to occur over and over again? Do you know what your customers, internal or external, think of the work your group produces? Have you seen work samples lately? Have you looked at copies of project reports or analyses your group has prepared recently?

If you can't answer "yes" to most—if not all—of these questions, then you're operating as a "hands-off" manager. Even if your group is empowered to make decisions for itself, you have a continuing responsibility to ensure that the work is being accomplished according to the company's standards and expectations. And if you don't know, you're not managing.

SOMETHING TO THINK ABOUT

How much involvement is enough involvement is a tougher question than it used to be. But remember the distinction we mentioned earlier between *knowing* something and *doing* something. You can probably never *know* too much about what's going on. It's easy to *do* too much, to meddle with a team that's already functioning efficiently and throw it out of whack. It takes real self-discipline for most managers who are in that position at least in part because they were good problem-solvers to know what's going on and yet not pitch in to "help" with the work. Resist the temptation. Knowing when to get involved and when to hold back is a lot of what makes the difference between an ineffective manager and a good one.

No. 103 You're Out of the Loop

You never find out how your workgroup is doing unless you get into trouble

THE SCENE

"But I thought you and everybody else was happy with the way we were processing the high-value claims," you sputter.

"Whatever gave you that idea?" Jim Chen, your boss, replies.

"We haven't heard a word from you or from anyone else that anything was wrong. We thought we'd have the worst ones done this week and be handling them on a routine basis by the end of next week."

"Well, you can forget that. I have a list of problems longer than my arm with the last dozen you've done. I can't understand why you'd think this was okay!"

You end the conversation as quickly as possible and call a meeting of your workgroup. You might be upset, but it is nothing compared to the way they are going to react.

POSSIBLE CAUSES

The organization uses the "if you don't hear anything, everything's okay" as the basic performance standard.

The oldest and most pervasive performance standard in the book. Also the worst.

Your boss doesn't understand the importance of good feedback.

He may be so used to "no news is good news" that he never thinks of anything else.

Your workgroup doesn't attempt to get feedback from its customers.

Have they been assuming that they know what their customers want without asking? Always a very dangerous way to go about things.

You didn't negotiate standards for your work before you started the project.

If you knew you wouldn't get feedback, why didn't you at least talk to higher management or the customer or someone and try to define what successful performance by your workgroup would look like?

> *Hint:* Not only *may* any and all of the four causes be involved, but all four of them probably are.

YOUR RESPONSE

If the organization uses the "if you don't hear anything, everything's okay" as the basic performance standard:

Does this sound familiar? It's how most organizations seem to run. And now you're realizing how poor this standard really is.

What do you do about it? In terms of changing the organization, not much. However, if you take each of the next three responses seriously and follow the suggestions with them, you'll do a great deal to help the situation.

If your boss doesn't understand the importance of good feed-back:

You start working on him today. You make it clear to him that you want every scrap of information on how your group might be falling short and you want it as soon as he gets it. You don't want him to "let things slide" in hopes the problem will go away. You want to hear it, you want to hear it without having him sugarcoat it, and you will listen to it and respond to it.

Now, make sure you mean it when you say you will "respond to" any concerns. Bear in mind that "respond to" doesn't mean "agree with," and it certainly doesn't mean "argue with" or "get defensive about." It means listen to the problem or complaint, understand it as fully as possible, and then do what's reasonable about it. If someone misunderstood something, clarify. If the person's expectations were wrong, help the person develop the right expectations. If you really did fall short, fix things as quickly as possible. That's what it means to respond.

When your boss passes on a negative observation to you, demonstrate responsiveness to the problem. Then demonstrate responsiveness to your boss. Report back on what you and the workgroup did. See if your boss is satisfied with your response. If not, find out what it takes and do it.

What does all this accomplish? It gives you great credibility with your boss, and it convinces him that you really mean it when you say you want feedback. And that will probably change everything, particularly if you couple it with the suggestions in the next response.

If your workgroup doesn't attempt to get feedback from its customers:

Time to change that, particularly if neither the organization nor your boss is concerned about good feedback. First of all, find out who your customers are. In this situation, who cares about how high-value claims are processed? There may be several units that care, and all of them may have different concerns. (It's simpler if you have only one customer, but don't be surprised if there are several.)

Then get organized to talk with your customers. In this case, you have a list of problems. You and a few members of your workgroup set the list in front of a customer and ask for more information on the problems. Do this with each customer. (If possible, take different workgroup members so that each one has at least one opportunity to participate in a customer visit.) Listen and take notes. Agree to respond by a specific date.

Then do what makes sense. If you need to change what your workgroup is doing, change. If you need to educate your customers, do that. Respond to every comment and respond in such a way that the customer can see that you're responding.

Be prepared: This may be frustrating. You may have to go back and rework what you've done, though you can also try to negotiate changing future products, if that makes sense. But do it. In the long run, your efforts will be rewarded, because the changes you make will save you work, make you more effective, and make your customers far happier.

If you didn't negotiate standards for your work before you started the project:

Many workgroups never think of this, but that doesn't make it right. Feedback is most effective when you know what the standards are. It's a lot easier to respond to "You said you'd pay no more than 75 percent on the dollar" than to "Look, I think we're paying too much."

This doesn't mean that you can necessarily negotiate very specific standards. In many cases, you can't. But you can get the best standards possible up front, and then you can improve on them as you get feedback. For instance, a starting standard might be "We expect you to negotiate every claim down." That gives your workgroup a guideline. Then you get the feedback: "You're not negotiating them far enough down." This gives you a chance to work on a new standard, which may turn out to be "Negotiate no more than 80 percent on the dollar unless there are special circumstances."

That's more concrete, and future discussion may help define "special circumstances."

Get the feel? Negotiate expectations going in, then get feedback against these expectations. It isn't a precise process. It may be sloppy. But, boy, does it beat any other reasonable alternative.

SOMETHING TO THINK ABOUT

Now that you've learned all this about getting feedback, apply it to your relationships with your workgroup. Has your guiding principle been "If I don't gripe at you everything's okay?" Stop. Have you been letting your workgroup get by without feedback from customers? Stop. Have you been letting them start projects with no agreement on the standard for a successful result? Stop.

Take every suggestion in this case and apply it within your workgroup. Give objective, straightforward feedback to all the members of your workgroup. If anyone would rather do without the feedback, tough break. Give it anyway, then discuss why the employee may be resisting it. Expect equally honest feedback from the workgroup on your performance and don't become defensive when you get it.

CHAPTER THIRTEEN

Getting It Right with Your Boss

No. 104 A Set-up for Failure?

He assigns you a high-priority project that you have no one capable of working on

THE SCENE

"But Rasheed, I don't have anyone who can do this."

"Then train someone to do it, or hire someone—just get it taken care of! Everyone else is overloaded, so yours is the only unit I can give it to. You have three weeks to get it done, and I want it done well. Any more questions?"

You shake your head, turning toward the door. No one in your organization has any experience at this, and there's not enough time even if someone did. It's going to be a disaster!

POSSIBLE CAUSES

Your boss has tremendous confidence in you and your unit.

As difficult as the project seems, it's a show of confidence in you that he gave it to you.

He's thinks your unit isn't as busy as some others.

He's not happy with your unit's level of productivity and believes you have more time than anyone else to devote to this project.

321

He is desperate.

Your unit is the best alternative he has.

> *Hint:* Worry about *why* your boss did it second. First, worry about how you're going to get it done successfully.

YOUR RESPONSE

No matter what your boss's reasons are, you need to make sure the job gets completed successfully. Here are some ideas:

Check first with each of your employees. Perhaps one or two of them actually know something about the project you've been given. You may be able to get it done with your own people. If you can, free them to concentrate on it.

Does another manager have someone qualified that you could borrow? Here's where the time you spend developing good relationships with other managers pays off. Perhaps a manager owes you a favor she can repay this way. If not, make it clear that if you can borrow one of her workers, you know you'll owe her one.

If no one in the organization can handle the project, can you hire someone temporarily to do it? This may not be as farfetched as it sounds; a tremendous range of talent is available for temporary work. If the person needs organizational knowledge, can you assign one of your employees to work with him and furnish this knowledge?

None of these will work? What can a team of your employees—perhaps with you as part of it—accomplish? Clearly, this will stretch all of you. You'll probably have to work nights and weekends. Look on it as a challenge, and make sure that your employees know that no matter what your boss's motive was, successfully completing the project in-house will be a real victory. (If you complete it successfully in-house, reward your people lavishly for their efforts. They'll have earned the reward.)

If he did it because he has tremendous confidence in you and your unit:

No matter how you complete the project, finishing it successfully will justify your boss's confidence in you.

There's another side to this. If you keep completing "impossible" projects, your boss may conclude that you and your unit can do *anything*. That's a great reputation to have—just make sure you and your employees are prepared to live up to it.

If he thinks your unit has plenty of time to work on the project, and other units don't:

Why would he think this? Maybe it's true. Perhaps, even though you think your unit is overloaded, it's really not carrying as great a burden as others. If that's the case, you'll just have to grin and bear it.

What if your unit is just as busy as the others? Why wouldn't your boss know this? Perhaps he hasn't seen evidence of your production—no regular reports of your progress, or no feedback from customers that would indicate what a good job you're doing. If this is the situation, you'll need to concentrate in the future on keeping him better informed about what your unit has accomplished.

But whether your boss's perception is accurate or not, you need to complete this project successfully and on time. Look at the ideas above on how to arrange that first. Concentrate on exceeding his expectations on this project, and then address the differences in your perceptions of your unit's workload.

If he simply is desperate:

Here's your chance to show that you can indeed come through for him. No one warms a manager's heart more than someone he can depend on in a real crisis. Use this occasion to demonstrate that he can always depend on you and your people.

SOMETHING TO THINK ABOUT

We've said it before and we'll say it again: One of your primary jobs as a good manager is to help your boss be successful. Even though you have to rearrange your own unit's priorities to meet his, do it.

No matter the reason your boss came to you in this crisis, it presents a real opportunity if you approach it properly. Certainly it's going to be difficult, perhaps almost impossible. Don't let that defeat you. Make up your mind to succeed, no matter what—and then succeed.

No. 105 A Bad Rap on Performance

She gives you a performance rating far lower than you think you deserve

THE SCENE

"But, Carmen, this is the lowest rating I've ever gotten," you say to your boss in dismay.

"I expected that you wouldn't like it, but it's the rating I'm giving you. If your performance improves, I'll be happy to give you a higher one next year."

There's obviously nothing you can do to change her mind. You pick up the paper and head for the door wondering what to do now.

POSSIBLE CAUSES

Your boss has been directed to give lower ratings this year.

Organizations often decide that ratings are too high in general, so they direct managers to give lower ratings to everyone.

Only a certain percentage of the ratings she gives can be good ratings.

Your performance wasn't that bad, but it wasn't as good as that of several others who're getting the higher ratings.

She's setting you up to get rid of you.

If you have a poor rating, this will be easier for her.

Your performance really was that bad.

There's nothing wrong with the rating. Perhaps it's even a little generous.

> **Hint:** These aren't four equally likely causes. The fourth one is probably the right one. You need to look at the other three first, though, to make sure you don't waste effort unnecessarily.

YOUR RESPONSE

If she's been directed to give lower ratings this year:

This requires some real sensitivity on your part. She may feel that it would be disloyal to the company to tell you this. She may also feel embarrassed that she had her authority limited. No matter what, she may not tell you what the situation is.

One way to find out whether this is the case is to ask her how you could have gotten a better rating. If she answers the question in great detail, you can be fairly sure that she developed the rating herself. If she's vague or evasive, she may be following a mandate from higher management.

If you conclude that this is the reason for the poor rating, let the matter drop. Accept the poor rating and then just do the best job you can. (You can take comfort in knowing that your performance really was okay and that this is just a bad break.)

If only a certain percentage of the ratings she gives can be good:

This is a lot like the situation above. The difference is that your boss has been told that only a certain *percentage* of her ratings can be high; the others have to be average or even lower. This happens often in organizations that believe that ratings should follow a "normal" distribution.

If this is the situation, there's no point in fighting the rating this year. Just make sure that your performance improves to the point that next year you'll get one of the high ratings. (You can console yourself with the same thought as in the situation before this one: Your performance really was better than your rating.)

If she's setting you up to get rid of you:

You're in a serious predicament, and you need to make a sound decision concerning what to do about it.

If your boss really doesn't want you in this job, there's not a lot of point in fighting her. See if you can't negotiate a mutually acceptable way to arrange your departure. Perhaps she can help you transfer to another unit or give you time off each week to do job hunting and then give you good references. In other words, if nothing you can do will make her want you in the job, don't try to hang on. Negotiate the best solution you can, then get a job somewhere they want you.

What if you don't want to leave, and you think you're being treated unfairly? The first step to take is to have a frank discussion with Carmen. Why does she want to get rid of you? Is there something you can do to change the situation? Keep in mind that the higher Carmen is in the organization, the less likely you'll be able to change the situation. And if she's the owner of the company? Go back to the preceding paragraph.

If you decide that you can't look for another job and Carmen sticks by the rating, you need to fight it however your company permits. It will help if you've not only done a good job but can *show* that you've done it. This is a risky course, but if you succeed you may prevent Carmen from doing anything like it again.

If your performance really was that bad:

As we suggested above, this is the most probable cause. You may not think your performance was that bad, but your boss does. Your task now is to perform effectively this year and make sure that your boss is aware of it.

Begin by finding out how your performance fell short. This is a perfectly proper question to ask your boss, as long as you're honest about it and not defensive. If she tells you, *don't argue with her.* If you believe she's wrong, leave it alone for now. Your present goal is to find out what she thinks.

Suppose your boss won't tell you what you need to do to improve? That's certainly not helpful, but it may happen. Accept it, and then see if someone else can give you useful information. Perhaps her secretary or assistant knows what Carmen expects from you and can tell you. Another manager who works for her or with her may be able to give you suggestions. If you know her boss and can't get information any other way, you might very discreetly see if he can find out for you. It doesn't matter whom you talk to, as long as you get accurate information.

Once you've found out what's wrong, correct it. If you really were performing well but she didn't realize it, do whatever you must to see that she realizes it this year. What if you weren't performing as well as you should? You know what to do about that. (Using this book and others like it throughout the year may help you improve significantly.)

What if you and your boss disagree on just *what* you should be doing or *how* you should be doing it? Start by answering this question: What's at stake here? If there's a principle or a matter of vital interest to you, it may be worth the disagreement and the low rating. Otherwise, it seems best to do what she wants done the way she wants it done.

Suppose you have a vital interest and you need to stand firm against your boss' expectations. Suppose she wants to reduce your authority or limit your freedom to make decisions. This is the time to have an honest discussion with her about your concerns. Perhaps you misunderstand her intent. Perhaps she didn't realize what's troubling you and is willing to change. Perhaps you can work out an alternative together. At the least, you'll have the matter out in the open, where you may be able to resolve it at some time in the future.

SOMETHING TO THINK ABOUT

Different managers have different perceptions about what constitutes good managerial performance. One manager may have a very hands-on approach and expect her subordinates to manage similarly; another manager may manage by exception and consider that more intensive involvement by her subordinates is a waste of their time. When the manager you report to changes, take time early in your relationship with your new manager to find out what she's looking for in your performance. You can do this by having a frank discussion with her as well as by your observation of her management style. Determine what her management style is and how well she's likely to tolerate differences in style among her subordinates. An early understanding of her expectations will reduce friction in the future.

No. 106 FEELING NEGLECTED

He gives a major new project that should have been yours to another unit

THE SCENE

You slam down the quarterly status report in disbelief. Sajni Naryan is working on the performance support enhancement that *you* suggested to your boss six months ago. Who does she think she is, taking over *your* project? But, then, she didn't do this on her own. Bud Jarvis, your boss, must have given her the assignment. Sajni isn't the sort of manager who builds her own empire by stealing from others. So why didn't Bud give the project to you? And what can you do about it now?

POSSIBLE CAUSES

Your boss may have had to make a decision between two close functions.

There may not have been any intention to keep you out of the project. Your functions and Sajni's just happen to overlap in this area, and Bud made a choice to go with her.

Your boss may believe that Sajni's group will do a better job.

In this case there *was* a conscious decision not to give the project to you. You've got a problem.

> ***Hint:*** Turf battles are seldom productive. You will probably never, by sheer strength of personality, be able to convince another manager (or your mutual superiors) that an assignment properly belongs to you. So fighting it out isn't usually a useful response to your boss's assignment of a project to another section. The way you get functions—and keep them—is by *demonstrating* that you can do the work, satisfy your customers, and meet your boss's needs better than anyone else can.

YOUR RESPONSE

If your function and Sajni's overlap in this area:

Talk to Sajni to let her know you're interested in the project and to offer her your assistance. Make it clear to her that you're not trying to take over. It's an area in which you're interested, and you'd like to do what you can to help her out.

Assuming that Sajni trusts you and accepts your offer at face value, give her whatever assistance she needs. In the course of this project, meet with her to work out specifically what the two of you believe are the limits of your respective organizations. Put your agreements in writing so there's less chance in the future that Sajni gets a project that should have been yours (or vice versa). If your company has a formal organization and functions manual, draft changes to that too. Then go, and have Sajni go with you, to your boss to present your proposal for splitting up the work.

Perhaps there are legitimate reasons for having two units assigned basically the same functions. (Maybe there's more work of the nature your units perform than can efficiently be handled under one supervisor.) In that case, you can't split the functions, but you'll still want to talk with Sajni to develop a mutual understanding that you'll work in tandem as much as possible—not in competition with one another.

After you and Sajni have come to a common understanding about how your units should interact, bring your boss into the conversation too. Let him know that you both prefer to work cooperatively rather than competitively. Suggest that at least some major projects be assigned to your units jointly and that you and Sajni will then assemble a team of employees from both units to work on them. That way both units will have the benefit, and ownership, of whatever good ideas are developed.

If your boss believes that Sajni's group will do a better job:

Your real problem isn't the project that got away. It's your poor performance record. You'll need to do some soul-searching about the causes for your boss's low opinion of your group. And once you know *why* your boss thinks less of your group than he does of Sajni's, fix it.

See Chapter 3 for ideas on organizational performance improvement, and Chapters 5 and 6 for help with various aspects of individual performance improvement.

Your boss is sending you a clear message here about his lack of confidence in you and your organization. Listen to it. For whatever reason, there have been times when you've failed to produce as well as he'd like. The only way you'll get the projects you want in the future is to show him *now* that you can perform.

SOMETHING TO THINK ABOUT

It's possible that it wasn't your boss who decided that the project should go to Sajni's group rather than yours. Maybe someone higher in the organization decided the question for him. Maybe a customer specifically requested that Sajni work on the project (or that you *not* work on it!). While the source of the decision differs, the root causes are the same as those described in the second cause and response above.

It's also possible that your boss gave Sajni the assignment because it's a high-visibility project and he's grooming her for advancement in the company. That's good for Sajni and too bad for you, but the question still remains: Why is he grooming *her* for advancement and not you? Maybe because of the low level of confidence he has in you and your unit? Sound familiar? See the second cause and response again.

In either case, there's no substitute for good performance. The best way to get the projects and recognition you want is to produce excellent results on the assignments you do get. That's what you expect of your employees and it's what your boss expects of you.

No. 107 Confusing Commands

She gives you vague assignments

THE SCENE

You walk out of your boss's office shaking your head in puzzlement. After 20 minutes of listening to her expound, you're still not sure what she wants. It could be anything from a marketing strategy to a technical report—all you know for sure is that it's something written and it's something about the new mutual fund accounts. But what? And by when? More and more often, your assignments come like the plots of a detective novel, a clue at a time and sometimes too late to prevent another fatality.

POSSIBLE CAUSES

Your boss may not know what she wants.

She may be thinking aloud and relying on you to put substance into her ideas. But even if she doesn't know exactly what she wants, she'll know it when she sees it, and she'll know it when she doesn't!

Your boss may have received the assignment from a superior, and maybe she's not sure what the assignment is.

The instructions she received may have been even less clear than the ones she's given you. She's added as much substance as she can, but basically you're both flying blind.

She may not be able to articulate her ideas clearly.

She may know *exactly* what she wants, but she's not good at conveying those ideas to you for execution.

> *Hint:* Sometimes, being a good subordinate means being a good mind reader. That's nothing unique to managers. You may have run across the same problem even before you were a manager. The difference is that back then, if you misinterpreted your boss's assignments, you were the only one whose labors were wasted. Now, if you misinterpret your boss's assignments, your whole unit may waste time on unproductive efforts.

YOUR RESPONSE

If your boss doesn't know what she wants:

If you can pull it off without making your boss impatient with you, ask her for the details she *can* provide about what she's looking for. Perhaps she's seen a product similar to the one she wants you to develop, or perhaps she knows of someone in another organization who's worked on something similar. Be careful about pressing for details, though. Your boss has probably told you as much as she knows of what she's looking for. Your pushing for more information than she has available is likely to embarrass her—and certain to irritate her.

Talk to other people whom you trust in the company about how they've handled similar situations. What kinds of things are usually important to your boss? Substance? Presentation format or style? Orientation to a specific audience? Then try to gear your products to those things you've identified as usually being important.

As soon as you have a concept and approach roughed out, go back to your boss for confirmation of the direction you're taking. Listen carefully to her criticisms. She may still not know exactly what she's looking for, but her initial reactions will tell you something about the things that strike her most forcefully. Then try again, and again, and again—until you get it right.

Don't be discouraged by this lack of specific direction. Things are going to be tough for a while, and you may begin to believe you can't *ever* please your boss. But little by little, you'll begin to get a feel for what she's looking for.

If your boss received vague instructions from her superiors:

As above, try to work out as many details with your boss as you can. Focus on the objective and goals of the assignment and on its intended audience. If there are people you know and trust in the company who've done work for the manager who's ultimately going to receive your products, consult with them for advice and hints on how to proceed.

Review company reports and formats to see how top management is used to seeing information presented. Look particularly at those portions of annual reports or publications that relate to the subjects you're dealing with. Model your product after the published items you've found.

Try to arrange to accompany your boss when she presents your proposals and drafts to her superiors. That way you can get first-hand feedback on how your product measures up to expectations.

You should also rely on your boss's advice as you proceed. *She's* the one higher-level management tasked with this assignment. You're the vehicle for getting it done. But if what you produce isn't what they want, she'll look just as bad as you do. So this is one time where it's clearly in your boss' best interest to help you succeed.

If your boss can't articulate her ideas clearly:

This situation is a little trickier than the first two, because in this case your boss *does* know what she wants and probably thinks you should too, because she's explained it to you. Chances are very good that she doesn't realize that she communicates poorly.

If your boss is someone with whom you have an open and trusting relationship, you can tell her directly that you don't know what she's asking for. Then make pointed inquiries until you get what you need.

If you don't trust your boss enough to be able to admit your confusion, go to trusted coworkers for advice. They'll probably know what your boss usually expects and accepts. What you've been asked for may be a routine report or product that you can easily put together—once you know what it is. For the long term, listen carefully as your boss gives assignments to *other* managers. Then talk to them about what they developed in response to the assignments. In time, you'll have picked up enough clues about what your boss's instructions mean to be able to interpret them accurately.

SOMETHING TO THINK ABOUT

Whenever you're having a communication problem with another person, whether it's your boss, a coworker, or someone who works for you, you should at least consider that the problem may be yours—not the other person's. Perhaps you're not asking the right questions. Or maybe you're filtering what you hear through your own view of things so that you can't see the other person's point of view. Particularly if there seem to be *lots* of people with whom you have communication difficulties, consider it a strong possibility that the weakness is in your listening skills, not others' communication skills. Look for training you can take on listening skills. Then take it and practice what you've learned.

No. 108 The Instigator

He keeps pitting you against another workgroup you need to work closely with

THE SCENE

"Well, this is the third month in a row that Andretta's workgroup has out-produced yours. What do you have to say for yourself?" Your boss, Frank D'Arecca, is visibly upset. This is the fourth time in the last two months that he's called you in to talk about your production compared to several others.

You try to reason with him. "I keep telling you, Frank, we just can't be competing with them. We rely on them too heavily, and the moment they think we're out to beat them they're going to make life really difficult for us. If you want us to compete, I can tell you about a couple of other workgroups we'd be glad to compete with. But we need to leave Andretta's group alone."

"No way! If you're not willing to get out there and compete with them, I'll find someone who will. Now you go back and think it over and come back in here tomorrow and tell me how you're going to beat them next month."

POSSIBLE CAUSES

Your boss is competing with Andretta's manager for a promotion.

He believes that if his workgroups maintain a higher productive rate than the other manager's workgroups he'll have a better chance at the promotion.

Your boss is naturally competitive.

No matter what situation he's in, he'll try to find someone to compete with.

There is an opportunity for healthy competition between work-groups.

Not all competition among workgroups that also have to cooperate with one another has to be destructive.

YOUR RESPONSE

If your boss is competing with another manager for a promotion:

No matter how conscientious your boss is, if he thinks he can influence his chances for promotion, he will probably do so. He has a powerful reason for looking better than his competitors for the job.

You cannot ignore this situation. Look carefully at the suggestions in the third response to see if you can set up a healthy competition with the other workgroup, remembering that Andretta's boss may be pushing that workgroup to produce for the same reason your boss is.

Suppose that healthy competition won't work. What then? You need to figure out the least harmful way to compete. Your planning will be easier if you have an idea when the job your boss wants will be filled. Are you going to have to compete for a month or two, or for no one knows how long? That makes a difference, perhaps a big difference, in what you do.

Do you know Andretta and can you work with him? Talk with him. See if he's in the same situation you are. Perhaps the two workgroups can engage in out-and-out competition if you and he meet regularly to ensure that events aren't getting out of hand. Try to find any way that will let each of you compete with the other that won't destroy the cooperation you need from each other.

If your boss is naturally competitive:

How is this different? Your boss isn't looking for a specific payoff (a promotion) from the competition. He just thinks he will get higher productivity from your workgroup if you're competing with Andretta.

Again, look at the next response for possible ideas. But also take a different tack at the same time. Schedule a meeting with your boss. Set the stage by assuring him that you want to give him what he wants. Then find out, in as much detail as possible, why he thinks your workgroup should be competing with Andretta's.

Is there some flexibility, despite his rejection of your offer to compete with other workgroups? Explore it. Identify the other workgroups and suggest why competing with them would be a good idea. Perhaps you and the managers of those workgroups can negotiate effective competition that won't interfere with necessary cooperation.

If there isn't flexibility, then lay out for your boss the disadvantages of competing with Andretta's workgroup. Perhaps you're dependent on his group for data or material, and it can disrupt your operations by delaying either. Or maybe you have to work together on certain projects that require skills from both your workgroups. Don't sound as if you're making excuses; present the case strongly but objectively. Then if he says, "Compete," you compete. (But when the harmful effects of the competition start showing up, you'll probably want to make sure he knows about them.)

If there is an opportunity for healthy competition between workgroups:

Even when workgroups must cooperate with one another, there may be some room for healthy competition. How do you find and define this room? Here are some suggestions:

- The two workgroups must agree that neither will do anything to make the other look bad. Without this basic confidence, the competition will become harmful in a hurry. Let each team do its best and win or lose on its own merits.

- The two workgroups must define as clearly as possible where they will compete and where they will not. In general, whenever one workgroup is a supplier or customer for the other, or reviews the other's work or performs in a similar role, competition needs to be strictly prohibited. In general, the more that either workgroup performs one of these roles vis-á-vis the other, the harder it will be to keep the results of competition from overflowing into the relationship.

- The two workgroup managers or other representatives must agree to meet regularly, to meet quickly if either thinks the other is breaking an agreement. Even very minor events can begin to erode trust rapidly if they're not brought out in the open, discussed, and resolved. Conversely, even what would be major problems can be resolved if they are caught and dealt with quickly enough and with good will on both sides.

SOMETHING TO THINK ABOUT

Over and over, we stress that your first job is to enable your employees to be successful because they get the work of the unit done, and that your second job is to contribute to your boss's success. Often you can accomplish the two of them together, often but not always. What do you do then?

Of course, the best answer is that you work very hard to find a solution that accomplishes both goals, allowing both your employees and your boss to come out as winners. Don't take this one lightly; with a reasonable amount of work and imagination, you often can find a solution that works for everyone.

What about situations where that isn't possible? Stop and ask yourself if you're really sure what your boss wants won't work, or if you're just not used to doing things that way. Your boss may be right, and you may be objecting just from habit. Don't ever do that. If you're going to disagree with your boss, make sure you've examined yourself and your response, thought the matter over, and decided that it's worth it.

No. 109 Job Insecurity
She's talking about abolishing your job

THE SCENE

"Don, could you come in here a minute," calls Josephine. "I've been looking over all these charts for the proposed reorganization, and the only one that seems to make sense to me is this one right here. But, see, it requires that your unit be split up between these other two sections. Gary would take one, and Georgia would take the other. I might be able to reassign you to a staff position. But when I'm getting so much pressure to flatten the organization, keeping your unit separate is just a lot of wasted overhead."

POSSIBLE CAUSES

Your boss may believe that the work will be accomplished more efficiently elsewhere.

She may have decided that the current organizational structure doesn't meet the company's real needs. Your job doesn't fit in.

The company may be faced with serious cutbacks.

Your job may be one of several that is being abolished. The restructuring that affects your unit may also affect your specific job.

Your boss may not be satisfied with the way you're doing the work.

If she doesn't want to confront you about your failure to meet her performance expectations, she can sidestep the issue by abolishing your job. That gets you out of the way, but without unpleasant confrontations.

> ***Hint:*** This situation looks extremely serious at first glance—and maybe it is. But the fact that your job is being abolished doesn't necessarily mean that you're going with it. Before you panic, take time to find out what's really going on. If your boss considers you a valuable employee, she'll do her best to find you another job in the company.

YOUR RESPONSE

If your boss believes that the work will be accomplished more efficiently elsewhere:

Talk to her about how the new organizational structure will work. What kinds of supervisory jobs will be available? Which ones could you be a serious candidate for? Which ones would you like to work in?

Make your bid for the jobs that you'd like under the new structure. Talk to your boss about your qualifications for the work and point out the strengths in your management style that have made you successful in your current job. (Your boss will know those already, but it doesn't hurt to do a little self-promotion right now.)

Whatever job you're assigned, accept it gracefully. If it's something you don't want, you're still free to look elsewhere. But it's a lot easier to find a job when you have a job. And by doing good work wherever you are, you'll get a better reference from your boss when you find a position you like better.

What if there is no position for you in the new structure? It may be because there just isn't enough money to support it. If there are five managers in your section and only four supervisory jobs in the new structure, someone's going to be left out. You need to find out why it's you. Do the workers who were placed have greater seniority? Are you not qualified for any of the new managerial openings? If you are qualified and have comparable seniority, what makes you a less desirable selection than your peers?

If there are sound reasons for your not getting one of the available jobs that aren't within your control (like qualifications or seniority), your situation is the same as for any other cutbacks. See the next response.

If the problem is your performance or your ability to work comfortably with your boss, the problem is much more serious. Not only are you out of a job, but you're not likely to get much help from her in finding another job. See the third response to this challenge.

If your company is coping with serious cutbacks:

Take comfort in the fact that there isn't anything "personal" about the situation. Lots of managers go through this. That doesn't find you a new job, but it does relieve you of any guilt you may feel.

Ask about outplacement services your company offers to help displaced workers find new employment. Talk to someone in your company's human resources department about your entitlements upon separation (such as severance pay, pay for unused sick days or vacation time, early retirement buy-outs available). Do some financial planning, with a professional consultant perhaps, to figure out how you could get by without your salary for a while.

Make a systematic plan for finding a new job. Identify commercial placement services if your company doesn't have out-placement help available or to increase your chances of finding a job quickly. Rely on friends and business acquaintances to help you find openings for which you can apply. Use the network you established during your employment to help you now in pending unemployment.

Don't panic! If potential employers think you're desperate, they're much less likely to consider you seriously. They'll figure you're going to take *anything* now just to get a job, and that you're likely to jump ship as soon as something better comes along. Stay calm, and plan your strategy. With a little planning, you may come out of this with an even better job than you left (honest!).

If your boss isn't satisfied with your performance:

It may be too late to save yourself, but it's worth one last try.

Talk to your boss about what she wants and expects and about what she isn't getting. Challenge 107 in this chapter has ideas on how to find out what your boss wants when she isn't clear in telling you. Then give it to her. Ask for feedback on how you're doing and what you could do to improve. Let your boss know you're serious about doing better work, and she may hold off on the decision to abolish your job until you've had a chance to prove yourself.

If you don't think you can meet your boss's requirements, or if she's not willing to give you another chance, it's better to quit than to be fired, because it will be easier to find a new job without the "black mark" of a previous firing on your record. Use the ideas in the preceding response to find a new job. Then resolve to perform better in your new organization.

SOMETHING TO THINK ABOUT

It's scary to think about being out of work, whether it's your fault or not. Even in these days of two-income households, many families rely on both incomes just to break even. Loss of one income may mean financial disaster. But it's important to realize that *no* job is absolutely secure. So it's best to plan ahead for financial setbacks. The six-month rule still applies. (Save at least the equivalent of six months' salary for a "rainy day.") And with the help of a financial consultant, there are even more things you can do to make your family more secure. You may not be able to avoid a decline in your standard of living, but with a little prior planning you can avert financial disaster.

No. 110 Insecure Boss

He thinks you're out for his job

THE SCENE

" . . . . and, furthermore, I intend to stay in this job until I retire or someone promotes me. You'll just have to wait until then to get it. If you want a promotion that bad, go find a job with a supervisor who's easier to fool!"

You stumble out of your boss's office, dumbfounded. Twenty minutes ago you made what you thought was an exceptionally good presentation to the corporate staff. You thought your boss would be proud of you; instead, he was furious—because he thinks that you did it as another step to get his job.

POSSIBLE CAUSES

You've been presenting yourself so that it makes you look good and your boss look bad.

He's drawn the logical conclusion that you want to get him out of his job and yourself into it.

You're innocent of the charges your boss is making; what you're guilty of is not paying any attention to how you're making him look.

Not quite as serious, but still bad.

You keep trying to make him look good, but he distrusts you.

No matter how hard you try, it always ends up this way.

> *Hint:* We've mentioned this before, but it bears repeating. One of your fundamental jobs is to make your boss look good. It doesn't matter what you think of him or how he reacts to your efforts; doing it is extremely important for your long-term success.

YOUR RESPONSE

If you've been presenting yourself so that it makes you look good and your boss look bad:

Oh, no. *You* couldn't be doing this. Before you jump to that conclusion, make an honest review of the matter. Do you talk to other managers so that it sounds as if you're succeeding *despite* your boss? When you make presentations, does the same message come through? How do you *feel* about your boss? (Scorn and arrogance show through pretty clearly, no matter how diplomatic you think your demeanor is.) Are there other ways you imply that you'd be even more effective if it weren't for him?

If there are, then stop. Stop now!

How you feel about your boss's competence is your own affair, but what you convey about your feelings to others isn't. He may get in your way, veto your best ideas, drive you crazy with nitpicking. That's your burden to bear, and it can be a heavy one, but it's not one you can share with the world in general.

Loyalty to one's boss is a fundamental rule of the organizational world. It may seem feudal, even dishonest. No matter, it's still the rule. You don't have to give him phony credit or flatter him, but it won't hurt to let him share the credit you get and to build him up. Who knows, if you start treating him like an effective, supportive boss he may begin to become one.

If you're innocent of the charges your boss is making, but guilty of his not paying any attention to how you're making him look:

All of the thoughts on loyalty in the previous response apply here. Presumably, you already knew how important loyalty is. You just forgot for a while.

Now it's time to concentrate on it again. Demonstrate loyalty clearly, but don't overdo it. The last thing you want is for your boss to think you're insincere about it. Make subtle changes in the way you present yourself and your work. Include him quietly but positively in the credit. Start slowly, then build on it until it becomes automatic.

Depending on the relationship between the two of you, it might also be appropriate to apologize to your boss for having created the misleading impression. If the relationship is at all strong an apology is proper.

If you keep trying to make him look good, but he distrusts you:

This is tough, so approach it carefully. Be as sensitive as possible. Are there particular times and/or situations that seem to reinforce his distrust? Can you modify what happens so that it's less threatening to him? Keep working on the problem; a number of small changes may start to turn him around.

You also need to have another concern: Is he undermining you? If he believes you're after his job, he may try to undercut you in the organization. Loyalty works both ways. If you give it, you have every right to expect it.

Is it possible to have a frank discussion with him? If you can, you might be able to negotiate the loyalty each of you expects from the other. That would certainly be desirable from both of your points of view.

SOMETHING TO THINK ABOUT

It's sometimes tempting to try to "show up" your boss, even to try to get his job. It may work, but it's dangerous. The manager who puts you in your boss's job is even likely to distrust you; after all, if you were disloyal once, won't you be disloyal again? Disloyalty is an almost sure way to trade short-term career success for long-run career stagnation.

The other side of that is the danger in working for a boss who doesn't show you loyalty. If that's the situation you're in, you may not have much job security, and what you have may be up for grabs every time he gets mad at you. Evaluate your situation carefully, and consider a job change. Although it may be disruptive, it might be the best step you could take to achieve your long-term career objectives.

No. 111 OVERLY INVOLVED BOSS

He "micro-manages" you and won't delegate any work of real significance

THE SCENE

"I just wondered how things were going on that Sylvestri case," Carl says as you walk into his office. "Have you had Lois look into those precedents I told you about? And have you been making Toni record all the time she's spent on the phone for this one? What about those statistics I gave you to review? Oh, and one other thing; let me look at that letter to the PrestoSync people before you send it out. Anything else you wanted to discuss?"

Not really, you're tempted to reply—just wondering what I have to do to get to run my own unit! But instead, you depart with a smiling, "No, sir" and go off to do Carl's bidding while the things *you* know need to get done sit for another day.

POSSIBLE CAUSES

Carl may have come up through your unit and still identifies with it.

This is a common problem. You know by now that supervisors tend to get very attached to the organizations they run. It's hard to relinquish control, even after being promoted to a higher-level job.

Carl may think that he's operating the way a manager should.

He may be reacting to the abuse of delegation he's seen by being too "hands-on."

Carl may not think you're doing a very good job managing by yourself.

This is another case where he perceives you as a poor performer.

> **Hint:** Although this is a difficult situation and *may* reflect Carl's dissatisfaction with your performance, it's much more likely that this is just the way Carl operates. Thats doesn't make it any easier for you to manage around him, but it should reassure you that Carl's probably not out to get you. You just have a difference of opinion about management style.

YOUR RESPONSE

If Carl came up through your unit and still identifies with it:

You have two tasks facing you: Convince Carl that you can do a good job running "his" unit (recognizing, of course, that you'll never match his achievements) and wean him away from the substantive work in the unit.

Begin by letting Carl know in advance every move you plan to make, before he has to ask. You're not asking his *permission* to take specific actions; you're letting him know because you are aware of his interest. Gradually begin to let him know about some less important items after the decision's been made and the action taken. Continue to discuss many items with Carl in advance, but offer to "take care of the details" so he won't have to be bothered. As time goes on, you should be handling more and more of the "details" without consulting Carl first. Let him know when your efforts are particularly successful—tactfully, so he doesn't feel that you're outshining his performance in the same job.

In order to achieve full delegation for running your unit, you will probably need to divert Carl's attention with other matters. (This is known as "managing your boss.") Bring problems to him that properly belong in his sphere—organizational issues, administrative matters, questions of interrelationships among units or with outside organizations. If you can keep him busy with these "big picture" issues (many of which will *never* be solved), he won't have time to meddle in the affairs of your unit.

If he still insists on getting involved to any appreciable degree in the substance of your work, try to limit his participation to specific areas. Maybe there's a cross-functional project team he'd like to head. Maybe there's a pet area he'd like to do some basic research in (research that you may or may not have a need for later). You should be able to channel his interests into areas that aren't an integral part of your unit's work.

What if he still insists on "micro-managing" your assignments? He's still the boss, and if he has the time and energy to do his job and yours too, there's probably not much you can do about it. You could make a tactful suggestion that he not work so hard, and leave more of the "grunt" work to you, but if he wants to get involved, you really can't stop him. Decide whether you can operate comfortably in that environment and, if not, start looking around for something better.

If Carl believes that he's operating the way a manager should:

Recognize that Carl's instincts aren't altogether bad. There are a lot of "high flyers" who are more interested in getting ahead and making themselves look good than in producing something of real value. Carl's "hands-on" approach shows he has a sincere interest in the good of the organization, and he's to be commended for that. At the same time, he's doing the job you're paid to do, and that makes your job even harder.

Much of what we said in the first response about convincing your boss that you can do a good job with the unit applies here too. Gradually assume more of the details of running the organization, at the same time that you direct Carl's attention to issues that are more properly handled at his level.

How well do you and Carl get along? Does he trust you? If you think he won't be threatened by the conversation, talk to Carl about his management style. Point out the extra burdens it places on him to do two managers' jobs and the difficult position you're in by not being allowed to make your own decisions. That little talk, coupled with your demonstration of your competence and willingness to attend to detail, may convince Carl to delegate more.

As above, the final decision about how much to delegate is Carl's. If he's not comfortable giving you greater freedom, it's a situation you'll have to learn to live with, or find another situation elsewhere.

If Carl doesn't think you're doing a very good job managing by yourself:

If Carl has reason to feel this way, your job is to prove to him that you can, and will, do much better. We've talked elsewhere about ways to demonstrate improved performance to your boss. See Challenges 105, 106, 109, and 110 in this chapter for ideas.

Changing Carl's mind is going to take some time. You can't just promise to do better and expect that you'll suddenly have full delegation. You'll need to demonstrate by continuing good performance that you can handle the job. You've already done something to raise questions in Carl's mind about your abilities. You need now to reearn his confidence.

SOMETHING TO THINK ABOUT

One of the real classics of management literature discusses this problem of delegation at great length. It addresses both ways you can use delegation to increase your leverage as a manager and techniques you can use to obtain greater freedom and delegation from your own supervisor. *Managing Management Time* by William Oncken is a "must" for any supervisor who wants to increase her effectiveness without increasing her toil.

No. 112 OBSTRUCTIVE BOSS

He refuses to support your decisions when they're unpopular

THE SCENE

"Now, Madeline, I know you mean well. I'd like to see your people produce more, too. But it's just not wise to fight over an extra 10 or 15 minutes at lunch. You can encourage them to get back on time, that's certainly okay with me. Writing them up for it, though, or docking their pay—that's just going too far. I want you to go back and tell Scott you've reconsidered and you're going to pull the warning out of his personnel file. I think everybody'll be happier that way."

It happened again! This is the third time *this month* that he's made you back down from an action because it was unpopular. How in the world does he expect you to maintain discipline and productivity if he undercuts you like this?

POSSIBLE CAUSES

Your boss believes that you rely too heavily on negative supervision.

He wants to see you develop more positive ways of motivating your employees.

He doesn't like to make employees angry.

For whatever reason, he believes that this isn't an effective way to handle them.

He doesn't want your unit to cause him any problems.

From his point of view, he has enough to worry about without your adding to it.

> ***Hint:*** One of the facts of organizational life is that your boss's managerial style puts limits on what you can do. If you push these limits too forcefully, he may lose confidence in you. The limits may be frustrating, but you can't avoid them if you want to keep his confidence. The challenge is to modify your style just enough that he's comfortable with it, while still dealing effectively with your unit.

YOUR RESPONSE

If he believes that you rely too heavily on negative supervision:

Look carefully at this alternative. If you think it may be the case, talk with him about it. You may have been leaning too heavily on "showing them who's boss" or "shaping them up." Ask your boss to suggest alternatives; then think them through carefully. Try them out and see what happens.

At the worst, you'll learn some new ways to supervise. They may not work in the current situation, but they might be just the ticket another time. At the best, you'll find they really do make your job easier.

We all prefer to handle situations in familiar ways. Unfortunately, the preference can all too quickly become a rut. Regardless of your boss's style, it's an excellent idea to try new ways of handling situations every so often. It keeps you flexible and growing.

If he doesn't like to make employees angry:

There might be any of several reasons for this. He may believe that you lose more from the anger than it's worth. He may need employees to like him. He may see himself as a kind person who doesn't upset anyone.

It doesn't matter why he reacts this way. If he doesn't want employees angry, you need to find ways to supervise effectively without making them angry enough to complain to him.

We don't have the space to talk at length about positive ways of supervising. Here are a few brief ideas.

- Make sure that employees get rewarded for doing good work, and not otherwise. Use praise lavishly for a job well done; spend a minimum amount of time criticizing poor work.

- Give clear assignments with clear standards for successful completion. That will be enough for most employees to do a good job. When one of them doesn't, provide objective criticism based on the standards.

- Be a leader. We know—that sounds hackneyed. It's not. A leader sets goals and gets employee commitment to work toward the goals. A really effective leader does this *with* his people; and his goals become everyone's goals.

- Above all—and this is hackneyed, too, but relevant—set the right example. Everything else you do is more effective if your employees see that you believe it enough to live it yourself.

If he doesn't want your unit to cause him any problems:

Some managers believe that they shouldn't have to handle problems from subordinate units. If a problem reaches them, they believe that the supervisor of that unit fouled up somewhere. Conversely, if no problems come to them, they believe that their subordinate managers must be supervising effectively.

If that's how your boss operates, work to make sure no problems concerning your unit trouble him. It's difficult. At the same time, it gives you the opportunity for real freedom in managing your unit. If you can keep problems out of his office, you can manage pretty much as you want. How often do you get a better deal than that?

The suggestions in the preceding response are applicable here as well. You also need to let your employees know discreetly that they'll be in big trouble if they complain to your boss before they've talked to you. That will give you the chance to take care of problems that arise (which, of course, you'll do).

SOMETHING TO THINK ABOUT

You can't build effective supervision around the idea that you'll never make employees angry. On the other hand, if you *consistently* make them angry you'll never have a really effective unit. What's the answer? Your management style should not make employees angry often; when it does, the issue should be an important one. However, the goal isn't to keep employees from being angry; the goal is to manage so that they do their jobs without the kind of intervention from you that makes them angry. That's good management.

No. 113 An Irksome Friendship

She's a good friend of one of your hard-to-manage employees

THE SCENE

You enter Jeanette Grimsley's office apprehensively and take a seat, wondering what kettle of hot water you've fallen into this time.

"Jon," she begins, "I've been hearing complaints that you're picking on Harold Schweibeck. Is there something wrong with the way he's doing his work?"

You knew this was coming. Jeanette and Harold have been friends since long before you came to this company. But Harold's been a problem for as long as you've been in the company too. And his continual bragging that "you can't touch me" makes it hard to demand anything of anybody else in the unit. But this is the first time Jeanette has actually confronted you about your attempts to tame Harold, and you're not sure whose side she's on.

POSSIBLE CAUSES

The question here isn't *why* Jeanette and Harold are such good friends (although knowing the answer *may* help you to view Harold in a somewhat different light). The real question is how you can get Jeanette to back your attempts to manage Harold without damaging her own relationship with him.

> ***Hint:*** A little empathy on your part will make it easier to understand this situation. Jeanette is in a difficult position. She's caught between the demands of the workplace and the expectations of the personal friendship she has with Harold. Unless things are orchestrated very carefully, she's going to lose on one side or the other. Either the work of your unit will suffer, or her relationship with Harold will suffer. Because the latter is likely to cause her more personal pain, it's not hard to see how she'll choose, is it?

YOUR RESPONSE

Regardless of the reason for the friendship between Jeanette and Harold, you still have a job to do. These suggestions may help you make things more palatable to Jeanette:

Make sure Jeanette knows exactly what problems you're having with Harold and how they affect your unit's ability to do the work. She may know Harold primarily from a social perspective. And if no one's complained to her before (with hard facts to back them up), she may not know what the problems are. Her attempts to protect Harold may spring from her lack of knowledge rather than a conscious decision to sacrifice your unit's productivity for the sake of her friendship with Harold.

In explaining the problems you have with Harold, focus on the impact they have on productivity and morale in your unit. Make it clear that these are not just differences of style or personality conflicts; they're problems that affect the unit's bottom line.

Suggest ways of dealing with Harold that won't require Jeanette's direct involvement. If you agree to take the heat from Harold while Jeanette takes the part of the sympathetic listener, she may be more willing to let you deal with the problem. Many managers have a stated policy of requiring their subordinates to deal with issues at their level without intervention. If Jeanette makes it clear to Harold that her involvement would violate a policy that she has already established, he may not blame her personally for all the "nasty" things you're doing to him.

If you can't gracefully arrange for Jeanette to remain uninvolved, you might suggest that Harold be reassigned to another unit that's not under her supervision. That would allow his new manager to deal with his problems without intervention and would take Jeanette entirely out of the line of supervision. The company could work out the problems with Harold, but Jeanette's friendship with him would remain intact.

What if Jeanette doesn't *want* to be uninvolved? What if protecting Harold, even at the expense of the company, is *exactly* what she's trying to do?

In that case, there's not much you can do about the situation except put up with it. If Harold's behavior or performance is intolerable, you might consider going over Jeanette's head. But you should weigh the consequences first. She will certainly be dismayed at your lack of personal loyalty to her and may remember it during later key events—like appraisal time, or when the next promotion comes up, or when unpleasant assignments have to be handed out. If she's angry enough, she may even try to get rid of you.

If it's Harold's performance that's at issue, there are probably some things you can do to minimize the damage he causes that won't upset him or Jeanette. Remove him from critical assignments; give him special projects to work on that will have high visibility with Jeanette, but with few other people. He may not do you much good in those assignments, but he won't do you as much harm either.

If it's Harold's conduct that's the problem, you need to evaluate just how bad his behavior is. Has he alienated key customers or suppliers? Is there potential harm to his own or others' safety or well being? In those cases, the problem is important enough to bring to the fore. Keeping on Jeanette's good side is *not* more important than the safety of your workers.

You may still be able to take some action without specifically involving Jeanette or openly ignoring her directions to you. Can you arrange for one of the other managers in the company, preferably at Jeanette's level or above, to observe Harold in action and put pressure on you, through her, to resolve the problem? If Jeanette sees that others are unhappy with Harold, particularly others who have influence over her, she may see the political necessity of dealing with the problem regardless of her social relationship.

If Harold's behavior is not intolerable, just annoying, do what you can to minimize its ill effects and put up with him as best you can. Your job isn't only to produce for the company, it's also to keep your boss happy whenever you can. So look on this as just part of the day's work.

SOMETHING TO THINK ABOUT

One of the advantages of a small company is the solidarity and "family" feeling that are easily fostered among managers and employees. One of the disadvantages is that those feelings frequently lead to friendships that extend beyond the office and can complicate management. In a larger organization, such friendships still develop, but when they do, there are more options. You can move people around to avoid potential conflicts of interest without damaging either person's career or opportunities for advancement. If personal relationships get in the way of company management more often than you'd like, maybe you're in the wrong environment. But if you like the feeling of being "part of the family," you should recognize that such conflicts are a price you may occasionally have to pay.

No. 114 INVISIBLE MANAGER SYNDROME

She bypasses you to your workgroup

THE SCENE

"Beatrice, why aren't you out in the bindery? You know that we have to get the pageant brochures out today."

"Oh, no—first we have to get the 1000 Club certificates printed."

"What ever gave you that idea?"

"Eleanor Schultz. She came by about an hour ago and told me to switch over to the certificates."

"Okay. Go ahead." You turn away, swearing under your breath. Once again, Eleanor has gone straight to your people instead of telling you what she wants done. It's a wonder that any of them pay any attention to you any more!

POSSIBLE CAUSES

Eleanor doesn't believe you relay her instructions accurately.

She's concluded that the only way your people are going to get the right directions is for her to give the directions to them personally.

You're often not around, so she's given up trying to find you to tell you.

It's easier just to go directly to your staff and tell them what to do.

She doesn't realize how disruptive what she's doing is.

She's not used to being a second-level manager.

She still thinks in terms of managing employees directly.

> ***Hint:*** This circumstance may reflect a broader lack of confidence in you. Keep that in the back of your mind while you're dealing with the specific problem. If your boss does lack confidence in you, that's by far the more serious problem.

YOUR RESPONSE

No matter what the cause is:

Instruct your people that if Eleanor or anyone else in higher management gives them instructions they're to tell you as soon as possible. They're to do what they're told, but they're to see that you know about it quickly. That way, you can at least keep up with what's going on. You won't be surprised when they're doing something different from what you told them to do.

Try to talk with Eleanor about the situation. See if you can find out why she bypasses you and how she looks at it. Remember that your primary objective is to listen; you can defend your position in a later conversation.

If she doesn't believe you relay her instructions accurately:

This one may take some work, but the solution is easy. It's probably best not to approach it head-on. Try to intercept Eleanor, so that it's awkward for her not to give you the instructions. Then listen carefully, repeat the instructions back to her, and make sure you understand them exactly. Then pass them on exactly. If you do it right, she'll begin to get the message and start dealing with your people through you.

You should also look at the reasons why you weren't getting the instructions right before. Did you get defensive if she seemed to be critical of you? Did you listen haphazardly, so that you got things confused? Just why did it happen? Is it happening in other situations, with other people?

Not listening carefully and fully is one of the worst habits a manager—or anyone—can have. If it's a habit you have, take advantage of this situation to rid yourself of it completely.

If you're often not around, so she's given up trying to find you to tell you:

She may have started off wanting to give instructions through you, but because you're often not there when she needs you, Eleanor's gotten in the habit of going directly to your employees. It saves her time and frustration.

The simplest solution, if it's practical in your situation, is to have an employee who generally takes over when you're gone. Ask your boss to deal directly with him if you're not around, and have him pass instructions on to the staff and let you know about them when you return.

If this isn't acceptable, having your employees tell you what instructions they received is the next best solution. You might also be able to time your absences from the work area so that you're less apt to be gone at the times Eleanor usually visits the area.

If she doesn't realize how disruptive what she's doing is:

She may have gotten into the habit of bypassing you and other supervisors because no one ever complained to her. She thinks it's okay with you. Or she may understand that you don't like it but not believe it interferes with anything.

This is where a good relationship with your boss is important. If the two of you can be honest with each other, you can bring the situation up with her. Ideally, she'll see how disruptive it is and agree to change.

This is another one of the many situations in which your ability to listen carefully and ask effective questions is important. Of course, this automatically means that you've learned not to be defensive.

If she's not used to being a second-level manager:

This is almost the same problem as the last one, but with a small twist. It's likely that no one has told Eleanor that bypassing managers and going right to their workgroup is disruptive because as a new second-level manager, she's been doing so only for a short time. That makes it even likelier that she'll listen if you bring it up to her.

There is one caution, though. If she's new, she may be very sensitive to any criticism of her supervisory style. You need to make it clear that you know she's just being conscientious. All you're asking is the chance to show her that she can come to you and get what she wants done.

SOMETHING TO THINK ABOUT

You have one solid argument for having your boss deal with your employees through you—no matter why she doesn't do so at the moment. If she passes her instructions through you, you can see that they're carried out. If she doesn't, you may not know exactly what she wants, and it may not get done. In other words, it will be easier for her to do her job if she works through you instead of bypassing you.

Make sure that's the case with any instruction your boss gives you. Be scrupulous in ensuring that she gets what she wants. If it's easier for her to get what she wants by going through you rather than around you, she will.

No. 115 Doing the Boss's Dirty Work

She tells you to fire a good employee whom she doesn't like

THE SCENE

Jimmy Czaki is a good, solid worker—not your best, but not your worst. Unfortunately, Norma, your boss, thinks he's a loud-mouth, basically because he questioned a remark she made in staff meeting a couple of months ago about parking assignments. It was, admittedly, a dumb thing to do. (Norma doesn't take questioning well.) Jimmy apologized, though, and things seemed to be going okay. But now every time Norma sees Jimmy in the company cafeteria, she gets all worked up again. Finally, this afternoon, Norma decided she'd had enough.

"Get that troublemaker out of here," she stormed. "Two weeks—max. Then I never want to see his smirking face again. Got it?"

You got it all right. But it's not fair to Jimmy or to you. He *is* a good worker. One question two months ago (and not a big deal at that) shouldn't get him fired.

POSSIBLE CAUSES

Norma may have observed things about Jimmy's conduct or performance that aren't apparent to you.

There may have been other incidents where Jimmy was indiscreet in his dealings with Norma, incidents that you're not aware of. If these are serious or frequent enough, Norma may have defensible reasons for wanting to fire Jimmy.

Norma may have just taken a dislike to Jimmy.

There may be no objective justification for her dislike and no real reason to fire Jimmy, other than that Norma told you to.

YOUR RESPONSE

If Norma knows things about Jimmy's conduct or performance you're not aware of:

Talk to Norma to find out what she's observed. Try to get specifics—times, dates, places, details of the incidents.

Given the information Norma's provided, what is *your* objective assessment of Jimmy now? Would you normally consider his errors in judgments grounds for dismissal? If so, take the information you've received from Norma and talk to your personnel department about the procedures your company requires in terminating employees.

If the incidents Norma has observed aren't things you'd normally fire an employee for, talk to her about your concerns. Find out why Norma considers Jimmy's behavior so unacceptable. If you feel strongly that Jimmy shouldn't be fired, make your case to Norma. You might even suggest that Norma herself notify Jimmy that he's being fired. But as long as Norma has objective reasons for the termination, she is the boss, and this is one time when your appropriate response is "Yes, ma'am." You can register your objections, but in the end, it's Norma's decision.

After Jimmy's gone and things are back to normal, you should take the opportunity to talk to Norma about her reasons for wanting Jimmy fired. If the two of you disagreed about the seriousness of what Jimmy did, you need to find out where your differences of opinion are. There will be other "Jimmys," and it's important for you to understand Norma's philosophy on acceptable and unacceptable behavior.

If Norma's dislike of Jimmy is irrational or unjustified:

Your first step should be to find out as much as you can from Norma about why she wants Jimmy fired. Depending on how reasonable a boss Norma usually is, you may be able to register your objections. But if Norma is likely to bear a grudge for your less-than-enthusiastic response, it's better to keep your objections to yourself.

As we said in the preceding response, regardless of how unreasonable Norma's instructions are, she *is* the boss, and you're expected to follow her directions. Just as you expect your workers to obey your instructions and question them later, Norma will expect you to do as she tells you.

Depending on how unreasonable you think Norma's instructions are, it might be a good idea to document your objections in a memorandum or other similar document. That way, if Jimmy fights his dismissal in a grievance or court of law, you'll be able to show that you were following instructions from higher-level management.

If Norma's reasons for Jimmy's termination go beyond bad judgment on her part, but instead are illegal, no amount of documentation will save you. If you believe that Norma's real motives for dismissing Jimmy are discriminatory or can be construed as such, you're better off refusing, keeping in mind the personal consequences. Let Norma's superiors know in advance that she wants you to fire Jimmy, and why. Then tell them that you intend to refuse, and your reasons for doing so. Keep in mind that you're taking a risk; they may not support you. In that case you'll have to make the unenviable choice between standing your ground at the risk of being fired, or complying with Norma's request and risking facing civil penalties for engaging in discriminatory conduct. It's not a pleasant choice, but by checking with Norma's superiors first, you'll know better where you stand.

SOMETHING TO THINK ABOUT

Interpersonal relationships between managers and workers, among coworkers, and between workers and their customers, are the fiber that holds organizations together and keeps companies in business. Although successful companies tolerate a wide range of employee work and personal styles, if you have an employee whose style is so far from the norm that he disrupts the rest of the group, consider that it may be better to let him go than to make the rest of your group accommodate him. However, make sure that your reasons aren't discriminatory. Try your best to help the employee fit in and become part of the team. (The suggestions in Challenge 5 should help.) But if he continues to be a liability to your team rather an asset, let him go.

Solution Checklists

Whenever you're faced with a challenge that doesn't exactly fit one of the situations we've described in the previous chapters, look here for hints on how to solve it yourself. These checklists will walk you through the issue and show you the steps to take to resolve it.

We've included seven different checklists that cover the spectrum of "people issues" you're likely to encounter as a manager:

Checklist #1: Performance Issues (either individual or group)

Checklist #2: Conduct/Behavior Issues (either individual or group)

Checklist #3: Acceptance Issues (when one or several of your employees isn't accepted by the group)

Checklist #4: Relationships with Your Peers

Checklist #5: Your Relationship with Your Boss

Checklist #6: Your Personal Issues

Checklist #7: Substance-Abuse

THE GENERAL CHECKLIST

Whenever you're confronted with a management challenge, these are the general steps you should follow to solve it successfully:

_____ State the issue specifically in terms of
  • its source (who's responsible for causing the situation to arise, not who's responsible for fixing it)

and

- the kind of issue it is (such as performance, behavior, and so forth).

_____ Ask questions and gather all the facts you need to make a decision.

_____ Identify the options available to you for resolving the issue, now that you know exactly what the problem is.

_____ Choose an option that you'll follow (or a series of steps if that's the best way).

_____ Consider writing down why you chose the option you did, particularly if you think you'll be called on to explain your decision or if the challenge is one that's likely to manifest itself again, perhaps in a somewhat different way.

_____ Implement your decision.

_____ Evaluate how well your decision worked. If the solution is one that you implement over a period of time, evaluate its success at specific points along the way. If it doesn't seem to be working out as you expected, go through the steps again to see if you can find a better approach.

The patterns that follow take you through the first three steps of this general problem-solving procedure. It's up to you as the manager to make the final decision, implement it, and evaluate its success.

Good Luck!

CHECKLIST #1:

Performance Issues

Answer each of these questions:

_____ Exactly what is the nature of the performance concern?

_____ Does the employee have basic self-management skills such as skill in organizing and prioritizing work and in sticking to deadlines?

_____ If not, look for formal training courses where the employee can learn those skills. Coach the employee. Set short, progressive deadlines to help the employee manage his work as he assumes greater responsibility for managing it himself.

_____ Does the employee have the technical work skills needed to complete his assignments?

If not, teach the skills through training (either formal or on the job), supplemented with practice and feedback. Assign a mentor to review the employee's work and provide continuing coaching. If the procedures are hard to remember or seldom used, consider devising a job aid to list the directions in narrative or a diagram. (Standard Operating Procedures [SOPs] are a kind of job aid too.)

_____ If training, practice, and feedback don't yield significant improvements, decide if the employee has the ability to learn the work. (Your human resources or training department may be able to help in this assessment.)

If he doesn't, transfer the employee to a job you believe he can do or terminate him.

_____ Does the employee have the interpersonal skills required to establish and maintain effective work relationships?

If not, use formal training to teach the skills or coach the employee. Provide regular feedback on his progress. If coaching and regular feedback and counseling don't result in improved performance, transfer the employee to work that doesn't require dealing with customers or clients and has minimal interaction with other workers—even if that means a cut in pay for your employee.

_____ Does the employee/organization have the tools necessary to do the work (such as supplies, materials, equipment, sufficient time)?

If not, remove the obstacles or devise ways to work around them.

_____ Does the employee/organization have a positive incentive for doing the work correctly and on schedule?

If positive incentives don't exist, design them into the system to the extent you can. At the least, remove any disincentives and make sure employees understand how their work contributes to the overall goals of the organization. (If you're not sure what disincentives might exist, ask your employees, "What gets in the way of your doing the best job you possibly can?" They'll tell you—maybe more than you want to know!)

Note: Look also at Checklist #7, Substance Abuse, to see if that could be the source of an individual employee's performance problem.

CHECKLIST #2:

Conduct/Behavior Issues

Answer each of these questions:

____ Exactly what behaviors is the employee/group exhibiting?

____ Is the behavior serious or merely irritating?

If it's merely irritating, caution the employee (or group) that the behavior isn't appropriate. Be prepared to live with most irritations, though, unless the behavior worsens or it begins to have a noticeable effect on the productivity of the unit.

____ Is the employee/group aware of the rules in this area?

If not, let her/them know what the rules are and warn of the consequences for not following those rules. Make a written record of the warning.

____ Is the behavior critical to the organization or to the safety and well-being of other people?

If so, your first action should be to stop the behavior. After the immediate situation is taken care of, decide on the corrective action. In a situation this serious, termination is likely to be the most appropriate remedy unless there are unusual or strong mitigating factors.

____ Does the behavior undermine your authority or the basic supervisor/subordinate relationship?

If so, consider moving the employee out of your unit unless there are strong mitigating factors.

____ Is the behavior something the employee (or group) has intentionally decided to do?

If so, and if it's serious (even though it's not critical to the organization or to employees' safety and doesn't undermine your effectiveness), you still need to take action strong enough to stop the employee and others from repeating the behavior. This may include retraining, reassignment, or some form of disciplinary action.

Note: Look also at Checklist #7, Substance Abuse, to see if that could be the source of an individual employee's conduct or behavior problems.

CHECKLIST #3:

Acceptance Issues

Answer each of these questions:

____ Exactly what is the issue that's arisen?

____ Are others failing to accept a worker because she is a woman or a member of a minority group?

If so, first make sure your workers know your policy, and the company's policy, on discrimination. Explain how you expect your employees to behave toward all their co-workers (for instance, including them in meetings and discussions that are relevant to their assignments). Model the behavior you expect of your workers, so that it's clear you practice what you preach.

Then work on changing the underlying attitudes that caused this problem. Examine off-the-shelf training materials. Discuss individual differences and individual contributions at staff meetings and other appropriate occasions. Arrange positive experiences for people of diverse cultures and backgrounds to work together.

____ Are others failing to accept a worker, not for discriminatory reasons, but because the worker irritates them?

Encourage your employees to work together harmoniously. Make the establishment and maintenance of positive relationships a part of each employee's performance discussions and see that all your employees understand the negative effects on their individual and group performance of failure to nurture those relationships.

____ Has one of your workers been accused of discriminatory behavior (including sexual harassment)?

If so, first get the facts. Talk to the employee who made the allegation, any witnesses he names, and the worker who's been accused. Take notes of your discussions. If you believe the employee is innocent, talk to the worker who made the accusation to explain why you believe he misunderstood the situation and advise him of the right to file a discrimination complaint. If you believe the accused worker did discriminate, take appropriate action, even if it means firing him.

CHECKLIST #4:

Relationships with Your Peers

Answer each of these questions:

_____   Exactly what is the challenge in the relationship between you and the other manager or unit?

_____   Is what this manager is doing (or failing to do) important to your effectiveness or the effectiveness of your unit?

_____   If it's not, just live with what she's doing. You have other, more important, challenges to conquer.

_____   If what she's doing (or not doing) is important, are good relations with her important to your personal effectiveness or the effectiveness of your unit?

If they are, forget trying to force her to change what she's doing. Instead, pick one of the following alternatives, which doesn't require you to confront her or try to compel her to change. If none of those alternatives will work, just live with the situation.

_____   No matter how important good relations are, do you currently have good relations with her?

If so, your best alternative is to work out a resolution with her.

_____   If you don't have good relations, or can't work out a resolution, do you have something to offer her in exchange for her cooperation?

If so, see if you can't strike a bargain with her. Even if your relationship isn't that good, you can probably make a deal.

_____   If you don't have anything to offer, is there another way beside confrontation to get what you want or need or to minimize the effect of what she's doing?

If so, try to work around the problem she's causing without forcing the issue.

_____   If you have no good alternatives short of forcing her to change, can you rely on your superiors and peers to support you if you try to force her to change?

If so, it's worth trying to exert some outside pressure on her to change.

If not, your only good alternative is to live with the situation.

CHECKLIST #5:

Your Relationship with Your Boss

Answer each of these questions:

____ Exactly what is the issue that's arisen between you and your boss?

____ Is it a problem because it will harm the company, harm you, require you to do something illegal, or something that would cause you to violate your personal moral standards?

If it's not one of these, why is it a problem? It sounds like a disagreement, which means that you may try to persuade your boss to do otherwise, but if you can't, you should do what he wants.

____ Is the problem that he wants to take (or wants you to take) an action that will harm the company?

If so, and if you trust your boss, discuss your misgivings with him. If he still wants to take the action after you've said your piece, do what he says.

If you don't trust him, decide whether it's important enough to force the issue. If not, do what he wants. If it is, use the following suggestions.

____ Is the problem that what he wants to do will harm you (hurt your career, make you look bad, and so forth)?

If so, and you trust him, discuss it with him.

If you're not satisfied with the results of the discussion, or if you don't trust him, see the following suggestions on forcing his hand.

____ Is what he wants to do (or wants you to do) illegal or something that would cause you to violate your own moral standards?

If so, and if you have effective connections with your boss's superiors, go to them with the situation.

If so, but you don't have effective connections, is what he wants to do serious enough to risk loss of your job? If not, do what he wants and then start looking for a job somewhere else, because his next request may be more serious.

If so, and the matter is serious enough for you to risk your job, you have no choice but to refuse to do what he wants and either threaten to make the issue public or give your resignation to your boss' superior. Needless to say, if you don't resign on the spot, you still need to start looking for another job—quickly.

(**Note:** There is a significant difference between an action that you consider to be immoral because it violates widely held moral standards and one that violates your personal standards. If it violates community standards, it may be easy for you to get support from others. If it violates your personal standards that most others don't share, they probably won't help you.)

CHECKLIST #6:

Your Personal Issues

Answer each of these questions:

_____ Exactly what is the issue that's arisen?

_____ Is your boss dissatisfied with your performance or generally unhappy with you?

If so, talk to her about what she wants to see changed. Then, if it's something you can fix, fix it. If it's something you believe you can't fix, or are unwilling to change, you should know by now that your boss will come out the winner. It's time to look around for another job or prepare to live with your boss's continuing dissatisfaction.

_____ Are personal problems interfering with your work?

If so, talk to your boss to let her know that there are outside influences that may affect your performance for a while. Let her know how long you expect the situation to last and try to work out some temporary accommodation that's acceptable to both of you.

Don't try to tough it out on your own. Your boss will notice the difference in your work, and she may assume you've just lost interest.

_____ Are you burned out on the job?

If so, try to find an interest, either on the job or in your personal life, that will revitalize you. Take some time off (no one's indispensable) to relax and reassess where you want to be and what you want to be doing. If you already have outside interests and the combined demands are overloading you, ease off. Give yourself some time to unwind and contemplate. If your dissatisfaction doesn't diminish in time, then consider whether this is really the right job for you. Get some professional help in identifying a career that will be more personally rewarding.

CHECKLIST #7:

Substance Abuse

A growing concern in the workplace is the impact of alcohol and drug abuse on employee productivity. Tremendous costs (many of them hidden) result from poor quality work, absenteeism, interpersonal conflicts, and other by-products of substance abuse.

There are several keys to identifying a substance abuse problem, but the primary indicator is change, including:

- Change in an employee's behavior
- Change in his patterns of work and absence
- Change in the way he relates to others
- Change in the quality of his work
- Change in the amount he produces

Most of the time, you *won't* be able to identify impaired employees by physical symptoms, some of which include:

- The odor of alcohol
- Dilated pupils
- Slurred or incoherent speech
- Disorientation
- Lack of muscular coordination (staggering, dropping things, shaking)

The clues will be much more subtle. And you won't recognize them if you don't already know what the employee's normal patterns are. Here's the checklist to follow:

_____ Get to know your employees' characteristics and patterns—the way each employee typically acts or reacts.

_____ If you notice a decline in work behavior or performance, talk to the employee about it right away. Evasion and denial are classic responses of employees with substance-abuse problems.

_____ Look for changes in other areas. If an employee has been calling in sick frequently, has his performance also deteriorated? Or is he more irritable in dealing with coworkers or customers?

_____ Identify the specific performance or behavior problem(s) affecting the employee, then confront him. Make sure he knows exactly what will happen if his performance and/or conduct don't improve. Having related the problem(s) to work requirements, you should then offer the employee assistance or referral if he believes he needs it. Don't accuse! Your concern is getting the work out. If the employee recognizes that he has a problem, he'll need your understanding and support. If he doesn't recognize it, none of your accusations will help.

_____ If your company has an employee assistance program (EAP), consult the coordinator for help in confronting the employee. If your company doesn't offer an EAP, locate community resources that can help.

_____ Then follow through. Whether the employee gets help or not, make it clear that you expect him to improve his performance and/or behavior. If he does, congratulate him and offer your continued support. Otherwise, take whatever measures are appropriate—including discipline or termination.

Index